CALLED ~~TO~~

CALLED TO ACCOUNT

RICHARD HIGGINSON

Eagle
Guildford, Surrey

Copyright © 1993 Richard Higginson

British Library Cataloguing-in-Publication Data. A catalogue record for this book is available from the British Library

Published by Eagle, an imprint of Inter Publishing Service (IPS) Ltd, 59 Woodbridge Road, Guildford, Surrey GU1 4RF.

All Scripture quotations, unless otherwise noted, are taken from the *Holy Bible, Revised Standard Version.*

Printed in the UK by HarperCollins Manufacturing, Glasgow.

ISBN No: 0 86347 074 2

CONTENTS

The smell of failure
A second prototype
New and old treasure
Short-term and long-term
Management by wandering around
Knowing what makes people tick
Gentle jesus, meek and mild?
The right man for the right time

The Triumph of the Cross

A knock-out blow
The relevance of redemption
Taking the blame
Risking a loss of reputation
Letting go
Resigning on a matter of principle
Making a clean sweep

Resurrection Power At Work

A resilient God
Fishing – the heights and the depths
Failing forward
A memorable breakfast
After Japan
Sharing the success
A different debate

The Neglected Source of Creative Energy

Two unsung heroes
Modern counterparts
Being on a high
An improbable transaction
Making connections
Girlies on the wall
Effective communication
Doing business across different cultures
In mint condition?
Spiritual treasure in clay pots

FOREWORD
by
Viscount Caldecote

Many books and pamphlets have been written recently on particular aspects of business ethics from a Christian point of view. But Richard Higginson has done a valuable service in writing such a wide-ranging book, which shows clearly how much wisdom there is in the Bible – both New and Old Testaments – which is relevant and applicable to business life.

The book is the outcome of much research and he shows an admirable understanding of real problems which arise in industry. But he also recognises that all too often there are conflicts of loyalty which not even guidance from Scripture can resolve, and that although there is seldom an ideal solution, as Christians we should conscientiously seek the best one and have courage to apply it.

Sometimes the book raises difficult issues and doesn't give a final resolution, because not all questions have a specifically Christian answer, for instance that of different types of ownership.

There is much sound common sense, as well as Christian virtue, in making time for quiet reflection which he advocates. I remember one Friday deciding that a manager should be sacked on Monday, but changed my mind when I reflected on the problem during the sermon in church on Sunday; and it turned out to be the best solution.

I would want to add some reference to the significant part which incentives play in business. For while they can be very beneficial, and even necessary in the successful conduct of business, they can be damaging, especially when too closely related to business rather than the long-term interests of the company. But this in no way detracts from the very real value of this book in facing up to some of the many issues in business life.

Its theme can best be summed up in the fifteenth Psalm, and in the final quotation in the book from Paul's Epistle to the Colossians: 'Whatever your task, work heartily, as serving the Lord and not men'.

Robin Caldecote

PREFACE

I can honestly say that writing this book has been a great delight. It has been an opportunity to bring together and set on paper ideas which have been germinating in my mind for the last four years. Let me explain the situation which has given rise to the book.

In 1989 Ridley Hall, an Anglican theological college in Cambridge, initiated a business-values project as part of its Ridley Hall Foundation for the study of faith and work issues. The catchy name given to this project was 'God on Monday', though it has changed more latterly to 'Faith in Business'. The project can well be described as a bold experiment in management development and theological education. The main focus of its programme is a series of residential seminars for people in positions of responsibility in business, commerce and industry. Based on the conviction that Christian faith is relevant to the world of business, these seminar weeks bring together small groups of business leaders in dialogue with theological staff, students and visiting speakers to explore in depth themes such as 'Values in Business Today', 'Issues of Leadership' and 'Managing the Dynamics of Change'. The intent and indeed the experience of these seminars is that through this combination of different types of expertise a realistic and authentic Christian perspective on business is being forged.

For the last four years a major part of my job has been to direct this project. The approach to business which I develop in the pages which follow is something which has steadily emerged during these years. Although this book contains the stamp of my personal ideas, there

is a sense in which it is a collaborative venture. My
training is in Christian theology and ethics; my direct
business experience is slight. Yet in the course of the
last few years I have done a great deal of listening
and a great deal of visiting. In writing, I have drawn
upon the insights of many men and women from diverse
business backgrounds. I trust that the very practical
nature of their concerns has kept this book down-to-earth
in character – while hopefully remaining true to my desire
to root business activity in an intellectually coherent
Christian theology.

It is impossible to name and pay tribute to all the people
whose ideas I have drawn upon in the course of writing.
However, I am particularly aware of what I owe to the
following:

Viscount Caldecote, former chairman, Delta Group
plc and 3i plc for kindly writing the Foreword;
James Allcock, Director of Gas Supplies at British
Gas, who read the script in preparation, asked pen-
etrating questions about my use of Scripture and
helped earth the case-studies in reality;
Jeremy Begbie, Lecturer in Christian Doctrine at
Ridley Hall, who led me into thinking further about
modern attitudes to work and the Protestant Work
Ethic;
Peter Benton, former Director General of the British
Institute of Management, for stimulating my ideas
about wealth creation;
Jacqui Blunden, former Ridley ordinand and now
Deacon at St Paul's Bedford, for the imaginative work
she undertook on 'liturgy and the work-place';
Bill Bolton, international consultant on science parks,
with whom I have talked much about company struc-
tures, technology and innovation;
Margaret Bowker, Tutor in Prayer and Prayer Coun-
selling at Ridley Hall, for valuable insights she
has shared about praying in the midst of a busy
lifestyle;
Hugo de Waal, Bishop of Thetford, former Principal

of Ridley Hall and the founder of the 'God on Monday' Project, who was instrumental in introducing me to the whole exciting area;

Richard Hobbs, Director of The Centre for International Briefing, for his fascinating seminars on doing business across different cultures (sadly Richard died in March 1993.);

Sandy Landale, management consultant from Worcestershire, who first put me on to the idea of a book on business focused round basic Christian doctrines;

John Lovatt, Managing Director of ACME Mars, who shared further interesting ideas along these lines;

Reid Murchison, businessman in Britain on a year's study leave, who commented on the script from an American perspective;

Christian Schumacher, management consultant, for his pioneering work on Christian theology as a resource for management;

Lady Judith Wilcox, Chairman of the National Consumer Council, for sharing the experience of success and failure in business so honestly;

and not least David Wavre, Managing Director of Eagle, for the enthusiasm and commitment he has shown in publishing this book and for his many helpful comments along the way.

My warm thanks go to all these and many others. Nevertheless, it should not be assumed that they would necessarily agree with all of the opinions expressed in these pages!

I am also grateful to various individuals who arranged for me to visit companies which are featured at various points. Thank you, therefore, to Ward Crawford (Trebor Bassett), Guy Douglas and Phil Phillips (Hewlett Packard), Nick Grant (John Laing), John Hougham (Ford), Les Johnson (British Nuclear Fuels), David Runton (FTL), and Clive Wright (ARCO Chemical), who all facilitated my research in a very helpful manner.

Along with certain named companies and individuals,

this book also features many case-studies where identification is less precise. Some of these are real-life stories where the individuals concerned preferred me to use a different name. Some are figments of my own imagination. Others comprise what seemed to me to be a suitable mixture of fact and fiction. Again I would like to thank all who have generously allowed me to draw upon their experience in this more anonymous form.

It may be that some who read this book will feel stimulated into entering into dialogue about ideas and opinions which are expressed in it. Alternatively you might like to hear more about the work of the Ridley Hall Foundation. In either case I should be delighted to hear from you. Please write to me at Ridley Hall.

To make the book reader-friendly, I have avoided the use of footnotes. Full details of all the books referred to in the course of the text can be found in the bibliography at the end. When quoting from the Bible, I have normally used the Revised Standard Version, but I have indicated when I have used other versions (either the New International Version or Revised English Bible) instead.

Finally, I would like to express heartfelt thanks to my wife, Felicity, and children Hannah, Daniel, Peter and Simeon. Throughout the writing of this book they have provided a rich source of encouragement, support, good humour and companionship. A fifth child arrived just as the book was in the final stages of preparation. We have called her Lydia, after that fine example of a New Testament businesswoman, the seller of purple goods from Thyatira (Acts 16:14).

Richard Higginson
Ridley Hall, Cambridge

CHAPTER 1

GRASPING THE NETTLE

The Gulf between Church and Business

This is a book intended for those in the fast track of business life – men and women who often have little time to read, but who recognise the need to step aside periodically in order to think. It is designed to meet the concerns of people in a number of different states of mind.

It is a book for those who want to face up to some fundamental issues in the business world which often go unaddressed. It is for those who find that personal faith and values are often difficult to relate to the way business seemingly has to operate. It is for business people who, looking back, know how they entered business but who are no longer sure of why.

Who else is the book for? It is for men and women who are sometimes confused by conflicting signs in the maze of management and the theory which surrounds it. It is for people who wonder whether the church is in the process of jettisoning orthodox Christian belief because it is irreconcilable with modern ways of thinking about the world. It is a book that attempts to bring together Christian theology and business practice in an exciting way.

Three little pen-portraits help to explain why I have written this book.

Taken for a ride?

Barry is thirty-two years old, a skilled mason who used to work for one of the big construction companies. He became increasingly frustrated, both by his own failure

to achieve promotion and by what he came to regard
as the low standards of behaviour characteristic of the
building industry in general and his own company in
particular. In the course of his work he saw evidence
of irregular payments made to secure contracts, safety
regulations which were openly flouted, and suppliers who
were delayed payment as long as possible. He tried to
close his mind to these things and tell himself they were
none of his business, but he couldn't.

Barry is married to Val and their first child, Laura, was
born eighteen months ago. The couple's contact with the
church hitherto had been almost non-existent, but the
arrival of a child prompted them to go along to their
local church and enquire about having Laura baptised.
The rector was warm and welcoming but emphasised
the seriousness of the vows that parents make in the
baptism service. Barry was not put off by this because he
hated doing anything half-heartedly. He felt challenged
to discover more about the faith he was proposing to
profess, joined a group for discussing 'Christian basics'
and one evening, stirred to his roots by an evangelistic
sermon given by a visiting preacher, announced to a
startled Val that he'd been converted.

For Barry, becoming a Christian had immediate effects.
He experienced forgiveness, peace of mind and a sense of
his energy and purpose for living having been dramatically renewed. He felt that life was beginning all over
again. To signal this new start he handed in his notice
at the construction company, and began work on developing plans for his own building company. These plans
developed with remarkable speed. He found a colleague
whose practical skills complemented his own, and secured
start-up capital from a bank with no problems at all. At
first Val was nervous about the revolution happening in
Barry's life, but as she began to grow into a quiet faith
of her own and noticed how much happier Barry seemed
to be, so her anxiety eased.

Barry wanted to make his a building company with
a difference. He had read of the growing popularity
of mission statements among larger corporations and

he decided to include one of his own in the literature
with which he launched the company. Included in an
impressive set of stated ideals was the promise that
'Suppliers will be paid promptly, in accordance with
agreed terms of trade'. His colleague Ron objected that
this could be a dangerous hostage to fortune but Barry
felt confident that God would honour him for the stand
he was taking. He did not intend to let others dictate their
trading practices to him but resolved to set an example
which he hoped would prove infectious.

For six months the business went exceptionally well
– even in the face of a recession which was gathering
pace. Barry and Ron soon found orders coming their
way. Customers were impressed by Barry's stress on
high standards which extended beyond being true to
his word to a high quality of workmanship. They took
on extra staff as the orders began to multiply.

But now, a year after Barry left the construction giant,
unmistakable problems have begun to appear. Barry and
Ron are getting the orders, but not the money. One
customer after another is making excuses for delaying
the payment of invoices. There are four which are giving
Barry particular concern.

A property development company with whom Barry
has a large contract reports that it has run into financial
difficulties because of the decline in the property market.
It says it cannot make further payments until its bank
has agreed to finance an overdraft. Another important
customer refuses to answer letters. When Barry tries to
ring him, his secretary always says that he's out or at a
meeting. The secretary promises that he'll ring back, but
he never does.

Then there is a couple on whose house Barry has
carried out a major extension. The couple separate just
before the work is complete and this leads to arguments
about who wanted the extension to be done and who
should be responsible for paying. Husband and wife
both put the onus on each other, with the result that
neither pays up. The fourth customer is a firm which
justifies delay of the signing of cheques on the grounds

that the crucial signatories are respectively ill and on holiday.

Barry and Ron could cope with one awkward customer, but not with so many. They wonder if their company has acquired a reputation for being a 'soft touch'. They are suffering from a nasty cash-flow problem, exacerbated by the promptness with which they seek to pay their suppliers. On average, Barry is having to wait sixty-five to seventy days for payment, and he makes it his policy to pay within twenty-five to thirty. He has exceeded his overdraft facility, and is beginning to get pointed letters from the bank manager asking him what he proposes to do about the problem.

For the first time since his conversion, Barry finds himself plagued by self-doubt. He hears the clash of conflicting voices. Ron argues that they have no option but to swallow their pride, explain the nature of the problem to their suppliers, and ask them to accept staged payment. Barry is reluctant to do this, because he says that he has put his integrity on the line. Val urges him to resort to a solicitor and get him to write letters threatening to take non-paying customers to court. Barry is reluctant to do this also, because he believes it somehow 'unChristian' and does not want to forfeit customer goodwill. When his faith is strong, he continues to believe that God will honour his habit of making payment promptly. But awake at night, he worries horribly about the prospect of his company going bust and the hopes he had for transforming business practice being exposed as foolish and naive.

Barry goes back to his rector, the trigger for his conversion, to discuss the dilemma with which he's confronted. But for all his friendliness and sympathy, the rector does not have any clear or practical advice to offer. He confesses himself a novice in the area of business, and leaves Barry feeling more confused than before he saw him. Indeed, Barry starts to ponder a more fundamental question: is it possible to practise Christian standards in the world of business? Is there so much cynicism and exploitation around that trying to operate differently is doomed to failure? Is he a sheep surrounded by wolves?

What counts as garbage?

Fiona is thirty-seven years old, single, and a partner in a leading accountancy firm in the City. She became a Christian as a teenager, and was active in the Christian Union at University. At that time she seriously considered whether God was calling her to full-time ministry, perhaps as a missionary, but her flair for maths and economics led her to start training as an accountant. Unlike many of her contemporaries, she passed her accountancy exams easily and became persuaded that her obvious talent for the job was a sign that God wanted her in this sphere of work. Joining her present firm when she was thirty, she has risen rapidly through the ranks and her average salary now stands at over £100,000 a year. She lives in a luxurious flat in a fairly exclusive London suburb.

Fiona is well respected and liked in her firm. As well as her technical skills she is extremely good at relating to people and is often asked to handle difficult situations, e.g., explaining to employees why they are being made redundant. She has overcome initial suspicion of her as a woman and can give as good as she gets in a well-humoured way when sexist banter flies around the office. Her winning way with potential clients regularly secures the firm more business. Fiona's skills are also recognised in the suburban church which she attends; she is on the church council and chairs an outreach committee. Unlike some of her single friends of the same age, she has no great hankering to be married, enjoying the freedom of her independent life-style. Yet during the last two years Fiona has become increasingly dissatisfied about what she is doing in life. Why?

The essence of Fiona's unease is a growing question about whether what she is doing in her job is of any real worth in terms of the kingdom of God. She has specialised in tax accountancy, and much of her time with clients is

spent discussing how their accounts can be prepared in
such a way that they pay as little tax as possible. Fiona's
firm claim to practise high ethical standards, and both
she and they take care not to encourage anything which
amounts to tax evasion. She is openly critical of the more
dubious practices which go under the name 'creative
accounting'. But there are times when she frankly tires
of conniving with the niggardly attitude to paying tax
which she encounters everywhere she goes.

Fiona is also growing uneasy about how wealthy she is
becoming. She tithes regularly, and is known for being
generous with both her time and her possessions, but
her savings, boosted by some astute buying and selling
of shares, seem set on a consistent upward curve. Fiona
eats out regularly and treats herself to expensive holidays
abroad. She enjoys the good things of life, but is beginning
to feel twinges of guilt about them. She sometimes worries
that she may be like the third type of seed described
in Jesus' parable of the sower, the seed sown among
thorns: 'they are those who hear the word, but the cares
of the world, and the delight in riches, and the desire for
other things, enter in and choke the word, and it proves
unfruitful' (Mark 4:18–19).

Another passage which has been on Fiona's mind
recently is Philippians 3. She finds herself challenged
by Paul's words: 'But whatever gain I had, I counted as
loss for the sake of Christ. Indeed I count everything as
loss because of the surpassing worth of knowing Christ
Jesus my Lord. For his sake I have suffered the loss of all
things, and count them as refuse, in order that I may gain
Christ . . .' (Philippians 3:7–8). Is she being called to give
up the gain of her comfortable job, and count it as refuse?
Or, as an American colleague of hers would say, garbage.
She recalls the idealism of her university days, when the
idea of 'giving up all for Christ' nearly led her to become
a missionary. Did she turn her back on a genuine calling
when she followed her present career?

Try as she might, Fiona cannot really view being a tax
accountant as a way of following Christ, or as counting for
anything significant in eternal terms. Nothing which she

is taught or she imbibes from her local church encourages her to make such a connection. There is much talk of 'ministry of the laity', but that is always taken to mean being a lay preacher, an elder, a church treasurer or a home-group leader; it is scarcely ever related to the world of work. In the weekly intercessions, prayers are often made for the so-called caring professions: teachers, doctors, nurses and social workers. People like Fiona who work in the financial sector never get a look-in. The preaching she hears is sound, thorough exposition of biblical passages, but few imaginative links are made with the modern world. Where does a job like accountancy fit into God's purposes? Fiona wishes she knew.

A cat among the pigeons

Miles is fifty-two, married and has three teenage children. He grew up in a strict Nonconformist family which was at the same time suspicious of worldly influences yet thoroughly involved in the world through the practice of trade. Miles accepted both Christianity and the legitimacy of participation in business uncritically. On leaving university he joined a multi-national company, one of the world's leaders in the gas, oil and chemicals industry. There he quickly built a reputation for being a resourceful innovator in start-up situations. After a varied career spent in different parts of the world, one not without its ups and downs, but on the whole very successful, Miles has just become a main-board director. His area of responsibility is Planning and Public Affairs.

Intellectually, Miles has moved some distance from the way he saw things as a young man. He has thrown off childhood taboos and is known as someone who loves nothing more than a good argument over a drink. He remains a committed Christian, though he has switched denominations, and preaches lively, provocative, theologically-questioning sermons in his capacity as a layman. Miles is also quite prepared to question some of the received orthodoxies in business, a characteristic which has sometimes led to confrontation with colleagues

in middle management but which has certainly had the
effect of keeping his mind fresh and his interest in
business very much alive.

The areas where Miles is apt to ask radical questions
are threefold.

The first is an ecological question, the responsibility
which a company like Miles' has in conserving finite
resources for future generations. He believes that along
with other energy companies, senior management in his
company have shut their eyes to the rapid depletion
of these resources for far too long. He would like to
see the company putting sizeable sums of money into
researching alternative sources of renewable energy. He
looks forward to the day when the company will be known
for its extraction and refinement of biomass, not oil and
gas. Miles is keenly aware of the growing sensitivity of the
public on 'Green' issues and he longs to see the company
taking pro-active measures not aimed merely at reducing
pollution, but revealing a genuine global concern.

A second area where Miles flouts conventional wisdom
is with regard to the company's pay structure, especially
in relation to its upper end. He does not believe the
company chairman should be paid £500,000 and main-
board directors anything upwards from £125,000. Miles
counts himself highly fortunate in having an excellent
secretary and regards it as flagrantly unjust that he
is paid ten times what she is. He knows the familiar
arguments, that these are the market rates and paying
such salaries is necessary to attract the top people, but
he only half-believes them; with directors setting their
own performance-related bonuses, well above the rate of
inflation, there is a strong sense of individuals feathering
their own nest. This is particularly hard to justify when
employees lower down the line are being asked to show
pay restraint. Miles wonders what the reaction would be if
he were to propose a self-denying ordinance on the board's
part for the coming year, nothing less than a pay freeze.
He decides ruefully that the answer would probably be:
send for the men in white coats!

The third area of controversy is the most fundamental

of all. It concerns what a company is actually for. Miles strongly reacts to the prevalent corporate philosophy that, whatever else a company may be for, maximising profits for the benefit of its shareholders is its main reason for being. Miles recognises the necessity of profit, indeed he has spent much of his career preoccupied with the size of profits, but he believes that to make the 'bottom line' the primary goal of a company is to stand logic on its head. The primary goal should be satisfying customers by providing an efficient, reliable service which enhances their quality of life. Whereas colleagues think in terms of customer service as the corporate means to increased profit as the corporate end, Miles inverts the relationship between the two: as far as he's concerned, increased profit is the means, and customer service is the end. He is convinced that if the company were to accept this, a major re-evaluation of attitudes would be necessary: one that might well be painful for the company, but would in time lead to a much sharper focus on customer needs and – ironically – increased profitability.

Miles is aware that a forthright statement of his unconventional views would create a stir on the Board. He is tactically astute enough to know that he needs to bide his time, make strategic alliances and think how he can present his arguments in the most persuasive manner. For his own satisfaction, as well as to defend his case against more philosophically minded colleagues, Miles wants to ground his thinking in a coherent theology. His intuition tells him that he is working along the right lines, but he wishes to establish clearer connections than he has yet come up with, between Christian theology and responsibility for future generations, differential pay structures and the question of corporate goals.

When he visits religious bookshops, however, Miles discovers that there is virtually nothing which is of any help to him. There are books which have much to say about economic systems, arguing strongly either for capitalism (providing a theological endorsement for wealth creation) or for socialism (talking much of God's bias to the poor).

There is very little which is engaged with business practice from a theological and ethical perspective and which address the dilemmas and pressures which arise for people working within those systems. Miles feels no option but to set about developing such a theology for himself, but he wishes that he did not feel so alone in the venture.

Bridging the gap

It is impossible to highlight the whole range of issues which this book seeks to cover in the course of three short case studies. But between them, Barry, Fiona and Miles do illustrate some key areas of concern. There is the question of what behaving as a Christian in a largely secular world actually involves, and whether too idealistic an approach is actually destined to fail. There is the question of what part apparently routine jobs have in God's purposes, and whether God actually calls people to such work. There is the question of whether there are some fundamentally wrong assumptions written into the way business usually operates.

The situations in which Barry, Fiona and Miles live and work are very different, but the experience of looking to the church and finding it wanting is common to all of them. Whether it is helpful pastoral support, affirmation of the type of work they are doing, connections between faith and business in Christian worship, or well-earthed theological writing – in every case they draw a blank. I have deliberately exaggerated in order to make a point, but the experience of many people in the business world is that this is an area of life which has been unduly neglected by the institutional churches. It was partly in response to this gap that Ridley Hall initiated the 'God on Monday' project.

In the work of the project and in what I have written here, I am regarding managers with a conscious Christian commitment as my main target of concern. This is not to deny the appropriateness of other people having a closer link with different groups in industry; for instance in

Britain, Industrial Mission has often had an orientation towards shop-floor workers and their concerns. But I am proceeding from the conviction that business leaders, though doubtless well-catered for in many ways, can constitute a particularly needy group. The burden of responsibility can fall very heavily upon their shoulders. As I have already intimated, the church often fails to show an intelligent, informed, understanding interest in the work which they do and the type of decisions they have to make. While for most employees the hours of work are being slowly reduced, the hours worked by managers are tending to increase. In an age when change happens so fast and market conditions are so unstable, so is the momentous nature of the decisions which they take and the processes which they set in motion.

Management, however, is a very broad term. It covers many different levels of responsibility. Team leaders on the shop-floor, engineers developing new technology, trade union leaders and product controllers all exercise responsibility, as well as finance directors and chief executives. I hope that all will find something to interest and stimulate them in this book. If people who are not in business read it so that they can relate more sympathetically to friends who are, that will be a welcome bonus! And if people who are not Christians read it because they are intrigued to discover how God and Monday can possibly relate to each other, all the better.

An exciting era

At the time of writing, the Western world lies unhappily in the grip of severe economic recession. Companies are cutting their losses, making redundancies and sadly, in some cases, going bust. Yet if one takes a long-term view, the present era is in many respects a very exciting one for business. Current problems should not blind us to underlying trends which are positive and hopeful.

First of all, there is the speed of technological development. Technology is able to perform functions today which would have been dismissed as idle fantasy a

generation ago. Electronic mail is revolutionising the
speed of communication within companies. There is a
human cost to advanced technology, because it leads to
massive job cuts in labour-intensive manufacturing, and
the new knowledge-based and service industries require
different skills and do not yet employ people in the same
numbers. But technology also makes possible exciting
ways of organising work differently. Telecommuters who
are equipped with their computer and fax do not necessarily have to go in to the office; they can do a lot of their
work from home or even their car, and this is good news
for able women who want to combine satisfying work with
keeping the family intact. Technological developments
are shaking up the labour force, demanding and enabling
a much greater flexibility.

Secondly, there is a pervasive trend in business today
striving for higher and higher quality. Japanese companies have set searching standards in this respect,
ironically learning the gospel of quality from an American
guru – W. Edwards Deming – who was a prophet without
honour in his own country until 1980. In Britain the
challenge of the Single European Market has helped to
improve quality, with the evidence of having attained
a high standard (BS 57570) becoming a crucial weapon
in jockeying for competitive position. Where a company
takes quality seriously, the philosophy is one not merely
of serving the customer but delighting the customer, so
perhaps we are all in for a good time in the future! Quality
becomes something for which the whole work-force, not
just a product inspector, takes responsibility, as illustrated by the widespread reorganisation of teams into
'Quality Circles'. In the best companies, it is a concept
which embraces every aspect of their activity: quality
in the standard of the product, quality in the service
to customers, quality in the treatment of employees. Of
course, in most areas of industry, there is still a trash-end
of the market, but it is generally getting smaller and even
there customers are demanding better value for money.

Thirdly, the formula for business success is becoming
much less stereotyped. Certainly, some of the world's

major corporations have continued to dominate their markets by working along hierarchical, bureaucratic, highly structured lines – though most are having to adjust their style in order to be able to respond to and initiate change fast enough. But there are some new players on the scene who have broken the accepted rules, yet pulled in the profits and brought new dash and colour to the business scene. Four brief examples from Britain in the 1980s serve to illustrate this. All are the subject of vivid biographies or autobiographies.

Alan Sugar, a poor Jewish lad from the East End of London, became a millionaire by making electronic goods at a price no-one could match. With his blunt, no-nonsense style of operating, and ruthless exploitation of cheap labour in the Far East, Sugar's Amstrad company made the personal computer available to a mass market. From a similarly impoverished background, but with a clear ideological aim, Anita Roddick has developed a company which produces cosmetics made from vegetable rather than animal ingredients, which are not tested on animals, and which avoid elaborate packaging. This downbeat, apparently unsophisticated approach has proved a roaring success, so that the Body Shop International now has offshoots all over the world. Richard Branson has proved that it is possible to combine aversion to conventional suits and a passion for daring stunts with being a successful businessman. Having made his name with Virgin Records, he then defied the wisdom which says 'stick to the business you know' by starting an airline, Virgin Atlantic – one that is now causing British Airways serious competitive concern. John Harvey-Jones, by comparison, was more from the mainstream of business, spending most of his working career with Britain's premier chemicals company, ICI. However, he still succeeded in cutting a dashing figure with his bold ties, shaggy sideburns, and commitment to making things happen. After playing a major part in pulling ICI's fortunes round during the 1980s, he achieved wider public recognition through the BBC's *'Troubleshooter'* programme, giving the benefit of his advice to certain selected, ailing companies. In short, there seems to be a new breed of charismatic business leaders, but what is refreshing is that no two seem to be alike.

Fourthly, business in the 1990s displays a growing sensitivity to ethical and spiritual values. This is not quite the same as saying that moral standards were bad and they're getting better, though that is doubtless true of some firms and sections of industry. It is rather that business is becoming much more conscious of the ethical factor. Sometimes the impulse comes from within, as company directors wake up to the fact that there is a moral component to quality as well as other dimensions, and it is actually more satisfying to act with integrity and treat other people with respect than to behave like two-faced swine. Sometimes the pressure comes from without, as companies find themselves obliged to demonstrate a high ethical profile with regard to the environment if they are to retain credibility in the public eye. This is the age of lead-free petrol, ozone-friendly aerosols, cruelty-free cosmetics, and – possibly – sulphur-free power stations. The 'greening of business' may be a case of too little, too late, but it is surely a process that is here to stay.

Openness to spiritual values is perhaps more difficult to substantiate, but it is a trait which reveals itself in various striking ways. There is a growing recognition that the culture or spirit which pervades a company is crucial to whether or not it functions well – and that there is something mysterious and undefinable about this. Many senior managers will admit that in a business world beset by so many uncertainties, they need a super-human source of power if they are to keep the show (not to mention themselves) on the road. It is interesting how the New Age movement, with its syncretistic, pantheistic approach to religion, is attracting growing numbers of business people on its courses. Orthodox Christians are apt to throw up their hands in horror and bewail the advances of heresy. A more constructive response would be to see the positive side of this development, to the extent that the popularity of New Age courses indicates business openness to a spiritual dimension to life, but to be unabashed about offering the resources of Christian faith and experience as a more satisfactory alternative. This is an exciting era, with many opportunities for Christian witness in business as well as in other ways. If Christians really are to prove a credible force in a business world brimming with possibilities for good, as well as for evil, they need to get down to some serious thinking about what their God and their work have to do with each other.

CHAPTER 2

FINDING A STRUCTURE

The Relevance of Credal Christianity

Companies in the 1990s are very much into the business of articulating their core beliefs and aspirations. Some call these statements expressions of corporate philosophy, some call them mission statements, others expressions of general business principles. They vary a great deal in form, but there is a similarity in content which runs through most of them. Statements of company philosophy articulate the values which the company seeks to embody (e.g., quality, mutuality, efficiency) and spell out the responsibilities which the company acknowledges towards various groups (e.g., shareholders, customers, employees).

Sometimes these statements have the feel of empty shells or hollow promises, because there is a major gulf between what the company says and what it does. But where a company takes them seriously, thoroughly educating their employees as to their meaning and importance, they have a very significant role to play. Expressions of corporate philosophy can provide direction and inspiration. In essence, they remind a company of its basic rationale and raison d'être, the structure of ideas which should undergird all it does. A company which loses sight of its organising beliefs soon lapses into a state of rudderless drift.

The fact that these expressions of corporate philosophy are often called *mission* statements, a word with clear religious connotations, is interesting. Indeed, I am often tempted to quip that these days there are more companies with mission statements than there are churches, which could be a sign that many of the latter are losing their

way. But the truth is that the church does possess
statements of organising belief which have helped to
restrict its falling into error, and which should provide a considerable impulse to mission. These are the
statements of the historic Christian creeds, notably the
Apostles' Creed and the Nicene Creed. Today these creeds
suffer from neglect; those congregations where they are
still recited tend to treat them as an opportunity for a
quiet yawn. But they continue to provide Christianity
with its essential structure of ideas. Whenever a radical
theologian dares to deny one of the credal statements,
like the virgin birth or the second coming of Jesus, it
invariably causes quite a stir.

What the creeds articulate is the overall shape of the
biblical story. They express fundamental truths about
the nature and activity of God and his involvement
with the affairs of humanity. They speak, succinctly but
memorably, about the origin of life (God the 'creator of
heaven and earth'), God's coming to earth in the person
of Jesus Christ ('for us men and for our salvation'), and
of our future destiny in 'the life of the world to come'.
The creeds give us a sketch of what theologians have
sometimes called *salvation history*. In them we find
an outline of the key events described in the Bible,
past, present and future, events which have momentous
significance for the human condition.

Theology and marriage

The import of the great themes of Christian theology is
much more readily appreciated in some areas of life than
it is in business. For an instructive example of where
Christians readily accept the relevance of a theological dimension, let us consider briefly the institution of
marriage. How does marriage look in the light of credal
Christianity?

The creeds direct us to begin with *God*, a God who,
according to Genesis 1:27, created man and woman in his
own image. Both sexes therefore reflect something about
God's nature, even if God transcends sexuality. Christians

moreover believe in God as Trinity: a God within whom
relationships exist, where different members of the Trinity
perform complementary roles, and where they interrelate in
a harmonious way. God himself provides a profound model
for a husband-wife relationship.

Turning now to the pattern of events revealed in
the Bible, a series of important observations can be
made about the phenomenon of marriage. First, the
institution of marriage is traced right back to *creation* and
to God's making human beings male and female. Genesis
2 pictures this as occurring in a two-stage process, first
Adam, then Eve. On his own, Adam is incomplete; he
lacks companionship, he lacks a helper. He also, of
course, lacks the capacity 'to be fruitful and multiply'
(Genesis 1:28). When Eve arrives on the scene, one can
almost hear Adam's cry of 'Whoopee!' prefacing his
remarks 'This at last is bone of my bones and flesh of my
flesh' (Genesis 2:23). There is a delight in his new-found
partner, a relish which probably includes the element of
sexual enjoyment. Adam and Eve come together in an
intimate relationship and from this Genesis 2:24 traces
the institution of marriage, with its three key ingredients:
leaving father and mother, cleaving to one's wife, and
becoming one flesh.

A theology of sexuality within marriage must therefore begin with a statement of its essential goodness.
It is a gift of God in creation. We feel the force of
this in the Song of Solomon, where the rich use of
metaphors from nature help to root sexuality in the
created order. But with the epoch of human history
known as the *fall* the intrusion of sin into the world, a
dark shadow falls over this as over other areas of life.
Genesis 3 depicts shame and embarrassment entering
into the sexual relationship once the fall has taken
place: Adam and Eve now cover their nakedness. The
harmonious, complementary relationship between man
and woman takes on elements of enmity (Genesis 3:15)
and domination (3:16). In the narrative portions of the
Old Testament, which may be taken as representative
of human history in this respect, human sin disturbs,

distorts and even destroys the marital relationship in
all sorts of ways.

It is not all doom and gloom. There are happy marriages
in the Old Testament, and touching notes of tenderness
and solidarity between husband and wife appear at
various points. But we encounter the discordant notes of
adultery, including adultery which involves incest, prosti-
tution and murder; polygamy, which is never condemned
as such but is shown as encouraging favouritism and
jealousy among wives; and divorce, permitted – according
to Jesus – as a concession to human hardheartedness.
Any theology of marriage needs to take seriously the
impact of human sin upon this area of life. The institution of marriage opens up great possibilities for human
happiness; it can also lead to untold horrors of human
misery. It is a sad fact how great a proportion of violent
crime is enacted between husband and wife, largely by
husbands on wives.

We move next to the saga of *redemption*, to the saving ministry of Jesus Christ. This is not the place for
a detailed discussion of Jesus' teaching on marriage
and divorce as revealed in his famous dispute with the
Pharisees. Christians in turn disagree about the small
print of what Jesus said. I simply want to concentrate
on the main thrust of Jesus' words. This was to compare divorce and remarriage (in general terms, whatever
'exception' he may have made) with adultery, i.e., as a
serious breaking of the vows of marital faithfulness.
Appealing to Genesis 2, Jesus recalled men and women to
the high standards of the creation ideal. He does not criticise the Mosaic permission for divorce, but effectively he
said: the law may permit divorce, but what is that to you?
You are joined together in the eyes of God and that is how
you should stay. Your marriage may run into difficulties,
but in the kingdom of God there are resources of forgiveness, love and grace which should enable you to overcome
these, to make the ideal of lifelong marriage into a reality.

That is marriage seen in the light of redemption. There
is a further spelling out of such a concept in Ephesians 5,
where the relationship of husband and wife is compared

to that between Christ and the Church, where there is a note of mutual submission and love, and where Christ's great act of self-sacrifice is seen as a model for the husband's attitude to the wife.

But at the same time as asserting possibilities for redemption in marriage, we have to acknowledge that the present era is one where sin persists alongside the capacity for transformation. Attempts to restore relationships are often frustrated, which raises the question of a continuing place for divorce. The hardness of human hearts makes this a seemingly necessary social regulation.

Finally, there is the perspective cast by our future hope (what theologians call *eschatology*) upon marriage. This contains a twofold thrust. On the one hand, the glimpse God gives us of the world to come serves to remind us that marriage has a limited role in God's purposes. It is a this-earthly institution. Jesus, in reply to the Sadducees' trick question, said that when the dead rise they will neither marry nor be given in marriage (Mark 12:25). There is a sense in which the New Testament relativises marriage within the context of a greater loyalty – a loyalty to Jesus Christ. In addition, the single person is presented as having an alternative vocation, being one who, as it were, points to the resurrection precisely because he or she is less absorbed by worldly affairs (so Paul argues in 1 Corinthians 7). On the other hand, a good marriage relationship also has eschatological significance, inasmuch as the human closeness and harmony which it represents provides a foretaste of the relationships which will exist more universally in heaven. In the words of Oliver O'Donovan, Professor of Moral and Pastoral Theology at Oxford University, 'Humanity in the presence of God will then know a communion in which the fidelity of love which marriage makes possible will be extended beyond the limits of marriage' (*Resurrection and Moral Order*, p. 71).

Virgin territory?

This excursion into marriage may seem a curious digression in a book devoted to the subject of business. I have

included it for two reasons. First, Christians engaged in
business are as likely as anyone else to be married. If they
occupy senior positions in management, their marriages
are particularly vulnerable to the stresses which the
demands and anxieties of work bring to bear upon our
closest relationships. A balanced, biblical perspective on
marriage does not provide a magic solution to such pressures, but it can help! Second, and more fundamentally, it
serves as an example where the full spectrum of Christian
theology is regularly given practical application. Little
that I have said in the previous section is particularly
original. Many books have been written on Christian
theology and sexual ethics. This is in striking contrast
to the area of business.

It is notable how, in the growing interest which exists
in the subject of business ethics, very little has yet been
developed by way of an identifiably Christian perspective.
Business ethics is an overwhelmingly secular phenomenon. Even where Christians have written on it, they
have been reticent about doing so on anything other
than a largely secular society's own terms. It is time
to redress this balance. While it is inappropriate to
expect Christians to have a different answer on every
or indeed most questions of business ethics, there should
be some coherence between the approach they adopt and
their overall theological perspective on life. The Christian
businessperson will not be flaunting Christian doctrine
at the meeting of every management team, but it should
provide a bedrock for the key elements in his or her
thinking.

Of course, business is not entirely virgin territory as
far as Christian thinking is concerned. This is evidenced
by two recent books on the subject of theology and
work, business obviously being a subset of that broader
category: *Work and Leisure in Christian Perspective* by
Leland Ryken and *Work in the Spirit* by Miroslav Volf.
The two books could not be more contrasting in their
theological emphases. Ryken's revolves round the notion
of *stewardship*: a staunch defender of the Puritan ethic,
he sees work as a sphere where one may exercise one's

God-given abilities in serving others and glorifying God.
He draws principally upon Old Testament material. Volf,
in contrast, takes as his starting-point the New Testament idea of God's new creation, and speaks much about
transformation, not just in people's attitudes towards
work but the structures within which they work. His
book is much more radical in tone.

The concepts championed by both of these writers are
valuable ones, and I shall draw upon them myself later
in the book. My objection is that as they stand, both
books suffer from theological imbalance. Each draws
upon certain important aspects of Christian theology
to the neglect of others. This is not untypical of those
who have written on the subject of Christianity and
business.

What I am attempting in the pages that follow is a
systematic exposition of Christian doctrine in relation to
the world of business. The relationship between theology
and business is explored, not just with regard to one or
two favoured ideas, but from the beginning of salvation
history to the end. In doing this, I have not followed either
the topics or the order of the historic creeds in a slavish
manner: that would be artificial. Nevertheless, there is
a chapter here devoted to every major theme in credal
Christianity. Only thus, I believe, can we come to a truly
satisfying integration of the life of faith and the world
of work.

What use is the Bible?

Such a statement of intent is all very well, but can it
actually be realised? Sceptical voices quickly arise. Is
there not a grave danger of distorting the essential
message of Christianity, of forcing the biblical writers
into the mould of management gurus when they were
clearly anything but that? If credal Christianity has as
its aim distilling the essence of the biblical story, it is
clear that the Bible will be for us a major resource.
This immediately raises the issue of its proper use. In
ecclesiastical and academic circles today, warnings about

misusing and abusing the Bible abound; the importance
of paying careful attention to the context in which the
biblical writers operated, our own late-twentieth-century
context, and the extent of the gap between the two,
is constantly stressed. Alongside the disciplines of Old
Testament studies and New Testament studies there is
now a third area of scholarship, *hermeneutics*, or the
principles of biblical interpretation. The whole business
of interpreting the Bible seems to have become very
complicated; so much so, that it is a wonder anyone still
has the nerve to read it expecting to discover God's word
for them today. The question: 'What use is the Bible?'
is no longer one that comes only from an unbeliever's
lips. It may well represent a very genuine inquiry from
a confused Christian.

There are indeed perils attached to interpreting the
Bible, especially when we come to consider the vexed
world of business. But the problems are not all of one
sort. Those Christians who still use the *Book of Common
Prayer* are familiar with the twofold confession: 'we have
done those things which we ought not to have done' and
'we have left undone those things which we ought to have
done'. Something similar applies to the area of biblical
interpretation. There are mistakes we make when we see
a passage which seems to speak very directly to business
but the connection is not as straightforward as we think
it is. These are errors ('sins' is too harsh a word) of
commission. There are also mistakes we make when
we fail to see that a passage which says nothing directly
about business could actually be of great relevance to it.
These are errors of omission. Which is the greater danger?
The answer will vary from person to person and group
to group.

Who's the real rascal: master or servant?

One biblical story which takes a business situation as its
scenario is the parable of the talents (Matthew 25:14–30).
A master who is going away on a journey entrusts his
property to three servants: 'to one he gave five talents,

to another two, to another one, to each according to his
ability' (25:15). A talent was a huge sum of money,
equivalent to 6,000 denarii, so that in terms of modern
purchasing power it represents several thousand pounds.
Through the practise of trade, the first two servants
double their quota of talents. When the master returns,
he is delighted with these servants and rewards them
with greater responsibility. In contrast, the third servant
buries his talent in the ground, giving as his excuse:
'Master, I knew you to be a hard man, reaping where
you did not sow, and gathering where you did not winnow;
so I was afraid . . .' (25:24–25). The master is thoroughly
disgusted and retorts that the servant should at least
have invested his money with the bankers, so that he
would have received the talent with interest on his
return. The parable ends on the sombre note of the
'worthless' servant being deprived of his solitary talent,
which is given to the servant who now has ten: 'For to
every one who has will more be given, and he will have
abundance; but from him who has not, even what he has
will be taken away. And cast the worthless servant into
the outer darkness; there men will weep and gnash their
teeth' (25:29–30).

It is striking how the affluent Christians I know who
are loudest in their affirmation of the capitalist system
gravitate very swiftly towards this passage. Often it
provides them with their main theological inspiration.
Taken at face value, Jesus' parable appears to lend
strong support to the practices of making as much money
as you can, banks lending money at interest, a hard,
even ruthless approach to the commercial world, and
the possibility that radical inequality of wealth between
persons may actually be their just deserts. It is a story
which, in the hands of some writers, has inspired a rather
ferocious work ethic, impelled as much by fear of what
happened to the third servant as desire to share in the
reward of the other two. Not surprisingly, it is said to be
one of Margaret Thatcher's favourite biblical texts.

A very different approach to the parable is found in
certain strands of liberation theology, the Latin American

and Asian style of thinking which champions those who are poor and sees the Christian Gospel as a summons to social and economic transformation. In the hands of C.S. Song, author of *Third Eye Theology*, the story becomes an exposé, presumably one conducted with a good deal of irony, of the evil practices endemic in so much commercial activity. The third servant is actually the hero of the story, because he refuses to go along with his master's dubious practices. Far from cowering in self-disgust at his low rate of return, he stands up to the king and shows him to be unjust and avaricious. The third servant has the courage to reveal the master's unacceptable face to him. Sure, he is made to suffer for his boldness, but that is Jesus being utterly true to life: such is the fate of those who go against the stream.

Flawed interpretations

We should not rest content with either of these approaches to the parable. Radically different though they are, both are guilty of two identical mistakes. The first is that they ignore the parabolic nature of the story. Jesus teaches about one area of life through the medium of another. A parable which presupposes a particular set of economic relations is not necessarily making a moral evaluation, one way or the other, of those relations. The details of Jesus' stories are often given in order to add colour and convey vividness; they should not be subjected to a process of thorough-going allegorisation. What we need to discover in each parable is the crucial point of connection or comparison which Jesus sought to draw.

In the parable of the talents, it is difficult to avoid the conclusion that the person of the master is meant, in some sense at least, to represent God. To evade this obvious conclusion is perverse. God is the one to whom we are all ultimately accountable. But that does not mean that all the harsh characteristics predicated of the master in the story are also true of God. Nor does it mean that Jesus was sanctioning a system of rapacious capitalism. Any encouragement which this parable seems to give to the money-making process needs to be balanced by the clear warnings given elsewhere in the Gospels about the snares of personal wealth.

The context in Matthew 25 provides an important clue to what the parable is all about. The story of the talents is one of three parables (the others are the ten virgins and the sheep and the goats) told by Jesus in the midst of warning his disciples about the unexpected nature of his second coming. Jesus wants his followers to be living in a state of constant readiness for his return. The first two servants in this story acted with responsibility and initiative; they took risks but they produced results. The most plausible interpretation of this parable is in fact implicit in the way that the word 'talent' has developed; for in English it indicates not a sum of money but a gift, aptitude or ability. God wants us to make the most of these abilities, whatever they are, and it would be a false circumscription of the parable's relevance to confine it to commercial abilities. The third servant failed even to develop his potential in the modest way represented by investing money at the bank.

There is a second flaw in the interpretations of this parable offered both by the comfortable capitalist and that system's radical critic. Each has a strong vested interest in the way their interpretation turns out. They find in the parable what they want to find. In contrast, we must be prepared to allow Scripture to stand over and against us, to challenge our convictions and expose our prejudices. If we are to acknowledge the Bible's authority, we should be ready to listen even when it speaks in voices that are unfamiliar and alien to us. In particular, the Bible resists human attempts to force it into the mould of any one economic ideology.

The eccentric employer

Another parable of Jesus which depicts employer–employee relations, the story of the labourers in the vineyard (Matthew 20:1–16), is even more prone to abuse by vested interest. This is the curious story of the householder who employs casual labourers at various different hours of the day (some all day, others as little as one hour), and who pays all of them the same wage – one denarius. I have heard different people attempt to draw lessons for industrial practice in three quite different ways. There is the chief executive's perspective, that the employer has absolute authority in this area, and therefore has the right to pay employees what he or she likes. Then there is the socialist shop steward's perspective, that all employees should be paid the same, whatever work they do or however hard they work. Finally there is the lawyer's perspective, that so long as an employer sticks by an agreement with an employee, no-one else has the right to complain. Whichever interpretation is chosen, the lesson drawn usually chimes in with the background of the person drawing it.

I shall not go so far as to urge that all such lines of interpretation should cease forthwith; they do, after all, stimulate the mind and encourage us to think again about accepted practice in the area of wage differentials. But by dwelling on the details of what is happening on the business front, all are in danger of missing the central message of the story. This is that God makes the same offer of salvation to us all, at whatever stage in life we repent. Because we human beings are set in a 'differentials' mode of mentality, God's generosity to those who turn to him late in life is apt to seem unfair to those who have served him throughout their lives. But this merely underlines the fact that his mercy transcends all human notions of fairness. Jesus was challenging his hearers, not so much (if at all) about current practice in the market-place, as about their understanding of and feelings towards God.

Making imaginative connections

Seeking to apply biblical material about business over-hastily is one pitfall. But there is another to which contemporary Christians in the West are, if anything, even more susceptible. This is to assume that there is

nothing of relevance to be gleaned from passages which
do not directly address a particular sphere of life – in
this case, business. The fact is that it is possible to
exaggerate the size of the gap between the Bible and
the modern world. Even where Scripture is silent in
terms of addressing a modern issue, there is plenty of
scope for an indirect or analogical approach. In their
book *Reading in Communion: Scripture and Ethics in
Christian Life*, Stephen E. Fowl and L. Gregory Jones
argue persuasively along these lines. They note that
the New Testament writers were not unduly worried
by historical discontinuities between the writings they
accepted as Scripture (the Old Testament) and their
situation; rather, they showed imagination in formula-
ting metaphors, drawing analogies and making connections to bridge the gap. They discovered secondary layers
of meaning in Scripture, lines of interpretation which
would doubtless come as a complete surprise if explained
to the original authors, but legitimate nonetheless. A
good example of this work of reinterpretation in action
is the first two chapters of Hebrews, where several
passages from the Psalms referring to (variously) God,
the Israelite King, and human beings in general, are
applied to the person of Jesus. The daring with which
the New Testament writers conducted this process is
indeed breathtaking at times.

Encouraged by their example, we should not be unduly
inhibited about relating and applying Scripture in a
fresh way to modern scenarios. If we truly believe that
as Christians we are people whose character is being
formed and transformed by the Holy Spirit, we can handle
Scripture, certainly with humility, but also – crucially –
with confidence. We will expect to find words of relevance
in the Bible, and the Spirit will stimulate our thought
patterns so that we make imaginative connections.

Powers and authorities

By way of illustrating this technique of applying Scripture afresh to our contemporary situation, I shall take

one of the great New Testament passages on the person and work of Christ, Colossians 1:15–20 (NIV):

> He is the image of the invisible God, the firstborn over all creation. For by him all things were created: things in heaven and on earth, visible and invisible, whether thrones or powers or rulers or authorities; all things were created by him and for him. He is before all things, and in him all things hold together. And he is the head of the body, the church; he is the beginning and the firstborn from among the dead, so that in everything he might have the supremacy. For God was pleased to have all his fulness dwell in him, and through him to reconcile to himself all things, whether things on earth or things in heaven, by making peace through his blood, shed on the cross.

Paul here presents the lordship and supremacy of Christ in a way which is awesome in its language and horizon-stretching in its scope. There are two particular phrases to which I wish to draw attention.

The first is the phrase which occurs in verse 16, 'thrones or powers or rulers or authorities'. Paul uses these words quite frequently, either in couplets ('powers and authorities') or on their own ('authorities'). The meaning attached to these phrases varies from passage to passage. In Ephesians 6:11–12, he is clearly referring to forces of spiritual evil against which the Christian is instructed to fight: 'Put on the full armour of God so that you can take your stand against the devil's schemes. For our struggle is not against flesh and blood, but against the rulers, against the authorities, against the powers of this dark world and against the spiritual forces of evil in the heavenly realms' (NIV). But in Romans 13:1 the reference to 'authorities' refers to those whom God has invested with political authority, and is thoroughly positive: 'Let every person be subject to the governing authorities. For there is no authority except from God, and those that exist have been instituted by God.' As an agent for the punishment of bad conduct, the ruler (potentially at least) is God's servant for our own good.

In Colossians 1 Paul appears to be using these expressions in an all-embracing way. He is referring both to powers in heaven and powers on earth, to powers that are bent on evil and to powers that have a potential for good. Caesar, Satan, angelic beings and a host of other agents who wield or are thought to wield authority were probably present in Paul's mind. He asserts that all find their origin in the creative activity of Christ, and all are subject to Christ's authority.

In our own day, we have become increasingly aware of the mysterious and formidable nature of power. We have become aware of the power which resides in the forces of culture. We are slowly coming to terms with the extent to which our behaviour and thought patterns are shaped by physical, psychological and sociological factors. Above all, we are recognising the power of the economic factor.

As we seek to apply this passage from Colossians to the modern world, it is entirely appropriate that we include economic forces in Paul's list of ruling authorities. What is the great power which shapes and moulds our lives today? Surely it is the market economy, which provides those of us who live in the West with goods and services in ever more astonishing profusion. In the 1990s, with the widespread collapse of socialist and communist systems, there is a sense of the market economy having established its authority in a hitherto unparalleled way. Of all economic systems, capitalism is clearly the most effective in creating wealth and in providing scope for business initiative and creativity. But it also has a downside: left to itself, the market system fails to distribute wealth in an equitable way, and like other systems, it has over the last two hundred years inflicted serious damage on the environment. The market economy is morally ambivalent, a major force for both good and bad. Ronald Preston gives powerful expression to this both in the title and the content of his book *Religion and the Ambiguities of Capitalism*.

Paul makes the claim that every power and authority

was created by Christ and for Christ. The vision of a
market economy which has been brought under the
authority of Christ, and is significantly changed thereby,
is a truly exciting one. It is something to inspire our
prayers, thoughts and actions. Such is the direction
in which a thoughtful reapplication of Scripture can
lead us.

The master welder

A second intriguing phrase is that in Christ 'all things
hold together' (v. 17). Paul pictures him as the one who
having created everything, then sustains it. Christ does
this both on the level of physics (upholding the constancy
of laws of nature, which makes possible the development
of science and the application of technology) and on the
level of metaphysics (providing life with its ultimate
meaning and rationale). Christ is the world's unifying
principle. But crucially, he is more than that: he is a
living person who helps us to hold our bit of the world
together.

   This is a very reassuring notion for the Christian in
business. He or she often feels pulled in lots of different
directions. The managing director of a manufacturing
company has to balance the complicated demands of
shareholders, staff, production engineering, design standards, safety requirements, cashflow, the customer who
wanted an order yesterday and the wife who is unlikely
to see much of him today. He often feels like a juggler
struggling to keep all the balls in the air, or a master
welder striving to forge effective links between the dis-
parate parts of his organisation. If all things hold together
in Christ on a cosmic level, there is hope for us yet on
a personal and corporate level. Colossians 1, like many
other parts of the Bible, contains unsuspected riches for
our daily encouragement and nourishment.

CHAPTER 3

UNDERSTANDING THE TRINITY

The God who Calls and Creates Community

Jim is forty-three, married and has four children. He is Production Director in a medium-sized electronics company. He has a reputation with his staff as a tough but fair manager, one who drives everybody hard but who cannot be faulted for his own effort and commitment. He sets groups and individuals clear targets, so all his staff are glad to know what's expected of them, though they wish he were a little more forthcoming in his praise when those targets are attained. On the other hand, Jim can be scathing in his criticism when mistakes are made, and he is an absolute stickler for discipline as far as the observation of company rules is concerned. If anyone is found on company premises the worse the wear for drink or playing short-cuts with safety regulations, the most number of warnings that he will give them is one, never two. All the same, he is admired for administering justice in a way that is transparently impartial. Jim has made it his business to ensure that nobody can accuse him of having favourites. Everyone in his sphere of operations, himself included, must prove that they are productive.

Most of the time Jim is the epitome of self-sufficiency and decisiveness: a man who knows his job backwards and is resourceful enough to find solutions when confronted by unexpected problems. But there are occasional days when he is anything but that. Jim has moments when he is crippled by self-doubt, desperate for affirmation and affection, and dithers about the making of decisions. His tactic then is to retreat from the production floor into his office, to bury his head in his hands, and make himself unavailable for half an hour or so. Usually he re-emerges into the fray as firm and decisive as ever, the crisis apparently quelled. But one day his secretary appears at the door of his office and is surprised to see tears streaming down his face. What is going on inside him?

The divine taskmaster

Jim is a Christian. He is regular in his churchgoing, systematic and generous in his giving, a man who spends long hours at work but always gets home in time to read a story to his children and say prayers with them. Jim has a very clear, uncomplicated view of God. God is the great creator who rules the world by law – physical laws and moral laws. He has made men and women to obey him and to work hard in making his earth a fruitful place. Human beings are by natural inclination disobedient, and repeatedly violate God's laws. In response to the crisis this created for God, he sent his Son, Jesus, in order to provide an example of what a perfect life of obedience comprises. Jesus' death on the cross satisfies the dreadful punishment God requires for sin. The slate having been wiped clean, we are therefore given a second chance to live obedient, productive lives in God's service. We must make the most of it, otherwise the eternal consequences could be severe.

Jim's understanding of God, which is faithfully reproduced in his personal style of management, is actually based on a passage in Jesus' teaching in Luke's Gospel.

'Will any one of you, who has a servant ploughing or keeping sheep, say to him when he has come in from the field, "Come at once and sit down at table"? Will he not rather say to him, "Prepare supper for me, and gird yourself and serve me, till I eat and drink; and afterward you shall eat and drink"? Does he thank the servant because he did what was commanded? So you also, when you have done all that is commanded you, say, "We are unworthy servants; we have only done what was our duty."' (Luke 17:7–9)

Although he might be reluctant to admit it, Jim's attitude towards God is that he can never do enough to please him. Jim may reach the targets he believes God has set for him, but he always feels that God wants something more. His model of God is that of the hard taskmaster. Wishing to pattern himself upon the character of God, he presents exactly the same image to his staff. He rarely thanks or praises them for their work, because he thinks a job well done should be automatic: it is simply a matter of performing one's duty. Much of the time Jim feels content with this model, and convinces himself, despite some evidence to the contrary, that his staff appreciate his style of management. But in those moments of crisis, Jim experiences sensations of terrible insecurity. He doubts everything: his own abilities, the purpose of his job, whether his wife loves him, and – most fundamental of all – his own personal salvation. If he will always remain an unworthy servant, how can a just and holy God possibly accept him? Jim knows no answer but to work even harder to try to prove his worthiness to God.

Jim's understanding of Christian doctrine and notion of God is not without some biblical foundation. God is holy, just and calls us to a life of costly service. But as it stands, Jim's view is seriously distorted. Jim's God is all justice and very little love; and the demands he perceives this God as making are stripped of the context Jesus was at pains to emphasise, the security of a forgiving relationship. Jim is desperate to establish his value with God, but the truth is that God has already shown how much he values Jim by dying for him. Jim is familar with grace as a theological idea but he has yet to savour it as a real experience – hence the urge to ground assurance in his own achievements.

The Protestant work ethic

What Jim's case illustrates is that there may be a connection, and not necessarily a healthy one, between our image of God and the way we practice our work. He fits in well with the thesis argued by the German sociologist and early management theorist, Max Weber, in his seminal book *The Protestant Ethic and the Spirit of Capitalism*, written in 1905.

Weber sought to show a link between certain Protestant beliefs and what he called the 'spirit of capitalism' which developed in the seventeenth and eighteenth centuries. He was intrigued by such attitudes as self-discipline, industry and thrift, the careful stewardship of time and money which led to considerable personal prosperity and with that, scope for commercial enterprise. Weber believed that these attitudes were encouraged by the teaching of certain branches of the Protestant Church about the nature of salvation. In particular, the Calvinist idea of God choosing some to be saved and others to be damned had a great psychological influence. Because one's eternal fate was seen as lying in the inscrutable will of God, this could lead to a state of chronic insecurity – for how can I be really sure that I am a member of God's elect? According to Weber, the answer that some Protestant Christians found was by working hard and accumulating wealth. They interpreted this as a sign of God's blessing, which in turn countered anxieties about their eternal destiny.

All this, of course, is highly paradoxical. A theological movement which strongly emphasises God's grace produces over a period of time adherents who attach a feverish significance to their own human works. Is such a thesis plausible? Weber's book has caused much controversy and his argument is almost certainly overstated. Capitalism wielded as much formative influence on the Protestant ethic as the Protestant ethic did on capitalism. But the fact is that characters like Jim really do exist. They see God as a hard-driving production manager and that is the model they copy in their working lives. They try to attain the elusive prize of peace with their maker through the delusory device of quantifiable achievements. Nor is this a trait found only in business. It is observable in many spheres of life, from the harassed housewife to the painstaking politician.

Nowadays it has become fashionable to deride the

Protestant work ethic. It is equated with an attitude
of workaholism, never knowing when to stop and failing
to appreciate our very real needs for rest and recreation.
This is a tendency which the Puritans had to some
extent, stemming from an exaggerated fear that Satan
finds evil things for idle hands to do. But it is as the
process of secularisation has taken root that the work
ethic has become a truly unattractive prospect. Jim
may be suffering – and making others suffer – through
his distorted view of God, but an impressive vein of
self-giving service still runs through his solid endeavours.
The manager who works all round the clock, believes that
money is the measure of everything and is motivated by a
naked egoism, possesses few redeeming features. He may
in some sense be heir to the Protestant ethic, but he has
moved an enormous distance from it.

Driven or called?

In its original form and context, the so-called Protestant
work ethic was an extremely positive contribution to
sixteenth-century thinking. The great merit of Martin
Luther's writing on the subject is that he broke down the
dichotomy between 'secular' and 'sacred' work. Luther
emphasised the great variety of occupations in which it is
possible to work hard and serve God. He saw the Catholic
Church of his time as giving the impression that only
the overtly religious occupations of priest, monk or nun
were truly pleasing to God; the rest were second-class
Christians. In contrast, Luther affirmed that the mother
suckling her baby, the maid wielding her brush or the
magistrate passing sentence were doing something of
real value if they performed these activities in response
to God's command and for his glory. Such teaching was
heady stuff in its day.

When our understanding of God is shot through with
the language of relationship, then a rather different
model from Jim's hard-driving production manager is
likely to emerge. An assurance of God's acceptance which
is grounded, not in our own achievements, but in the

depths to which he has reached to demonstrate his love for us, can release us from that chronic insecurity which has such damaging psychological effects. Luther's dominant image is not of a God who *drives* in relation to work but of a God who *calls*. It is from him that we derive the idea of secular work as a vocation. Luther thought that almost every sphere of activity can be a genuine vocation in which the individual can serve his or her neighbour and please God. He considered there were just a few occupations which were beyond the pale, notably robber, prostitute and (for some of his life at least) usurer. Like Calvin after him, Luther invested even the most apparently mundane of jobs with God-given significance.

This teaching still has enormous relevance, particularly for Christians working in business in the modern world. Whether the job that they do is highly repetitive or even if it is technically very sophisticated, it is easy to be misled into thinking that such work has little value in God's sight. Alternatively, there may be an uneasy feeling that, in its very essence, the job is morally problematic. Take Fiona, the tax accountant we met in chapter 1. She abhors what she regards as the miserly attitude of many of her clients towards the payment of tax. She especially dislikes the hypocrisy of those who combine a ready acceptance of 'diddling the taxman' with loud condemnations of 'scroungers who exploit the social security system for all its worth'. Yet she knows that by the efficient and knowledgeable way in which she performs her job, she is materially assisting them to pay as little tax as possible.

Fiona's dilemma is a very real one. From a managing partner's point of view, Fiona might appear too morally sensitive for it to be sensible that she continues in her present position. God's perspective is almost certainly different. It is only if people like Fiona stay in their morally ambiguous situations that the world can be changed, little by little, for the good. She is obviously constrained in the extent to which she can perform a prophetic, challenging role. But there will be occasions when she can point out inconsistencies of attitude, warn of the dangers of sailing close to the wind, and set an example in terms of transparent honesty. In itself, there is nothing disreputable about being a tax accountant. Individuals and companies often have highly complex financial affairs, and they require specialist professional advice in order to know exactly what tax they should pay. There is injustice in the phenomenon of too much tax being paid, as well as too little. Bringing clarity and order to a company's financial affairs is a crucial attribute in business, and Christians like Fiona are performing invaluable service when they do their job well. But there is no disputing the emotional strain and psychological cost that may be involved in doing so. It is a tough life, constantly rubbing up against selfish attitudes and hypocritical postures. Yet that may be precisely what the cost of discipleship means for someone with Fiona's particular abilities.

Obviously, it is possible that God may call the Fionas of this world into other areas of service. Luther's understanding of vocation is rightly criticised for being too static. A key verse for him was 1 Corinthians 7:20: 'Each one should remain in the situation which he was in when God called him' (NIV). Luther, taking this out of context (which is Paul's advice on whether to marry with the end of the world being expected shortly) interpreted this too woodenly, to mean one occupation for life. But the fact is that God can call us to many different spheres of activity within a lifetime. Indeed, the changing patterns of work within the Western world increasingly point in this direction.

In particular, it must be acknowledged that the ordained ministry is the richer for the presence of people who have held down responsible jobs for several years before going into full-time Christian leadership. But I sometimes feel it is a pity when individuals make this move just when they are getting into positions of significant influence. The church needs to offer more support and encouragement for those of its members struggling to offer a positive witness in corporate situations where their scope for manoeuvre is limited. This support should consist not just of the occasional prayer or a patronising pat on the back, but teaching from the pulpit which affirms the diversity and complexity of Christians' callings. There are indeed those who are *called to account*.

A false antithesis

Miroslav Volf criticises Luther's teaching on vocation on a number of other scores also. He thinks that this understanding of work tends to be indifferent towards alienation at work and has been misused ideologically to glorify dehumanised work. This may well have been a tendency, but there is no intrinsic reason why the concept of vocation should lead to such a consequence. Volf wishes to replace vocation with the concept of *gift*, which he thinks has a much sounder New Testament basis. Passages like Romans 12 and 1 Corinthians 12 teach that all Christians have been equipped with gifts which are to be used for the benefit and building-up of the church. Clearly, many of these gifts (e.g., teaching and administration, mentioned in Romans 12:7) are of wider relevance also. People with well-developed skills in interpersonal relationships or clarity and vividness of communication are invaluable in a business context. Volf thinks that it is the matching of gift to task which should guide Christians in their choice of career, not a dubious notion of divine calling.

Clearly there is an important point here. Where a sense of vocation is unaccompanied by any evidence of possession of the necessary attributes (whether it be pastoral sensitivity for a clergyman or manual dexterity for a craftsman), an individual ought to ask himself, in all seriousness, whether his understanding of God's purpose for him might be mistaken. But ideally vocation and gift should be complementary concepts. There is no need to play one off sharply against the other, as Volf does. Indeed, there is reason to think that gift by itself is an inadequate sustaining motive. We can all think of situations at work which everyone finds uncongenial, tasks for which nobody will claim a gift. Who except a sadist enjoys telling a group of employees that their services are no longer required? Yet the fact is that there are times when for the company's good, or because the nature of work has changed, people have to be made redundant. Someone has to be the harbinger of bad news. Usually it falls to the line manager or the personnel manager; it is part of the job expectation that they perform this function. For a Christian, seeking to discharge this unpleasant responsibility faithfully, sensitively and as truthfully as she can, the conviction that God has called her to this particular job may play a very important part in steadying the nerves and carrying her through.

The Trinity – puzzle or profundity?

If models of God are significant for the way in which we work, and the model that Jim has is – generally speaking – a destructive one, what understanding of God ought to be guiding us? I suggest that the answer lies in taking seriously the truth of God as *Trinity*.

Many people have difficulties with the doctrine of the Trinity. Fundamentalist Christian sects dismiss it as unbiblical because the word 'Trinity' never actually appears in the Bible. Orthodox Christians accept the idea, but tend to regard it as a strange mathematical formula which defies adequate explanation. For a clergyman or lay preacher the task of giving the sermon on Trinity Sunday is regarded as the ultimate challenge.

In the light of this it might be tempting to regard the Trinity as a piece of baggage better jettisoned, an acquisition which has proved of doubtful value in the conglomerate of Christian teaching. Yet nothing could be further from the truth. The doctrine of the Trinity was not something invented by the early Church out of a desire to be awkward. On the contrary, it is a profound truth which those Christians felt bound to articulate in order to make sense of their exciting experiences.

The first disciples began with a belief in Yahweh, the one true God of Israel, about whom they had been taught from their mothers' apron-strings. Then they joined up with this man Jesus, who wasn't just a dynamic, charismatic personality but who taught the crowds, forgave sins, calmed storms and healed the sick with the authority of God himself. All the same, it took the very special event of the resurrection to drive the disciples to the outrageous conclusion of calling this very earthy man God in person. (I shall say more about this in chapter 10.) Then, after Jesus was raised and had left them for good, the disciples found – somewhat to their surprise – that they were actually able to carry on Jesus' work. They had the courage to preach in the teeth of fierce opposition, the faith to heal a crippled man, and the capacity to forge a committed community of people out of a set of individuals plucked from diverse and seemingly incompatible backgrounds. The disciples realised that an event which Jesus had predicted would happen had happened. The Holy Spirit had come upon them, to dwell in them, guide them and inspire them.

So here we have the germs of a doctrine of the Trinity. God the Father, the one, true, holy, indivisible God, creator and sustainer of the universe; God the Son, God made manifest in a particular, historical, tangible human person; and God the Holy Spirit, God living and active in lots of hitherto very ordinary people. How this one God could be present in these three very different ways is what the doctrine of the Trinity is all about. Some theologians may have made it less intelligible than others, but let us not forget it was the spectacular events of Easter and Pentecost which forced the early Church to take it on board.

It is in fact a great shame that the Trinity is rarely mentioned in church except on Trinity Sunday. If we could only stop thinking of it as a puzzle and be content to accept it as a glorious part of God's being, we would find that it can teach us much about life in all sorts of ways. That includes the area of business.

Mirroring the life of God

Christian Schumacher, son of the famous thinker and writer E. F. Schumacher, is a management consultant,

widely used by major companies like ICI, who finds the
key to understanding industrial processes in the doctrine
of God the Trinity. Discerning this represented a sudden
dawning of light which brought to fruition long years of
intellectual search.

The first important point Schumacher hit on was that
though there is clearly overlap between what they do,
the different members of the Trinity tend to be associated, both in the Bible and in Christian tradition,
with different types of activity. Analysis of this reveals
a basic pattern which is common to most human activity, business included. Every business operation needs
planning: careful, imaginative, creative planning. God
the Father shows this *par excellence*. Every business
operation needs *executing*: someone prepared to roll up
his sleeves and go out and do what needs to be done,
effecting transformation of the situation which has been
planned. No one has done that more dramatically and
decisively than Jesus the Son. Every business operation requires *good communication*: someone who will
co-ordinate the efforts of planner and executive, explain
what is going on in the maelstrom of the market-place,
and help to evaluate what it is that has been achieved.
This is a more diversified brief but the Holy Spirit is
certainly equal to it!

Analogies of this sort can become strained. We should
not push this one too far. But it is potentially a very
exciting thought that in our normal sphere of business
operations, we are in a sense mirroring the life of God.
As we partake in the regular cycle of planning, executing
and evaluating, we reveal ourselves to be creatures made
in the image of God – not just any God, but a Trinitarian
one. There is a pattern present in the world because it
was there in God first.

Whole work

Schumacher takes his Trinitarian analogy a stage further.
It is important not to romanticise people's experience of
work, but to recognise that many find work frustrating

and unfulfilling, even soul-destroying. Schumacher traces this to the fact that, since the Industrial Revolution, much of our work has been organised in such a way that it has a deformed character. For work to be satisfying, it needs to partake of all three elements of planning, doing and reviewing. Individuals and groups are too often treated as mere functionaries, instead of being given responsibility for applying creative and critical thought to their activities. Schumacher advocates the organisation of companies into small workgroups so that all may experience the satisfaction of 'whole' work.

In addition, the nature of each group's activity needs attention. Job satisfaction is likely to be less when employees are performing merely peripheral or cosmetic operations, like storing things. Jesus did not simply perform a function; he transformed a situation. The memorable moments at work are when a situation is transformed: when oil is found, a new garment designed or a crucial contract secured. These of course are the initial stages, and often the most exciting. The oil then has to be drilled, the clothing made and the deal carried out. There is satisfaction, too, in seeing the desired process of transformation through to its conclusion. Episodes in which transformation occurs are easiest to identify, of course, where the focus is on a company's core activity. It is more difficult in the sphere of ancillary operations, which no company is able to manage without. But there is often scope for streamlining an organisation so that every individual and group partakes less of tedious, trivial activities, and is more involved with the fundamental process which gives meaning and purpose to the whole enterprise. This principle can extend right down to the matter of a manager giving a secretary some responsibility in the drafting of letters and not treating her simply as a dictating machine.

Togetherness

There is another lesson to be learnt from the Trinity, one which is less developed by Christian Schumacher. It is a rather obvious point but a vital one. The God we worship as the Trinity is a God who relates well within himself. Father, Son and Spirit operate together as an immaculate unit. The internal harmony of the Trinity is a yardstick by which to measure our own 'togetherness' as people – both individually and corporately.

There is a swift objection to such a statement: harmony is all very easy for God, but it is much more difficult for us. Isn't the quality of relationship which exists in the Trinity far beyond any thought of emulation? The answer to that is both yes and no. Through becoming man in Jesus, and exposing himself to the very real temptations of being human, God allowed that unity in divine purpose to be subject to the most severe strain. If Jesus had submitted to any one of the three temptations in the wilderness God's plan for rescuing humanity would have been in ruins. In the Garden of Gethsemane, daunted by the prospect of an agonising death, Jesus asked for the cup of suffering he foresaw to be removed. But this was qualified by the words 'not what I will, but what thou wilt' (Mark 14:36).

So the operation pulled through, partly because there was a fundamental unity in purpose (Jesus understood the part his death would play in the Father's design) but also because there was a relationship of love within the Godhead. We get glimpses of this precious three-way relationship from time to time in the Gospels. At the baptism of Jesus, the Holy Spirit marks him out as special, while the voice from heaven says 'This is my beloved Son, with whom I am well pleased' (Matthew 3:17). In John 14 Jesus traces the essential continuity between the three persons of the Trinity: 'And I will pray the Father, and he will give you another Counsellor, to be with you for ever, even the Spirit of truth . . .' (14:16–17). Their three roles interlock without any sense of dissension or competition.

All this is very different from the position we often see in industry. In many companies, promising young executives are pitted against each other in order to stir them into working longer hours, grabbing a bigger chunk of the market, and wringing more profits out of their share of the business. In his fascinating book, *Odyssey: Pepsi to Apple*, John Sculley shows how the internal rivalry which was cultivated within Pepsi-Cola helped to produce aggressive performances in the market-place and contributed to Pepsi catching up with Coca-Cola in the so-called 'Cola Wars' of the 1970s. Elwyn Thomas' and Mike Woods' *The Manager's Casebook*, which seeks to teach management theory through persuading the reader to identify with the various executive directors of Vulcan, an imaginary computer company, is equally revealing in this respect. Most of the managers' attention and creative energy goes into jockeying for position amongst and against each other. They are preoccupied with forging tactical alliances, covering their backs and boosting their personal prestige within the organisation, to the neglect – so it appears – of the company making a corporate mark upon the wider world.

Yet business does not have to be like that. Where management teams have mutual confidence in their respective abilities, mutual trust in their relationships, and mutual agreement about their objectives, a different atmosphere altogether is possible. Most groups of managers take a considerable time to reach that position; the directors of Vulcan do eventually pull together, but it takes – plausibly enough – a full three years.

Companies as communities

However, the aims of a management team clearly go much further than establishing a mutuality of spirit among themselves. They want to see that spirit reproduced in the company as a whole. This is a more demanding objective still, but again it is not so idealistic as to be beyond hope of earthly realisation. At its best, a company is not far removed from Paul's vision of the church as a body, with every member playing his or her part, and love (perhaps translated in a corporate context into the language of friend and colleague) giving ballast and movement to the whole.

I saw a vivid picture of such a company in action when I visited FTL, a one-hundred-strong engineering firm in West Yorkshire which makes industrial hoses. The atmosphere it conveyed was purposeful and convivial: in short, it evoked a strong sense of community. Much of the credit for this lies with David, the company's founder and chairman, who is a committed Christian. He makes it his habit to walk round the factory regularly, knows all the workers by name, and is accessibility personified. Another key figure is Kathy, his personal assistant, who has grown beyond that job to take on the role of personnel manager as well. In what is a very flat management structure, she plays a crucial role as coach to the leaders of the various production teams. She possesses the invaluable knack of getting alongside people in a gentle way and helping them to sort out problem areas.

It was in the teams on the shop floor that the community spirit of the company was most strikingly evidenced. Christine, the leader of a predominantly female team, had eyes which shone as she spoke affectionately of her team as a happy family. The warmth of relationships is shown by the fact that they regularly come in twenty minutes early in the morning to have a good chat before settling down to the workbench. But these Yorkshire women are no dewy-eyed sentimentalists. They are quite capable of giving a good rollicking to a member of the team who is letting the others down by failing to pull her weight. They pay keen attention to production levels, and they know who to elect as a good leader.

In an age when so many of the localities where people live have lost all sense of community, when inner cities can be areas where people fear to go out and suburbs are full of people trapped in highly privatised lifestyles, a company which creates community in the work-place is doing something of priceless value. Churches must not fall into the trap of thinking they hold a monopoly of this commodity. Indeed, when people are living alongside each other every day, rather than bumping into each other after a weekly service or even sharing together in a homegroup, there is greater scope for discovering that unity of fellowship which comes through whole-hearted dedication to a common task.

We need to take to heart the message that God the Trinity is a personal being who both embodies community and is in the business of creating community. The model that David, the chairman of FTL, has of God is a rather different one to that which motivates Jim, the production manager with which this chapter began, and it seems to make for much healthier relations in the work-place.

CHAPTER 4

ADDING LIFE TO ORDER

The Wonder and Risk of Creation

Where were you when I laid the earth's foundations?
Tell me, if you know and understand.
Who fixed its dimensions? Surely you know!
Who stretched a measuring line over it?
On what do its supporting pillars rest?
Who set its corner-stone in place,
while the morning stars sang in chorus
and the sons of God all shouted for joy?

Does the rain have a father?
Who sired the drops of dew?
Whose womb gave birth to the ice,
and who was the mother of the hoar-frost in the
      skies,
which lays a stony cover over the waters
and freezes the surface of the deep?

Do you know when the mountain goats give birth?
Do you attend the wild doe when she is calving?
Can you count the months that they carry their
      young
or know the time of their delivery,
when they crouch down to open their wombs
and deliver their offspring,
when the fawns growing and thriving in the open
      country
leave and do not return?
(Job 38:4–7, 28–30; 39: 1–4, REB)

These excerpts form part of the answer God gave to Job in response to the questionings of that tormented man. They emphasise the beauty, wonder and attention to detail of God's work in creation. Job chapters 38–41 are well worth reading in conjunction with Genesis 1: the poetic splendour of these passages evoke admiration and awe at the magnificence of what God has made.

Cosmologists today are apt to describe the origins of the universe in rather more prosaic terms. The most widely accepted hypothesis of how it all began is the big bang theory. According to this, a series of rapid reductions in the temperature of the universe brought about the transformation of particles of energy into the elements of matter. Stars, galaxies and eventually various successive forms of life duly followed.

On the face of it, these two accounts do not seem to have much in common. Ancient Middle Eastern cosmology speaks of a world which sprang dramatically into being a few thousand years ago. Modern Western cosmology tells a story of simplicity evolving into complexity over 15 billion years. It adduces a range of scientific evidence to argue its case.

The cosmic architect

However, there is no reason why Christians should see acceptance of the big bang theory as a threat to their faith. Many who have studied the origins of the universe carefully are convinced that it is shot through with the evidence of Mind. Only a very special universe could support life on earth, and that is precisely the universe we inhabit. As John Polkinghorne points out in *Reason and Reality: The Relationship between Science and Theology*, quite small variations in any of the fundamental specifications of our world would have made it sterile. This is true, not only in terms of getting it off to a good start, but also of its continued history and its detailed process (e.g., the chemistry of carbon and the properties of water). It is a wonderful, life-sustaining fact that the several different layers of the atmosphere provide suitable temperatures

on the surface of the earth, shield us from the impact of
cosmic particles, and block lethal ultraviolet radiation.
To believe all this could be so by mere chance is less
plausible than the view that there is indeed a cosmic
architect – namely, God.

Both the ancient and modern cosmologies actually
suggest a God with a marvellous foresight in planning, a
truly painstaking eye for detail. From the Old Testament
we derive the impression that sophisticated life-forms
emerged ready-made, seemingly at a snap of God's finger-
tips. The story of evolution indicates a rather more
patient God who 'endowed his world with a potentiality
implanted within the delicate balance of the laws of
nature themselves' (*Reason and Reality*, p. 78). Who is
to say that the latter is any less impressive than the
former?

The design plans involved in God's great feat of cosmic
architecture are the embodiment of a profound *wisdom*.
Proverbs 8 expresses this thought in a charming way
by picturing wisdom as God's master craftsman (8:30).
'I was there', says Wisdom personified, in the midst of
all the marking of foundations and establishing of limits
which were a necessary part of God's creation. Christians
have seen fit to identify this figure with Christ, not
surprisingly in view of Paul's description of Jesus as the
'wisdom of God' in 1 Corinthians 1:24.

An initiative laden with risk

Yet for all the excellence of God's planning, his act
of creation was an initiative laden with risk. For he
created a world in which the balance of forces needed
to sustain life and make it pleasurable is very delicate.
Imbalance, threatening life and causing destruction, is a
constant danger and a persistent reality. To some extent
(philosophers of religion argue about how much), God has
allowed the world to make itself. We need not therefore be
surprised if it contains ragged edges and imperfections.
Austin Farrer, asking himself the question, what was
God's will in the Lisbon earthquake of 1753, replied

that the elements of the earth's crust should act in accordance with their nature. It is difficult to think of a more satisfactory answer. Marvel at the essential goodness of God's creation should not blind us to the fact that there are forces within it which are inhospitable, even hostile.

In our own day, the equilibrium of the conditions supporting life on earth is being disturbed in a hitherto unparalleled way. The ozone layer which filters out harmful ultra-violet radiation from the sun has been punctured by chloride gas, released from the chlorofluorocarbons (CFCs) used in fridges and aerosols. Carbon dioxide and other 'greenhouse' gases are accumulating in the atmosphere and trapping heat near to the earth's surface. Rising sea levels are likely to result. As areas of natural habitat are destroyed, so the diversity of living plants and creatures is shrinking fast. The fragile miracle which is planet earth is in grave peril.

The fact that this is so relates – ironically – to the crowning achievement of God's creation, the making of human beings. The ecological balance has been radically altered by the creatures whom God designed to continue and further his work. But it was precisely in doing so that he took his second great risk. God created a being with the alarming capability of destroying the whole operation.

Venturing into the unknown

The creation of something new is a common experience in business, and one of the most satisfying. It is very exciting to be given the responsibility of starting from scratch, of operating in a greenfield situation. There is the opportunity to stamp your particular ideas on the process; hopefully, if the operation succeeds, people will notice and credit will come your way. Being in at the start usually carries with it power and influence. It is interesting that in Colossians 1 the same word *arche* is used to mean both 'power' (v.16) and 'beginning' (v.18). The two ideas were closely linked in Greek thought, and the same is true today.

The other side of the coin is that to take the initiative is to accept risk. Every businessman who has started a new company, headed a new project or even championed a new idea knows that. More new companies fail to survive their first year than go on to prove a success. There is never any shortage of people waiting to say 'I told you so' when some bright idea proves impractical or unmarketable. It is not surprising that employees who are principally concerned to survive until retirement keep their heads down and their acts of initiative to a minimum. Not everybody has the temperament to be a risk-taker.

There are of course ways of reducing risk. Detailed, meticulous planning, the sort of planning that went into God's design of the human eye or the passage of the seasons, is one of them. Attracting a talented team, individuals who have distinctive skills but can work well together, is a second. Thoroughly researching and testing the potential market is a third. But when we take initiatives in business, there is bound by very definition to be some element of venturing into the unknown. We experience vulnerability because we make ourselves critically dependent, in certain areas, on the response of others.

I spent a fascinating day behind the scenes on a building site in Leicester, watching the construction of a new shopping centre. Here the initiative in an act of creation lay with the firm of property developers. But it was striking how many other parties were involved in what was going on: a major construction company with responsibility for overall site management, numerous sub-contractors carrying out specialist tasks, the firm of architects who had designed the centre, quantity surveyors checking on the state of the foundations, and retailers large and small to whom shopping units were being let. When all these different parties are working together in a smoothly integrated process, the effect is very impressive. But the reality often falls short of that. Grit gets into the machine. Materials are not delivered on time, the architect changes his plans, job specifications prove more difficult to put into effect than anticipated, and fire authorities demand the inclusion of extra fire escapes. Because there are penalty clauses attached to late completion, any delay becomes the subject of fierce debate. Which of the various parties is to blame for the fact that work is running a month behind schedule? Contracting work out to other people is the name of the game, but it entails enormous hassle. What started as a process of well-intentioned co-operative endeavour easily degenerates into a situation resembling corporate war.

In many working situations of this type, a setback takes place which is quite unexpected. One of the retailers in the shopping centre under construction had requested an unusual feature in their unit, a centrally positioned escalator. A month before my visit, this retailer had gone bankrupt. The property developers were now experiencing severe difficulty trying to find a replacement retailer willing to incorporate this distinctive, already constructed feature into their premises.

Human creations, just like God's, are full of pain and struggle along the way. We put ourselves into the hands of others, who cannot always deliver the goods as quickly as we would like. Along with many other qualities, considerable measures of patience, determination and negotiating skill are required to see the job through to completion.

Betrayal in the boardroom?

Nor is it the case that being the moving spirit behind an organisation guarantees one control over it indefinitely. There are many stories like that of Martin, chairman of a high technology company in the south east of England which expanded rapidly during most of the 1980s. Martin is a talented scientist. He developed the initial technology on which the company was based, and is proud of the reputation it acquired, not only for being in the forefront of technological development, but also as a caring company with excellent staff morale. For the first five years he combined the roles of chairman and managing director, but in 1985, recognising that the management skills in the company needed strengthening and that he himself was suffering from over-work, he brought in an experienced businessman, Norman, as managing director. However, Martin remained in a full-time executive role as Chairman.

For the first three years the arrangement appears to work well. The company's sales and profits are set on a steadily growing curve, and a successful share offer marks its launch as a public limited company. But then it is hit by the recession, rather earlier than most hi-tech companies at a comparable stage of development. 1989 sees a slump in profits, a small reduction in dividend, and Martin coming under an increasing amount of pressure from voices both inside and outside the firm. There are three main problem areas.

Firstly, a small subsidiary company, started in France in 1988, is causing Martin a major headache. With the advent of the Single European Market in view, it seemed to make sense to have a base in Europe, but a substantial siphoning of profits from the British operation is proving necessary to get it satisfactorily established. Questions about whether or not the company should continue in this direction are being asked.

Secondly, relations between Martin and Norman are becoming increasingly strained. Norman has requested a clearer delineation of the roles of chairman and managing director. He argues that Martin should stick to the areas of product strategy, making contacts and public relations, whereas Martin cannot help but be interested in questions of financial detail and handling people. Norman feels that Martin is getting in his way, while Martin feels that Norman is trying to marginalise him.

Thirdly, the company is lagging behind in its Research and Development programme. It has expanded its range of products to six, all linked to the original technology; the life expectancy of the product range is estimated to be another four years. What is going to happen after that?

Martin is aware of an increasingly restless spirit among the Board of Directors, but it still comes as a major shock when, at a meeting early in 1990, the Board tell him that

they think he should resign. They propose a restructuring
of roles at the top with Norman being given full responsibility for the day-to-day running of the company as chief
executive and a high profile outsider being brought in as
non-executive chairman. They tell Martin that they think
his main skills lie in the scientific area and say that they
would be very happy to continue using him on a contract
basis as a technological consultant.

Martin feels that his baby is being snatched away
from him. That which he lovingly brought to birth has
expressed its independence of him in – to his eyes – a
totally insubordinate manner. More famous names than
his (Steve Jobs of Apple, George Davies of Next) know
what it is like to be the founder entrepreneur who is
sacked. It can be a necessary, if painful, step for a board
of directors to take when such a person stands in the way
of the company's future progress. But there is no denying
the pain of the creator-parent. It is an anguish close to the
heart of God, as the following passage from the prophet
Hosea makes clear:

> When Israel was a child, I loved him,
>   and out of Egypt I called my son.
> The more I called them,
>   the more they went from me;
> they kept sacrificing to the Baals,
>   and burning incense to idols.
>
> Yet it was I who taught Ephraim to walk,
>   I took them up in my arms;
>   but they did not know that I healed them.
> I led them with cords of compassion,
>   with the bands of love,
> and I became to them as one
>   who eases the yoke on their jaws,
>   and I bent down to them and fed them.
> (Hosea 11:1–4)

I take the story of Martin a stage further in chapter
9. In the meantime, there are further fruitful areas

of comparison between divine and human creativity to
explore.

Stability – the springboard for change

There is no mistaking that the sequence of events described
in Genesis 1 has a logical order about it. God creates night
and day, heaven and earth, land and sea, sun and moon. He
puts into place the essential building-blocks of his universe,
creating the conditions for a more exciting act to follow.
Then he sets about filling his earth with life: vegetation,
fruit-bearing trees, sea monsters, winged birds, cattle and
creeping things. Last of all he creates men and women.

The writer of Genesis telescopes the whole saga of
creation into six memorable action-packed days. We now
believe that the process probably took billions of years. No
matter, the important message is the same: the creator of
the universe took pains to install a sound structure before
turning his hand to something truly inventive.

Modern management literature is full of talk about corporate culture. It analyses the different styles of management and operating which permeate different companies.
One of the most instructive discussions occurs in John
Sculley's *Odyssey: Pepsi to Apple*. Sculley was chief
marketing man at Pepsi during the 1970s, and President
by the time he was thirty-eight. Having been instrumental in raising Pepsi-Cola to the big league, a corporate
giant alongside Coca-Cola, Sculley was then lured away
to become Chief Executive Officer of the up-and-coming
Apple Computer Company. It was a difficult decision to
leave, but Sculley was eventually persuaded to move by
the line: 'Do you want to spend the rest of your life selling
sugared water, or do you want to change the world?'

What Sculley discovered in Apple was a company
with a culture diametrically opposed in almost every
respect to that he had experienced previously. At Pepsi,
board meetings were elaborate in their formality and a
means of reinforcing pecking order in the organisation.
At Apple everyone dressed informally and arguments
were wide-ranging and unpredictable. Apple, too, had a

major corporate rival in IBM, but unlike Pepsi, thought
in terms of developing sharply differentiated products
and of creating a whole new generation of customers.
Sculley came to understand the difference as one between
second wave and *third wave* companies, Pepsi being an
outstanding example of the second wave, industrial age,
and Apple being an equally outstanding example of the
third wave, information age.

Sculley sums up the difference in terms of a series of
contrasting management paradigms:

Characteristic	Second Wave	Third Wave
Organisation	Hierarchy	Network
Output	Market share	Market creation
Focus	Institution	Individual
Style	Structured	Flexible
Source of strength	Stability	Change
Structure	Self-sufficiency	Interdependencies
Culture	Tradition	Genetic code
Mission	Goals/strategic plans	Identity/ directions/values
Leadership	Dogmatic	Inspirational
Quality	Affordable best	No compromise
Expectations	Security	Personal growth
Status	Title and rank	Making a difference
Resource	Cash	Information
Advantage	Better sameness	Meaningful differences
Motivation	To complete	To build

(*Odyssey: Pepsi to Apple*, p. 95)

Most of these contrasts are self-explanatory. By 'genetic
code' Sculley means an imprint of the company's identity which is evident in all that it does, but may be
expressed in a great variety of ways. Unlike tradition,
it is forward-looking. The genetic code at Apple consisted essentially of the vision of its founder, Steve

Jobs: a society in which everyone was able to make use of a highly-powered informational tool, the personal computer. In seeking to realise that vision, it is engaged in a restless search to make its existing products as obsolete as quickly as possible. Like many other companies of its type, Apple is constantly seeking to present the customer with 'meaningful differences' which will prompt further purchasing.

Sculley thinks that though second wave companies have their strengths, third wave companies are the emerging form, not only for hi-tech companies, but for all institutions. This is because the source of their strength lies in their readiness for change. They are willing to adapt to changes in social habits, customer interests and the economy. Their organisation is highly flexible, often relying on a network of independent business partners.

The pace of change in business today is without doubt inexorable. Those who glory in past success and rest on their laurels are soon knocked out of their complacency. A good example of this is the Swiss watch industry, which prided itself on its elegant watches made according to traditional mechanical design. The development of new electronic digital watches, spearheaded by companies from Japan, took the industry almost fatally by surprise. The opening up of world markets, the breakdown of cartels (official and unofficial) and the ingenuity of technological development are combining to put a premium on rapid change which was not true of the industrial scene thirty years ago.

If readiness for change is a condition of survival, a key question for companies becomes how to encourage an innovative culture. The answer seems to lie in creating an atmosphere where new ideas are welcomed rather than stifled, where people are actively encouraged to experiment with alternative ways of doing things and to test new products in the market-place. Often there is just no way of knowing if something will work unless you try it. No scientific process of investigation can tell you in advance; it is all down to unforeseen contingency factors. But the willingness

to innovate means you are able to take advantage of
it.

Nevertheless, it is possible to take 'thriving on chaos'
(the catchphrase used by one famous management theorist, Tom Peters) to a rather ridiculous extreme. Putting
all its emphasis on new products and new processes, a
company can end up in a confused condition wasting
vital reserves of energy and seeing nothing through to
its proper conclusion. It is a mistake to try to change
everything at once: most people are by nature quite
conservative, and they need reassuring signs of stability
amidst the change. Often an unwavering commitment
to core values (comparable to Sculley's genetic code)
will serve both employees and customers in good stead
during a radical reorganisation in corporate affairs. If a
company has built up a well-earned reputation for the
care it demonstrates for its employees or the speed with
which it carries out repairs, it would be most unwise to
jettison this for the sake of spurious short-term goals.

Riding the whirlwind

There is a special onus on the business leader in the
midst of all this. He or she has a responsibility to stay
calm and be selective about major strategic innovations.
Peter Benton, former Director General of the British
Institute of Management and one-time Managing Director of British Telecom, is fond of citing a telling passage
from Addison's poem about Marlborough at the Battle of
Blenheim to illustrate this disposition:

> 'Twas then great Marlborough's mighty soul
>   was proved,
> Calm and serene he drives the furious blast,
> Rides in the whirlwind and directs the storm.

There are echoes here of the closing chapters of Job, for
it was out of the whirlwind that God spoke. To demonstrate cool discernment and serene unflappability when
market conditions are unstable is surely a God-given

attribute. Marlborough himself was a focus of stability at Blenheim. Similar individuals are needed in leadership positions today.

John Sculley experienced crisis two years after his move to Apple. Having expanded rapidly through 1984 and 1985, the company found itself lumbered with computers it was unable to sell in 1986. This temporary loss of strategic direction was partly due to a deterioration in Sculley's relationship with Steve Jobs, an episode which ended with Jobs leaving the company. Sculley then knew he had to act fast to save Apple.

One important lesson which Sculley draws from this crisis experience is the importance of not panicking. He gives this advice:

> Only concern yourself with those things that you can do something about. The things you can't do something about shouldn't keep you awake at night. To keep a clear head, it's important to get some time off alone. You need perspective from the crisis. I gained it by getting up each morning at four-thirty for a long run on the road in the cold darkness. (*Odyssey: Pepsi to Apple*, p. 267)

Although Sculley gives no evidence of any Christian commitment, this is impressive advice which the Christian manager does well to emulate. Concerning oneself only with the things one has power to influence is fully consonant with an attitude of trust in God. 'Therefore do not be anxious about tomorrow, for tomorrow will be anxious for itself. Let the day's own trouble be sufficient for the day', said Jesus (Matthew 6:34). Nevertheless, each day does require concerted attention, and a period of quiet reflection is an admirable way to start it. For many Christians, a disciplined pattern of prayer at the beginning of the day provides a still centre which is crucial to their peace of mind. This may well be quite short – Sculley's 4.30 a.m. start reveals a man of unusual constitution! But spending time in quiet with God, whether it is in the bedroom or while walking to catch the train, helps to give a sense of perspective and an objectivity in the making of tough decisions. Christians have their own spiritual resources for riding the whirlwind.

When Sculley comes to describe what he actually did to avert the crisis, it is striking how much he drew on his experience at Pepsi. He introduced a much more functional type of organisation, appointing the most disciplined and experienced executives to the most important control jobs. He was also prepared to cut costs in a decisive way, cutting deeper than appeared necessary at the time; this involved closing a plant in Texas. For all his apparent conversion to a third wave style of company, Sculley acted in a second wave manner when the chips were down. While he still invested boldly in research and development as a sign of his confidence in Apple's future, he imposed financial discipline on an organisation which had begun to spend money like water.

Newton and Einstein

Stability then is the precursor for change, discipline the context for the taking of initiative. It is as true of our own acts of human creation as it was of God's creation.

An interesting analogy can be drawn between Sculley's second and third wave style of companies and the two dominant scientific approaches of our modern age, those associated with the names of Newton and Einstein. In the seventeenth century, Sir Isaac Newton formulated the laws of motion and gravitation. This understanding of the action of forces on bodies made possible the vast array of mechanical innovations characteristic of the Industrial Revolution. The emphasis lay on order, predictability and principles of sound construction.

The Newtonian approach is still recognised as valid for velocities and dimensions which fall within our normal experience. But at the beginning of the twentieth century physicists started to explore dimensions of reality untouched by their Newtonian forbears. Albert Einstein (in company with other notable physicists) showed that Newton's laws do not account for velocities approaching the speed of light and dimensions on a subatomic scale. Here we encounter phenomena that are not so amenable to straightforward explanation. Light has been shown to have a dual nature, behaving as a wave under certain conditions and as a particle under other conditions. Quantum theory explains the behaviour of atoms, but it makes allowance for the unexpected, having discovered that this part of the physical world is so sensitive to disturbance that less probable events are apt to occur. Physical reactions take place with potentially creative results, but there is a higher degree of uncertainty or randomness about them than scientists brought up in a Newtonian school of thought could ever have imagined. Here the emphasis lies on relativity, unpredictability and creative power.

Science has to harness the insights of both these intellectual giants. It cannot credibly turn its back either on Newton or on Einstein. A nuclear power station is able to function because both Newton and Einstein were correct: the one provided the principles which enable the plant to be safely constructed, the other helped to explain how a nuclear reaction takes place. A similar synthesis is required in the realm of business. Stability is a springboard for change, order needs to be saddled to creativity. Exciting new initiatives can then take place.

CHAPTER 5

MANAGING PLANET EARTH

The God-given Role of Humanity

In Christian theology, human beings are said to be made in the *image of God*. It is an important concept, though the actual phrase occurs only a few times in the Bible: most famously in the creation story ('God created man in his own image, in the image of God he created him . . .') but rarely thereafter. What does it mean, and what are its implications?

First, it is important to be clear that humanity as a whole bears the image of God. It is not the preserve of those who have Christian faith. Two key biblical passages speak of human beings in general as warranting respect and protection precisely because they have been made in the image of God. In his covenant with Noah, God warns against the shedding of human blood because he has made man in his own image (Genesis 9:1–6). In James 3:9, there is a similar warning against violence of the tongue: 'With the tongue we praise our Lord and Father, and with it we curse men, who have been made in God's likeness' (NIV). The lesson is plain: all human beings possess a basic dignity because they were created in God's image, and that dignity should be respected. In this sense 'image' may be thought of in terms of a divine *stamp*: a mark that has been indelibly stamped on a person, and which communicates the message 'Beware – this is sacred ground!' For the Christian in business this provides a reminder that everyone (janitors, secretaries and part-time workers included) is to be treated with respect.

Second, the *content* of the image of God is not to be reduced to any particular human attribute. The great theologians of the past tended to locate it in terms of such characteristics as human rationality, moral responsibility or awareness of a spiritual dimension to life. Contemporary theologians have preferred to speak of other attributes (arguably ones rooted more securely in the immediate context of the key reference in Genesis 1:26–27), like human relatedness, the capacity to be creative or stewardship over the rest of creation.

But why should the divine image not take in the entirety of the human person? The different views all have something important to say in what they affirm, but they are narrow – even reductionist – when they seek to exclude rival interpretations. All these characteristics are present in human beings, though clearly, particular capabilities will be more developed in some individuals than others. What should also be true is that each is enhanced by the experience of becoming a Christian.

At this point it is important to note another way in which the word 'image' is used in the Bible. Human beings can be seen as the image of God inasmuch as they *mirror* God, i.e., they reflect God in his goodness and glory. They can only be such a mirror if they are turned towards God and living in a fundamentally right relationship with him. Because human beings are sinful and have rebelled aginst God, most of the time they offer a very poor reflection of God to one another. In short, the divine image is marred.

This 'mirror' way of understanding is essential in order to make sense of most of the New Testament references to the image of God. Paul speaks of our human need to be changed into an authentic divine likeness. Christ is the one perfect image of God: 'He is the image of the invisible God, the firstborn over all creation' (Colossians 1:15 NIV). God's purpose is that we should be conformed to the likeness of his Son (Romans 8:29), so that we are instructed to 'put on the new nature, created after the likeness of God in true righteousness and holiness' (Ephesians 4:24). The new self is being renewed in knowledge, in the image of its Creator (Colossians 3:10). The implication of all this is that human beings comprise a pale shadow of the divine image until God's redemptive work takes effect in them.

When a person becomes a Christian, therefore, changes can be expected in such areas as these:

* Sharpening of the mind
* Sensitising of the conscience
* Exploration of life's spiritual dimension
* Developing one's relationships with God and other people
* Spurred creativity
* Deepening of concern about the environment

The progress we make in each of these areas does not constitute an actual claim to the designation 'image of God'. But it does say something about how faithfully we are reflecting that image.

Rulers of creation

The last of the qualities mentioned above, relating to our stewardship of creation, is especially relevant to the area of business. It is therefore appropriate to consider it further.

Many biblical scholars observe that in Genesis 1–2 we appear to have two distinct accounts of creation, the one starting at 1:1 and the other at 2:4. They reflect different theological interests and emphases. One difference is the account they give of humanity's place in relation to the created order. In Genesis 1, men and women are told to 'subdue' the earth and 'have dominion' over living creatures. The Hebrew words used are quite violent in tone; there is a clear implication that if nature is to satisfy human needs, considerable force may have to be exerted upon it. This is an unpopular text with many ecologists because they feel it has encouraged human beings' exploitative and destructive instincts *vis-à-vis* the rest of creation. They wish that Christians down the ages had been guided rather more by Genesis 2,

where the picture of man is much more suggestive of the
caretaker. God gives Adam the twofold charge of looking
after the Garden of Eden and naming the animals. The
atmosphere here is that of friendly benevolence, not a
struggle for survival.

In the present ecological crisis, it is not surprising that
many Christians feel more comfortable reading Genesis
2:15–20 than Genesis 1:28. Alternatively they try to
remove the violence from the language of the latter
and reinterpret 'dominion' in benevolent terms, as a
responsible discharge of office with the welfare of one's
subjects firmly in view. The effect of that is to go some way
towards harmonising the two accounts. A more honest
response is to acknowledge the distinctive nuances of the
two accounts and say that each has something important
to say about our relationship with the natural world. It
is sentimental nonsense to imagine that some element
of subduing the earth is unnecessary. Pests have to be
controlled, wilderness needs to be tamed, water has to be
found. The human explorer who ventures into the desert
or the jungle experiences nature 'red in tooth and claw'.
But this is not the whole story. In his role of gardener,
man has the leisure and opportunity to cultivate and
classify. His relationship with creation can then be more
that of companion, rather less of master.

Psalm 8 sheds further important light upon this issue:

> O Lord, our Lord,
>   how majestic is thy name in all the earth!
>
> Thou whose glory above the heavens is chanted
>   by the mouth of babes and infants,
> thou hast founded a bulwark because of thy foes,
>   to still the enemy and the avenger.
>
> When I look at thy heavens, the work of thy fingers,
>   the moon and the stars which thou hast
>   established;
> what is man that thou art mindful of him,
>   and the son of man that thou dost care for him?
>
> Yet thou hast made him little less than God,

and dost crown him with glory and honour.
Thou hast given him dominion over the works of thy
    hands;
    thou hast put all things under his feet,
all sheep and oxen, and also the beasts of the field,
the birds of the air, and the fish of the sea,
    whatever passes along the paths of the sea.

O Lord, our Lord,
    how majestic is thy name in all the earth!

God has made man *ruler* of creation. There is no mistak-
ing the language of royalty in this psalm. Human beings
have animals, birds, fishes and by inference the rest of
God's creation as their subjects. It is strong language.
Without doubt Psalm 8 stands closer to Genesis 1 than
Genesis 2.

At the same time, we should note the magnificent
paradox this psalm contains. On the one hand the writer
proclaims that man is 'little less than God'. On the other
hand he is lost in wonder that the God who made heaven,
moon and stars should even think about human beings.
The psalmist proclaims our smallness and our greatness
in consecutive breaths. After spelling out the scope of
human rule he returns at once to the theme of God's
majesty. Psalm 8 is a song to instil humility, not to
prompt arrogant human aggrandisement.

The concept of human beings as rulers of creation
should be affirmed, but with two cautionary notes. The
first is that as rulers we are not absolute, but accountable.
'The earth is the Lord's and the fullness thereof', is how
another psalm begins (24:1). It is God's gracious provision
to us as a dwelling-place, and should be treated with
respect. The second is that in the New Testament Jesus
radically reinterprets the notion of ruler. Contrasting the
rule that he embodied and his disciples should aspire to
with the rule exercised in the Gentile world, he said that
'whoever would be first among you must be slave of all.
For the Son of man also came not to be served but to serve
. . .' (Mark 10:44–45). There is indeed a legitimate place

for human beings *serving* the sheep, the birds and the
fishes. In our own day the most practical expression of
that may well consist in decontaminating land, cleaning
up the air, and ceasing to pollute the sea.

Tapping the world's resources

A crucial part of the task of managing creation is the
judicious utilisation of the world's resources. God has so
constructed the world that most of its resources require
some process of extraction, conversion and refinement
before they can be of benefit. This is true both of resources
which lie above the earth's surface (cotton to make shirts,
sugar to make sweets) and those which lie below (coal and
gas to provide warmth and energy). Here lies the essence
of manufacturing industry. The more sophisticated the
industry, of course, the more processed is the nature of
the primary materials, such as the micro-chip in the construction of computers. Many of the heavy manufacturing
industries have passed their heyday, but it is erroneous to
think we will ever change to a wholly service economy. As
long as human beings survive on planet earth, they will be
endeavouring to develop material resources in ever more
efficient and ingenious ways.

In terms of world history, it has taken human beings
a very long time to learn to tap these resources. In 1787
the French chemist Nicolas Leblanc devised a method of
producing soda, the first chemical to be used on a large
scale (in glass and soap manufacture). The principle of
electromagnetic induction was discovered by Michael
Faraday in 1831, and electricity first used to light streets
and public buildings in the mid-1870s. The first oil
well was drilled in Pennsylvania in 1859. But once the
industrial revolution was truly under way, it spawned
invention after invention. The last two hundred years
have seen a fantastic flourishing of technological creativity. Business has provided the medium through which
scientific research and development have been tailored to
human needs and desires. In the wake of manufacturing
industry has come a whole sphere of ancillary services,

notably financial services which have provided venture
capital and helped to manage the element of risk.

Western culture, and British society in particular,
has always had its share of critics who are inclined to
denigrate the process of industrialisation and to take
the marvels of technology for granted. They bemoan
much of what has happened in the last two centuries
as a flight from a wholesome, simple lifestyle into an
obsession with material possessions. Christians often go
along with this critique of materialism but they need to
beware of hypocrisy in doing so. Do we really regret the
advent of the washing-machine which eliminates long
hours of tedious labour (especially housewives' labour)
or the telephone which quickens communication? It is
true that an ever greater profusion of material goods
stimulates the motive of greed, and sometimes leads to
individuals stockpiling possessions which they never put
to meaningful use. But what industry ceaselessly tries to
supply is an improved version of what has gone before,
the replacement of what is becoming obsolete by a new
product which serves the customer significantly better.
It is obvious that for the purposes of an author, and
many others besides, a word processor represents an
enormously valuable advance on even the most sophisticated typewriter. We should be grateful for products
which genuinely add to the quality of our lives. There
is no reason why those who make them, or even those
who advertise them, should be objects of scorn.

What do we mean by wealth creation?

The notion of adding value to original resource provides
the most satisfactory way of understanding the concept
of *wealth creation*. Few phrases in recent times have
been more contentious than this one. Associated in most
people's minds with the 'enterprise culture' of the 1980s,
it has been advocated boldly and attacked fiercely. Yet
much of this debate has been sterile in character; the
pugilists have been talking past each other. The crux
of the problem has lain with the lack of agreement over

what the phrase 'creation of wealth' actually means. Even those who line up together as supporters of wealth creation often differ significantly in their definition.

On the one hand, there are those who understand wealth straightforwardly in terms of money. A wealthy person is understood as someone who has plenty of cash in the bank or the financial assets to realise it. 'Creating wealth' tends to be an abhorrent notion to those who think it is principally a matter of making rich people even richer, with the gulf between them and the poorer end of society widening. This was after all a trend which tended to characterise the 1980s.

To make the simple equation: wealth = money is therefore to be assured of a negative reaction in some quarters. But as with technology, so it is worth warning against a perverse snobbery with regard to money. The simple fact is that you can do constructive things with money that you cannot do without it. Money funds public hospitals and schools; it pays for agricultural tools and irrigation systems in the Third World. When people gasp at the big profits made by some leading companies, they tend to forget the contribution these companies make to society through the tax they pay. A thriving business sector is good news for those who administer public services because it means more money can come their way through the Treasury. Peter Morgan, Director General of the Institute of Directors, and a staunch defender of wealth creation, understands wealth not in terms of individual wealth or personal riches, but the material prosperity of the general population.

Nevertheless, wealth is not a straightforward synonym for money. In most people's minds it means something broader. The question is how broad. Miles, the unconventional director whom we met in chapter 1, has a very radical understanding of wealth. He thinks that it is anything which contributes significantly to human wellbeing. A personnel director who introduces an excellent system of staff appraisal creates wealth, as does the course designer who creates a delightful golf links. Extending this principle to the national scale, the scenery of the Alps comprises an important part of the wealth of Austria; a free democratic system is the wealth for which people shackled by rigid totalitarian set-ups long. Then there is the category of spiritual wealth. Miles is fond of quoting the 'unsearchable riches of Christ' (Ephesians 3:8) as a wealth which out-compares all others.

Clearly, Miles has an important insight here. 'Wealth' is sometimes used in this broader sense, and there are many things in life we value greatly to which it is impossible to put a price. But if we make this general use of the word 'wealth' into its primary or normative use, we are liable to create linguistic confusion. Wealth should not be equated with the wider concept of wellbeing. In most people's minds, it is always likely to retain a strong financial connotation.

The concept of 'creating wealth' as 'adding value to original resource' has the advantage of drawing on both these contrasting ideas, while being hamstrung by neither. It acknowledges that creating wealth is about making money: a company that markets a product successfully will do that. But it is also about adding to the quality of people's lives: a company that turns out a really useful product will do that also. Making a profit and serving the customer are two different sides of the same coin 'wealth creation'. Eliminate either one, and you have something which is a pale shadow of true wealth. There are other valuable things which a company can do (such as providing satisfying employment, the sort of working atmosphere described at David's firm in chapter 3) but these do not – strictly speaking – constitute wealth creation.

The cost of industrial progress

Nevertheless, we should not speak about adding value to resources too glibly. The critics of modern industrial society do have a valid objection on their side. The fact is that in extracting, refining and developing material resources, human beings have often destroyed value as fast as they have added it. In the course of firing the

power-stations which keep our homes warm and our
factories light, electricity generation processes make the
air steadily more polluted.

Acid rain from power-stations in Yorkshire drifts across
the North Sea and kills trees and fishes in Scandinavia
and Germany. Nobody marks this down on the debit
sheet of the electricity company, and the damage done
is difficult to quantify, though those who specialise in
environmental audits are improving techniques of doing
so. But clearly it illustrates that wealth creation has a
double edge. The benefits brought are real (the electricity
generated from the power station makes possible the
performance of life-saving operations) but they also entail
considerable costs.

The environmental situation we find ourselves in today
is full of ironies and complexities. We already possess the
technology to solve some of the problems we have created.
Technically there is no difficulty in removing sulphur, the
exporter of acid rain, from power-stations, but the cost
involved is formidable. So far Britain has shown much
less willingness than (West) Germany – a country in
this respect more sinned against than sinning – to instal
a systematic desulphurisation programme. Initiatives of
this type need to be taken nationally (the electricity
companies cannot be expected to bear the cost on their
own) but spending taxpayers' money on such programmes
is not the issue on which elections are won.

Some environmental issues are difficult to evaluate
because, as yet, there is relatively little agreement about
the essential facts, let alone what should be done about
them. Meteorologists argue about whether the recent
rash of hot summers provides proof of global warm-
ing or falls within the cycle of natural variability. In
investigating specific issues of environmental concern,
one becomes aware of the disparity in accounts of what is
going on. Environmental pressure groups paint the worst
possible scenarios, while vested interests try to persuade
the public that there is nothing to fear.

This tendency is strikingly evident in the ongoing controversy surrounding the use of nuclear power. The areas

where interpretation of the empirical data is disputed include:

Economics What are the true financial figures? Is nuclear power an irresistibly cheap or prohibitively expensive form of energy? Can it only survive through hefty state subsidies? How do its costs compare with those of using existing or alternative sources of fuel?

Technology What are the arguments for and against reprocessing nuclear fuel? Is this to be applauded because it represents recycling on a massive scale, or spurned because it is cheaper to make new fuel out of freshly mined uranium? How prolific are the supplies of uranium?

Safety How does the safety record of the nuclear industry compare with that of other industries? Is there or is there not a significant incidence of leukaemia in the surrounding location of nuclear power stations? Does the threat, however remote, of another Chernobyl, decide or muddy the argument?

Waste Disposal What are the respective dangers posed by low-level, intermediate-level and high-level waste? Are the processes which have been devised for containing them satisfactory? What about the risk of accidents in transit?

All these areas of concern warrant close and detailed attention. Very often people jump to hasty conclusions because they are prejudiced in one direction or the other. On one side nuclear energy is too easily tarred with all the negative and destructive associations bound up with nuclear weapons, while the creative possibilities offered by the interaction of neutrons and Uranium 235 atoms are ignored. On the other side, the effort and ingenuity exercised in developing the industry to the state where it is today can blind its defenders to the cost involved in sustaining it.

We live in an age when serious issues are regularly

trivialised, where the media contributes to polarisation
on matters of major concern because it forces moral
protagonists into boxing corners to fight each other. In
this climate it is not easy to get at the facts, to make
evaluations objectively in a cool-headed way. But that
is a very important part of the Christian's calling. In
our moral judgements as in other areas we need to heed
Paul's words in Romans 12:2: 'Do not be conformed to this
world but be transformed by the renewal of your mind,
that you may prove what is the will of God, what is good
and acceptable and perfect.' 'Prove' in this context has
the meaning of 'discern', 'identify through a process of
weighing and testing'. A renewed mind chews issues over
carefully and prayerfully. It neither eschews fashionable
opinion automatically nor follows it slavishly. The gift
of sober judgement is crucial to discharging the task of
managing planet earth in a responsible fashion.

CHAPTER 6

FACING THE REALITY OF SIN

The Residue of the Fall

Robert Jackall is an American sociologist who decided to make a study of the world of corporate management. He wished to examine the work that managers do, the intricate social contexts of their organisation, the manner in which they strive for success, and the habits of mind they develop. Above all, Jackall wanted to investigate the occupational ethics with which managers survive and flourish in their world. His concern was with what actually went on, down at the desk or out in the field, as distinct from the ethical stances publicly professed by the company.

Jackall had considerable difficulty finding companies willing to co-operate with him in his research. But he eventually found three large companies which were willing to allow him to carry out extensive interviews with managers at a wide variety of levels. The three companies were in textiles, chemicals and public relations respectively. Jackall records and analyses his findings in *Moral Mazes: The World of Corporate Managers*. It is an astutely observed, brilliantly written book.

Jackall shows how on one level, American companies are highly bureaucratic. Bureaucracy is characterised by close attention to details and orders, an adherence to standardised procedures, thorough written documentation of daily business in well-maintained files, and impartial, fair treatment under the law. But this is not the whole story. Features of personal loyalty, favouritism, informality and operating outside the law also permeate the corporate ethos. The outshot is a hybrid bureaucracy which bears comparison with the courts of European

royalty. The individual survives and flourishes by curry-
ing favour with powerful officials up the line who stand
close to the ruler.

Jackall portrays a world in which managers are obsessed
by an all-consuming desire for promotion, and a corrosive
anxiety about their perception by those who matter in
the company. It is a world which presents a comfortable and benign exterior to the outside world. Corporate
headquarters are notable for their plush carpets, potted
trees, fine pictures, leather upholstery and attractive
receptionists. Enquires from the public are dealt with
eagerly and politely. The inner reality of this world,
however, is one of tension and conflict. Few managers
are openly at war with their colleagues, and it is crucial
never to show public disloyalty to one's immediate boss.
One needs to be seen as a good team player. But to
stay on the ascent, managers are constantly vying for
positional advantage. They take every opportunity to
mark themselves out as different and seek the organi-
sational limelight.

Working in a company can easily assume the character
of playing a game – albeit a game people are taking
desperately seriously. Learning the need to exercise strict
self-control, they cultivate the trick of masking both
emotion and intention behind a bland, agreeable public
face.

> In a world where appearances – in the broadest
> sense – mean everything, the wise and ambitious
> manager learns to cultivate assiduously the proper,
> prescribed modes of appearing. He dispassionately
> takes stock of himself, treating himself as an object,
> as a commodity. He analyses his strengths and
> weaknesses and decides what he needs to change in
> order to survive and flourish in his organisation. And
> then he systematically undertakes a programme to
> reconstruct his image, his publicly avowed attitudes
> or ideas, or whatever else in his self-presentation
> that might need adjustment. (*Moral Mazes*, p. 59)

Covering your tracks

The result, in Jackall's view, is a highly narcissistic type
of person, one who is constantly re-examining his own
performance as if glancing in a mirror. In this world,
appearances count for more than reality. Managers recognise that there is often precious little justice in who gets
promoted and who doesn't. Contingent and capricious
factors determine much in corporate life. Judgements
made about managers' performance can be lamentably
superficial. Whoever is currently in charge of an area may
be counted responsible for a financial deficit even if he or
she has inherited others' mistakes. Others become adept
at starving their part of the business of important capital
expenditure and thereby giving a misleading impression
of high returns. But precisely because life is often unjust,
it is crucial to manipulate appearances as much as
possible. When the company hits trouble and blame
starts to be apportioned, you run fast and you cover your
tracks. In order to eradicate oneself from trouble-spots
satisfactorily, it is necessary to have established strategic
alliances, but in such a way that one has never committed
oneself irrevocably to somebody else's personal fortunes.
Changing tack without losing face is the name of a very
demanding game.

Jackall thinks that in such a climate the principal
managerial virtue becomes an essential, pervasive and
thoroughgoing *pragmatism*. He relates two incidents in
the companies he investigated of individuals who made
moral protests about dubious practices. One, who worked
in a company's medical department, sought to draw
senior managers' attention to the fact that most of the
textile workers had suffered substantial hearing loss
as a result of the high level of noise experienced in
the mill. The other was a company accountant who
came across a number of financial irregularities (bribery payments, doctored invoices and misappropriation
of pension funds) in the course of his work. Both found
themselves treated with a mixture of indifference and
hostility; one decided to leave his company and the

other was fired. The latter came to the sad conclusion
that 'What is right in the corporation is what the guy
above you wants from you. That's what morality is in
the corporation' (*Moral Mazes*, p. 109). When Jackall
interviewed others in the organisations about the fate
which befell these two individuals, they expressed very
little sympathy. They saw the violations which upset the
company whistle-blowers as commonplaces of corporate
life. Even when they acknowledged matters of principle
were involved, they thought business was all about a
trade-off between principle and expediency. There was
a ready acceptance that, in this trade-off, expediency
usually wins.

It would be dangerous to take Jackall's account as a
standard description of business. His sample of companies was small, and they were limited to the United
States. Nor can it be denied that many of the attitudes
and habits he describes are found in other spheres of life
also. Both the academic and ecclesiastical worlds have
their share of manipulators and unscrupulous operators.
Indeed, my experience of the three different areas –
university, church and business respectively – leads me
to the conclusion that business often compares well with
the other two in terms of direct, honest communication.

Nevertheless, those with extensive experience of corporate life, in Britain as well as America, know that the
phenomenon described by Jackall does exist. Pockets of
the business world can develop where people practice the
arts of deception and dishonesty so often that it becomes
part of their constitution. In this situation, truth itself
can be a card which is played to catch the other person
out. There is a true story of two company chairmen
who once met on Liverpool's Lime Street station. 'You
bloody liar!' growled one at the other. 'You told me
you were coming to Liverpool today so I assumed you
weren't!'

This is not the way that companies ought to operate.
When human beings are preoccupied by their image
in the mirror, they have become curved in on themselves. That is precisely the way in which Martin Luther

defined sin – *incurvitas in se*. The companies investigated by Jackall demonstrate this unattractive dimension of human nature run rampant. They display our
fallenness.

Marks of the fall

For a variety of reasons, many people have difficulty with
the Christian doctrine of the fall. Who can take seriously
an ancient story which features a talking serpent and God
walking in the cool of the garden? Why the emphasis on
shame about sex, a factor which assumed sinister dimensions with St Augustine's influential understanding of
our sinful nature as being transmitted through the very
act of intercourse by which human beings are conceived?
And if we accept the evolutionary hypothesis to be correct,
surely we recognise that the evils of conflict, disease and
disaster were present in the unfolding history of the world
long before human beings arrived upon the scene?

Genesis 3 does indeed present real problems for the
modern mind. Perhaps the most serious is the nature of
the particular command which Adam and Eve disobeyed.
In creating human beings in his own image, God gave
them the ability to make meaningful choices in the moral
realm. He did not desire the unthinking conformity of
the robot. Men and women are able to discern good
from evil and so they have freedom to choose. If this
standard theological argument is correct, and surely it
is, why should knowledge of good and evil be presented
as a temptation?

But despite the problems, Genesis 3 still has power to
probe and convict. It does touch on fundamental truths
about the human condition. I shall pick out three and
show their particular relevance for business.

Self-aggrandisement

The first is contained in the answer to the question: what
was sinful in the desire of Adam and Eve to eat of the tree
of the knowledge of good and evil? Genesis 3:5 provides

the clue. The key phrase in the serpent's beguiling words
of temptation is 'you will be like God'. Adam and Eve,
prototypes of every human being who has come after
them, rebel against their creaturely status. They seek
equality with their creator. They assume pretensions
above their God-given station.

Corporate business provides many examples of human
hubris. As in other spheres of life, people can become
corrupted by power or success, and start to behave with
an arrogance which brooks no opposition. They aspire to
be gods in their own empire. Some chairmen or chief
executives pride themselves on the fear they create within
their organisation. Subordinates are cowed into submitting to the leader's everyday whim: 'When he sneezes,
we all catch colds,' is how one of the managers in Jackall's
study described the thrall exercised by his chief executive
officer.

Self-aggrandisement of this sort can have sinister
results. Brady, the accountant whose case Jackall docu-
ments, discovered an elaborate system of detailed financial reporting which went all the way to the top. He
eventually realised that this had been established not,
as the chief executive intended to portray, to eradicate
financial irregularities, but so that he could oversee
and authorise them. The misappropriation of a leading
British newspaper's pension funds starkly illustrates the
excesses sometimes perpetrated in the wake of a highly
dictatorial style of leadership.

Such arrogance can also affect the making of strategic
decisions. In some sectors of industry, companies feel
they have to prove their might by taking over other
companies at periodic intervals. In the heady years of
the 1980s this powerful flexing of industrial muscle
almost became a ritual requirement as far as the stock
market was concerned. But the number of takeovers
which subsequently proved successful was strikingly low
– no more than 30 per cent, according to one estimate.
Many of these takeovers were devoid of business logic.
Often, too little thought had been given to whether
different companies were compatible, or – where clear

differences had been recognised – of how disparities in corporate culture were to be handled. There is the sad phenomenon of asset-stripping, where the most valuable parts of a newly-acquired company are sold off, in order to finance the debt incurred in buying it. I am not suggesting that mergers and takeovers should be a no-go area. Where resorted to selectively, they have a part to play in strengthening the position of one company and rescuing the fortunes of another. But they carry with them a temptation to personal and corporate vainglory, symptomatic of the condition of human fallenness.

A second key story about the origins of human sin appears in Genesis 11. Whereas Genesis 3 portrays individuals succumbing to temptation, this describes a more corporate act of aggrandisement.

'Come, let us build ourselves a city, and a tower with its top in the heavens, and let us make a name for ourselves, lest we be scattered abroad upon the face of the whole earth.' (Genesis 11:4)

This was a well-planned operation. So keen was this ancient community to build a lasting monument to themselves that they used bitumen and brick which had been burnt in a kiln, rather than simply dried in the sun as was common. But they too were guilty of wanting to 'be like God'. Interestingly, a gnawing sense of insecurity seems to have lain behind this: 'lest we be scattered upon the face of the earth'. In attempting to shore themselves up against that danger, they unwittingly brought that exact fate upon themselves by way of divine judgement.

Are there present-day parallels to the story of the Tower of Babel? Does something of the same desire for a name and the same niggling insecurity lie behind the drive towards opulent company headquarters, wasteful as these often are of space and money? There are extravagant edifices in the commercial world which have been made to look like statements of hollow pretence, when

the weakness of their underlying financial foundation
has been exposed.

Sexual alienation

It is not only the relationship between human beings
and God which goes awry in Genesis 3. It is also the
relationship between man and woman. Although Adam
and Eve remain partners, they now experience feelings of
alienation from one another. Part of God's judgement is
that the woman will encounter the man's way of relating
to her in the form of 'rule' (3:16). Whether or not there
is a natural tendency for men to exercise leadership in
the relationship anyway, this is now experienced in an
authoritative – and with that, potentially exploitative
– mode.

Lorraine is an attractive nineteen-year-old secretary
with curly dark hair and a well-endowed figure. She has
been working for her present boss, Ron, who is a sales
manager, for the last three months. At first she liked
working for Ron because he showed a personal interest in
her, and took her into his confidence about the problems
he faces both at work, where he is under pressure to meet
very demanding sales targets, and in his marriage, where
he and his wife appear to be quite unhappy. But now that
Ron thinks that they have established a good working
relationship, Lorraine feels that he is beginning to take
liberties with her. He has twice asked her to work consid-
erably beyond her normal hours, disrupting her plans for
evening activities. He is also making flattering comments
and physically touching her with increasing regularity.
The latest and most alarming incident happened last
week. As she was typing at her desk, he came up behind
her, slipped his hands over her shoulders and told her
what lovely breasts she has. When Lorraine said 'please
don't do that', he stopped caressing her, but she feels
that it won't be long before he tries again. She feels sorry
for Ron, but doesn't want to get sucked into an affair.
Lorraine is a shy girl and is hesitant about complaining to
anyone else in the company, because she thinks that Ron

will deny anything improper, and she may jeopardise her
continued employment there. She feels frightened and
vulnerable.

Lorraine's predicament is not unusual, nor is it new.
The threat of sexual harrassment is found in one of the
loveliest stories in the Old Testament, the book of Ruth.
Upon returning to Bethlehem with her mother-in-law
Naomi, Ruth offers her hand in the barley harvest,
gleaning the fields after the reapers have been over
them. She comes to the field owned by Naomi's relative
Boaz, who notices a new face among the gleaners.

> Then Boaz said to Ruth, 'Now, listen, my daughter,
> do not go to glean in another field or leave this one,
> but keep close to my maidens. Let your eyes be upon
> the field which they are reaping, and go after them.
> Have I not charged the young men not to molest you?
> And when you are thirsty, go to the vessels and drink
> what the young men have drawn.' (Ruth 2:8–9)

The potential hazard of Ruth's situation is underlined
by the fact that when Naomi hears of where Ruth has
worked, she says 'It is well, my daughter, that you go out
with his maidens, lest in another field you be molested'
(2:22). It is a sad commentary on the extent of sexual
alienation between human beings, especially the lack of
self-control and respect shown by men, that women often
do have to seek safety in numbers in this way.

The problems are not only physical ones. Although the
situation is slowly improving, women are frequently the
victims of low pay or are unfairly passed over when it
comes to promotion. Aspiring female managers have special hurdles to surmount when it comes to the projection
of image. Jackall noted this in his research. If a female
executive projects a warm, engaging femininity, she is
apt to be seen by her male colleagues as a 'fluff-head'
and dismissed as inconsequential. But if she copies these
same colleagues and assumes a public severity in her
demeanour, she runs the risk of being labelled a 'cal-
culating bitch'. A company may well have an excellent

equal opportunities policy on paper, but sexual prejudice
dies very hard in practice.

Shifting the blame

A third feature of the Genesis story which rings bells is
the way the culprits pass the buck. Adam blames not only
Eve, but even, by implication, God himself: 'The woman
whom thou gavest to be with me, she gave me fruit of
the tree, and I ate' (Genesis 3:12). The woman blames
her tempter: 'The serpent beguiled me, and I ate.' It
is very difficult to say: 'I was to blame. I did it, and
I'm sorry.'

This is a tendency within business which we have
already noted. None of the different parties on the
construction site in Leicester were willing to accept
responsibility for delays which took place. The managers
interviewed by Jackall were involved in elaborate games
of buck-passing, trying to ensure that they got the credit
when things went well and were nowhere to be seen when
things went wrong. This trait was well in evidence in some
of the financial scandals which rocked life in the City of
London during the 1980s. Directors, chief executives and
managers further down the line all sought to duck their
share of the blame.

Passing the buck is a natural human tendency which
is reinforced in a professional climate where admitting
mistakes can either be highly detrimental to one's future
career or can render one's company open to expensive
legal claims. The cost of allowing accountability to rest
with me, or my company, seems frighteningly high, so we
seek to shift it. It is understandable, but it is dishonest.
Disowning responsibility is another demonstration of our
fallenness.

Whatever we may think about how the fall actually
took place, the evidence for the fact that we are sinful,
fallen humanity cannot be refuted. It is important not
to get hung up on the word 'fall'. It is possible to use
it without being irrevocably committed to the literal
nature of the Genesis story about taking the forbidden

fruit. The word should instead be understood as a piece of theological shorthand. It refers to the fact that human beings have indeed fallen far short of their high calling. They deviate from God's purposes for them and his world in a great variety of ways. Self-aggrandisement, sexual alienation and shifting the blame are not the only deviations practised by human beings. But they do stand out very prominently, both in the Genesis story and in our modern world.

Commission or bribe?

We must not take a simplistic attitude to sin. Sometimes it is genuinely difficult to see how we can avoid doing something which is – in some sense – wrong. Each of the various alternative courses of action open to us appears flawed, and our minds may be honestly vexed as to which of the different possibilities is least flawed. The fallen nature of our world is evident, not just in wilful acts of wrongdoing, but in the pervasiveness of evil which is built into particular social and economic arrangements. Extracting oneself with clean hands from some of these situations verges on the impossible.

The area of questionable payments is a good illustration of moral murkiness. Stuart is Chief Sales Executive for a motor company which specialises in the export of lorries and trucks to Third World countries. The firm has been struggling recently and there is the prospect of large-scale redundancies back home if more orders are not secured soon. Stuart is currently trying to secure a £200m. contract with a West African government. He reckons that if his tender succeeds, this could avert the loss of five hundred jobs, for a year at least. But Stuart isn't dealing with the government directly. He is acting through an agent who will present the company's case to the relevant government minister, and this agent is demanding a payment of 9 per cent for his services.

The situation is not a new one to Stuart, nor to the Board of Directors who are well aware of the context in which he conducts negotiations. They know that

they cannot do business in certain countries without
the services of an agent, who knows the language, the
relevant institutions and the government departments
intimately. Cultivating close relationships through acts
of generous hospitality may well be an accepted part of
that business culture. In this setting, an agent performs
a crucial commercial function and Stuart has no objection
in principle to paying him as a percentage of the value of
the contract.

However, Stuart is surprised at the size of the payment
which this particular agent is demanding. When he
questions the figure of 9 per cent, the agent refuses to
concede any ground and intimates that a rival firm is also
interested in the tender and is prepared to make such a
payment. Stuart regards this firm as inferior to his own,
both in terms of the quality of its vehicles and its moral
standards. He feels caught on the horns of a dilemma.
Should he pay the agent what he is demanding? When he
refers the matter to his Managing Director, Eric's reply
is forthright: securing the contract is crucial, and Stuart
should be ready to offer the agent 10 per cent in order to
outbid the rival firm. Much as Stuart hates the thought
of losing the contract, it is an answer he receives with a
heavy heart.

What constitutes a bribe? According to one dictionary
definition, a bribe is 'an inducement improperly influencing performance of a public function meant to be gra-
tuitously exercised' (*New Dictionary of Christian Ethics*,
p. 65). In some African countries customs officials expect
small sums of money to be given them when freight is
loaded or unloaded. These are often known as *customary*
payments: they do not confer special privileges, but tend
to be regarded as an acceptable way of augmenting small
incomes in those particular countries. Such payments
are a less than ideal method of operation, but it may
be impossible to do business in some parts of the world
and not resort to them at times. A *special* payment, in
contrast, secures the payer a benefit which is thereby
denied to anyone else. Many people pass through customs
controls; only one company, normally, wins a particular

contract. Putting money in the pocket (or more likely the Swiss bank account) of the government minister who decides the destination of a contract is an unfair way of securing competitive advantage. It is difficult to avoid the conclusion that it fits the definition of 'bribe' cited above.

Where does paying an agent fit in this analysis? Is the practice a special payment at one remove, or more akin to a customary payment? Normally agents demand a standard fee; in that respect they treat all companies bidding for tender in the same way. In demanding an unusually high figure, and seeking to play off one company against another, this agent is departing seriously from customary practice. If Stuart's company complies with his demand, there could well be three serious moral consequences: fanning the flames of greed in the agent, financing an improper use of the money by the agent, and sparking off a destabilisation of operating conditions within that country. They would be well advised to find another agent – quickly.

What help does the Bible have to offer on this subject? In the Old Testament the Hebrew word *shohadh* is variously translated 'gift' or 'bribe' depending on whether or not the context implies disapproval. In Proverbs 18:16 the effects of a gift are simply described: 'A man's gift makes room for him and brings him before great men.' But the usual context is one of condemnation:

> You shall take no bribe, for a bribe blinds the officials, and subverts the cause of those who are in the right. (Exodus 23:8)

> You shall not pervert justice; you shall not show partiality; and you shall not take a bribe, for a bribe blinds the eyes of the wise and subverts the cause of the righteous. (Deuteronomy 16:19)

> For I know how many are your transgressions,
>   and how great are your sins –
> you who afflict the righteous, who take a bribe,
>   and turn aside the needy in the gate. (Amos 5:12)

Most of the biblical references condemn bribery in the
context of the law-court. There payments to officials are
improper because they threaten the impartial administration of justice. The business situation is not quite the
same. But perhaps the most important question for a
Christian embroiled in a scenario like Stuart's to ask is:
what is just or fair in this situation? Is the payment I am
considering making a species of injustice? It is a question
which may not cut very much ice with Stuart's Managing
Director, but it is one he needs to resolve in his conscience
before God.

Mixed motives

Moral ambiguity is not only characteristic of practices
like questionable payments, where differences in culture
cloud the issue to some extent. It is a reality which
penetrates to the heart of the whole business enterprise.

Some would go further and say that the fundamental
motive of business, especially in the way it operates in
a market economy, is that of selfishness. People are in
commerce and industry for their own interests, and we
need to reckon with them on that basis. No one has
expressed this view more succinctly than Adam Smith:

> It is not from the benevolence of the butcher, the
> brewer, or the baker, that we expect our dinner,
> but from their regard to their own interest. We
> address ourselves, not to their humanity but to
> their self-love, and never talk to them of our own
> necessities but of their advantages. (*The Wealth of
> Nations,* Book I, p. 119)

It has to be said that, far from trying to dispel this view,
businessmen often appear to be at pains to reinforce it.
Captains of industry pride themselves on their devotion
to the bottom line. Even when they speak about other
objectives, they are usually quick to subordinate them
emphatically to the motive of profit. The famous assertion
by IBM's Thomas Watson Jr ('Our early emphasis on
human relations was not motivated by altruism but by

the simple belief that if we respected our people and helped them to respect themselves, the company would make the most profit') is a rather depressing illustration of this. The organisation Business in the Community, which encourages companies to give a certain proportion of their profits away to worthy causes in the community, does so with the argument that this will boost the company's reputation and redound to its benefit. 'Good ethics means good business' is the adage with which business ethics institutions seek to persuade companies to take an interest in the subject.

The professed dedication to financial ends is so widespread that where unusual individuals like Anita Roddick claim to be in business for other goals also, they are apt to be greeted with scepticism. But I would like to turn this sceptical approach on its head. I believe that many people in business are less one-sided economic creatures than they like to admit. In other words, they are not motivated only by goals of profit and self-interest. They genuinely care about satisfied customers, fulfilled employees, or a less polluted environment. Often they will take the morally right course of action, not just because it pays them in the long run, but simply because it is the right thing to do, or because they would lose their self-respect if they didn't. Sadly, the general corporate atmosphere often inhibits them from saying this.

The fact is that people work in commerce and industry for a variety of motives. Expressing and developing a talent, being part of a close-knit team, and enjoying the satisfaction of making something new, all enter into it. Profit is a very strong driving force in some; the ideal of service wields greater influence in others. The mix will differ from person to person and company to company. Miles' view, already cited in chapter 1, is that the common understanding of the relationship between profit and service needs to be reversed. For him, increased profit is the means, efficient customer service is the end. As the representative of a company which deals in oil and gas, he wants to maintain the value of its share price so that the company can continue to keep the

public warm in winter. It is plausible to endorse this as
the Christian view, because service lies at the very heart
of Christian discipleship. But four qualifying comments
need to be made.

First, Christians have to live in the real world. Unless
they choose to form their own exclusively Christian company (a course of action which has its own problems) they
are likely to find that most of their colleagues do not share
the same degree of altruism or idealism. Miles' colleagues
in senior management do not see the company objectives
quite as he does. But they are not so far apart in their
thinking that it is impossible to work together. In this
situation Miles' 'Christian' view jostles for attention with
other more profit-driven views.

Second, the gulf between business and other types of job
is less great than is often imagined. Are surgeons or top
civil servants guided more by ideals of public service, or by
the handsome salaries which are theirs to command? As
with business leaders, the answer is probably a veritable
mixture. Certainly the desire to feather one's own nest is
not confined to the business sector.

Third, there is a level of self-interest which is entirely
right and proper. It need not be a matter of embarrassment at all. A man who seeks promotion and a higher
salary is likely to be doing so not just for his own sake,
but for the wife and family he wants to support. On a
corporate level, profit is an essential constraint in the
disciplines provided by the market system. In the long
run, it is the only sure way of continuing to attract
fresh capital. Without profit, there can be no expansion,
no investment in new jobs, techniques or products. A
company must look after its own interests if it is to
survive and flourish.

Fourth, the dual motives of profit and service need to
be linked in a coherent whole. In chapter 5 I suggested
that the concept of wealth creation, understood as adding
value to original resource, provides the key to doing so.
When value is added in the eyes of the customer, money
is transferred to the hands of the producer. Mutual satisfaction can then take place. This is no more intrinsically

selfish than the joy which a devoted couple bring to themselves as well as each other in the act of making love. Mixed motives are not necessarily a bad thing.

The basic legitimacy of business endeavour must be affirmed. But as in the bedroom, so in the boardroom: human sinfulness repeatedly rears its ugly head. The signs that we live in a fallen world lie all around us.

CHAPTER 7

APPLYING THE BIBLE AFRESH

The Lessons of History

The choice of doctrinal themes which I have treated thus far will come as no surprise to those familiar with tomes of systematic theology. Following the doctrines of God, creation, humanity, and the fall, incarnation, crucifixion and resurrection can confidently be expected around the next corner. I shall indeed pass on to these momentous New Testament themes in due course. But in a book concerned with the subject of business, it would be remiss to ignore the great bulk of Old Testament material which stands between humanity's fall and Christ's incarnation. If we are looking for material in the Bible which deals explicitly with the economic domain, it is the Old Testament, especially the Old Testament law, which is undoubtedly our most prolific source. There is much here that warrants careful consideration. Commenting on it also provides the opportunity to develop further some of the preliminary observations about the use of the Bible made in chapter 2.

In the Old Testament law, obedience to God in matters pertaining to their material welfare is a vital element in the call to the Israelites to be a holy people. References to treatment of employees and conduct in business come thick and fast, though often they are mixed up with regulations on many other spheres of life, from the trimming of beards to the avoidance of wizards. Leviticus 19 provides a good example both of a seemingly random collection of miscellaneous commands and of some typical economic concerns:

And the Lord said to Moses, 'Say to all the congregation of the people of Israel, You shall be holy; for
I the Lord your God am holy. Every one of you shall
revere his mother and his father, and you shall keep
my sabbaths: I am the Lord your God. . . .

When you reap the harvest of your land, you shall
not reap your field to its very border, neither shall
you gather the gleanings after your harvest. And you
shall not strip your vineyard bare, neither shall you
gather the fallen grapes of your vineyard; you shall
leave them for the poor and for the sojourner: I am
the Lord your God. . . .

You shall not oppress your neighbour or rob him.
The wages of a hired servant shall not remain with
you all night until the morning. You shall not curse
the deaf or put a stumbling block before the blind,
but you shall fear your God: I am the Lord. . . .

You shall keep my statutes. You shall not let your
cattle breed with a different kind; you shall not sow
your field with two kinds of seed; nor shall there
come upon you a garment of cloth made of two kinds
of stuff. . . .

When you come into the land and plant all kinds
of trees for food, then you shall count their fruit as
forbidden; three years it shall be forbidden to you,
it must not be eaten. And in the fourth year all their
fruit shall be holy, an offering of praise to the Lord.
But in the fifth year you may eat of their fruit, that
they may yield more richly for you: I am the Lord
your God. . . .

You shall do no wrong in judgment, in measures
of length or weight or quantity. You shall have just
balances, just weights, a just ephah, and a just hin:
I am the Lord your God, who brought you out of the
land of Egypt.'

(Leviticus 19:1–3; 9–10; 13–14; 19; 23–25; 35–36)

Reading a chapter like this is a strange experience.
Some of these laws seems strikingly relevant, and can

be applied more or less as they stand. Employers should
not exploit their position of power by delaying payment
of wages to employees. Standard measurements should
be used so that customers are not in any sense short-
changed. Other laws belong very clearly to a different culture, and it is far less obvious how we should apply them
or even whether we should seek to apply them at all.

For example, the law on gleaning makes sense in
an overwhelmingly agricultural community as a simple
way of making provision for the poor. It requires fresh
thought to make it applicable to the urbanised industrial
societies of the West. Perhaps Marks and Spencer, with
their custom of giving away produce which is left at the
end of the week free to charitable organisations, provide
as close a contemporary parallel as it is possible to find.
One is tempted to add that it well befits a firm with
Jewish origins to follow this practice. On the other hand,
Leviticus 19:19 (forbidding 'a garment of cloth made of
two kinds of stuff') has clearly passed them by; my
St Michael's shirts are 65 per cent polyester and 35
per cent cotton! And what are we to make of the law
about planting and eating fruit? One can hardly expect
companies which have carried out takeovers to abandon
all thoughts of making a profit from their new enterprises
for a full five years.

Leviticus 19 illuminates a truth which, deep down, all
Christians know: that when it comes to the contemporary
application of the Jewish law we are all highly selective.
But we vary, both in what we select and in the principles
of interpretation which underlie our selections. There is
a genuine difference of opinion in Christian circles about
the relevance of the Old Testament law to present-day
economic affairs.

Jubilee ethics

One of the boldest attempts at applying the Old Testa-
ment to modern society is found in the work of Michael
Schluter, Director of the Jubilee Centre in Cambridge.
Reactivating the Extended Family: From Biblical Norms

to Public Policy in Britain, which was co-authored by
Michael Schluter with Roy Clements, outlines the theoretical basis for this. Starting from Jesus' words in
Matthew 5:18–19 (about the permanence of every 'jot and
tittle' in the Law), they argue that the Old Testament law
provides a *normative model* of political economy, which
is as relevant for an unregenerate society now as it was
then. The nation of Israel included among its number
sinful and unbelieving people, and the Mosaic law, while
embodying high ideals, does make some allowance for
human hardness of heart. Schluter and Clements are
critical of those who restrict the usefulness of the Law
to a few general principles. This fails to do justice to the
richness of the details of the Old Testament law, which
are worthy of close attention. They feel that modern
society would do well to emulate ancient Israel in a
number of particulars.

First, Schluter and Clements argue that there is much
to be learnt from *kinship* institutions in the Old Testament. The smallest recognised institutional form was the
three-generational (what they call 3-G) family. Parents
accepted their responsibility to look after grandparents,
who probably lived close by, in separate houses but on
the same plot of land. The clan, which was based on
wider kinship ties, provided a further vital support-role
for the 3-G family. Schluter and Clements contrast this
with the modern West, where the family is defined as a
nuclear (two-generational) unit, where different members
of the family are often widely scattered, and grandparents
tend to be looked after by the state rather than their adult
children. They see this as symptomatic of a decline in
relationships in our society. They suggest policies to
reactivate the extended family by, for example, the state
giving financial incentives to the family to care for its own
members, and the development of new house construction
with 'clusters' suitable for extended family use.

Second, Schluter and Clements attach great significance to the fact that each family had a plot of *land*. 'The
land-holding system which God gave Israel in the Law has
as its objective that every 3-generational family and clan

should own a piece of land in perpetuity' (*Reactivating the Extended Family,* p. 13). Joshua chapters 13–19, which superficially looks like one of the most tedious sections of the Bible, is actually significant in this respect: it describes the systematic sharing-out of the newly-conquered land, tribe by tribe and clan by clan. Some movement in landholding was allowed, as is clear from Leviticus 25. But effectively, it was only a matter of leasing out land for a limited time, because in the fiftieth ('Jubilee') year every bit of property was returned to its original owner. The seriousness attached to the permanent ownership of land in Israel is well illustrated by the incident of Naboth's vineyard. When King Ahab tries to persuade Naboth to give him his vineyard (offering him either an alternative vineyard or money), Naboth replies in a state of high indignation: 'The Lord forbid that I should give you the inheritance of my fathers' (1 Kings 21:3).

Seeking to apply this, Schluter and Clements believe that in society today every family, as a right, should own a piece of property. They advocate a system of universal owner-occupation, recognising that this would require either compulsory purchase of much currently rented accommodation or a building programme specifically to assist those who are not owner-occupiers at present. In order to ensure that there would be no reversion from this, they propose that those selling houses could be required to show that they were using the funds obtained towards the purchase of another dwelling.

Third, Schluter and Clements believe that the effect of the landholding system in ensuring long-term site residence of the 3-G family and the clan would have encouraged the persistence of kin-based forms of *economic activity*. They do not find any evidence in the Old Testament of economic activity being heavily concentrated in large cities or particular regions. Restrictions on land markets would have made today's urban pattern a non-starter. The strong roots which people had in town and region probably helped produce a spread of business activity to match the distribution of population.

Following on from this, Schluter and Clements wish
to see active efforts made to promote the small family-
business sector. They suggest tax relief could be given
to equity earnings in firms belonging to members of a
person's extended family. They think there is a case
for demerging some large companies and for providing
incentives to companies to open new plants in regions
of high unemployment, thereby reducing migration out
of the area.

Schluter and Clements believe that applying the Bible
afresh in the twentieth-century world would actually
result in a distinctive socio-economic system:

> Looking at the OT Law from the perspective of the
> quality of relationships as its primary goal, and
> family and kinship as its central institutions, pro-
> vides many disparate laws with a centre of gravity,
> a unifying theme. From this perspective, the Old
> Testament Law can be seen to have a high degree
> of internal consistency. Thus, if Capitalism is a
> system organised in the interests of capital, and
> Socialism in the interests of society, then OT Israel's
> ideology might best be described as *Relationism*
> as this word points towards both the underlying
> goal of the quality of human *relationships*, and the
> institutions of kinship, as blood-relatives are often
> referred to as 'relations'. (*Reactivating the Extended
> Family,* pp. 20–21)

Turning the clock back?

I believe that the Christian church owes Michael Schluter
a debt of gratitude for the service he has performed in
redirecting attention to the Old Testament as a source
for social ethics. The Jubilee Centre which he directs has
done sterling work as a pressure group on issues such
as credit and debt and Sunday trading. Yet I do not
believe that the position he and Roy Clements expound

in *Reactivating the Extended Family* represents the right way forward. It is too wooden a method of interpreting the Old Testament for today.

Important though the Old Testament is, it must for the Christian be seen in the light of the New. The New Testament does not place anything like the same emphasis on the categories of family or land as we find in the Old Testament. This fact alone should prompt caution about enshrining either as the basis of a socio-economic system.

Of course, family households continue to exist in the New Testament era. Paul gives important ethical teaching in the so-called 'household codes', spelling out the responsibilities of husbands, wives, parents, children, masters and slaves (Ephesians 5:21–6:9; Colossians 3:18–4:1). Jesus affirmed the financial responsibility of adults to support their ageing parents; indeed, he warns against neglecting this under the guise of religious fervour (Mark 7:9–13). But there is also a sense in which the New Testament sharply relativises the institution of the family. Jesus subordinates loyalty to fellow-members of one's family under the obligations carried by a more fundamental loyalty to him (Luke 9:59–60; 14:26). He warns that the effect of his coming will be that some members of a family will decide for him, others against him. Jesus actually experienced scepticism rather than support from his own kith and kin (Mark 3:20–21; 6:4).

In the New Testament church, the people of God no longer comprise a succession of self-contained extended family units. The boundary between belief and unbelief cuts right across this most basic of institutions. The fellowship which Christ creates is a fellowship between those who are *unlike* (e.g., Matthew the tax-collector and Simon the Zealot) as much as it is between those bound by loyalties of kin (e.g., the fishermen brothers James and John). It expands, even explodes, traditional notions of friendship and obligation based on geographical locality and blood relations.

Land, too, loses its theological significance in the New

Testament. Disciples of Jesus find their personal identity in him, not in their family plot. Jesus talks of followers who have 'left house or brothers or sisters or mother or father or children or lands, for my sake and for the gospel' (Mark 10:29). In Acts 4:32–36 we read that those who possessed lands or houses sold them, and brought the proceeds to the apostles so that they could distribute to all in need. No doubt in time the church reverted to a more conventional pattern with individual members owning their own piece of property. But the book of Acts and the epistles convey the strong impression of a pilgrim people, with individuals like Paul ready to live a rootless existence in the cause of spreading the Gospel, and a recognition that Christians' true homeland is in heaven (Philippians 3:20–21; Hebrews 11:13–16).

The New Testament gives us little material to go on with regard to characteristic forms of economic activity. But the focus it contains on breaking down conventional barriers (especially that between Jew and Gentile) makes me question whether the small-scale family business should be regarded as the normative style of arrangement. Christianity created a body of people with a unified purpose which (at its best) overrode the cultural divisions of the day. Large multi-national companies now are attempting something very similar. Of course they have their own dangers, such as the possibility of individuals feeling lost and anonymous within the impersonality of a big organisation. But multi-nationals can also breed internationalism as opposed to nationalism, tolerance as opposed to narrow-mindedness, and the potential for personal growth and development as opposed to its frustration. The larger scale which is characteristic of modern societies brings ethical and cultural gains, not just losses.

Schluter and Clements seek to move too directly from the Old Testament economy to the present day. They neglect the important role played by the New Testament as a *filter*, refining, reinterpreting and revolutionising what is there in the Old. They are also in danger, both of presenting an unduly romantic picture of what went on in the Hebrew agricultural economy, and of taking an overly jaundiced view of what happens now in the modern industrial economy. The close proximity of relatives is not always conducive to happy and supportive relationships. Conversely, modern technological advances like telephones and motorways mean that families can still function meaningfully as extended networks even when they are separated by factors of distance.

The threefold categorisation of the Law

The Old Testament law does have valuable lessons to impart in the sphere of business. But we need to exercise a good deal of discrimination to determine what aspects of it are of continuing relevance. The most helpful way of looking at the Law remains the threefold categorisation used by the Reformers. They saw the Law as comprising three different types of material, ceremonial law, moral law and civil law.

Many scholars today object to this categorisation, on the grounds that the Old Testament itself makes no such distinction. Different types of law are all mixed in together. Thus in Leviticus 19 the seminal statement 'love your neighbour as yourself', highlighted by Jesus as one of the two most important commandments, is followed by the apparently trivial verse which forbids the bringing together of different types of cattle, seed and clothing (Leviticus 19:18–19).

This objection, however, is not decisive. The crucial point is not how the Israelites understood the Law, but how Christians should, in the light of distinctions made in the New Testament. The case for saying that substantial sections of the Law come under the heading *ceremonial,* or 'ritual', and are no longer binding upon the Christian, receives strong support from the New Testament. According to Mark, Jesus declared all foods clean when he asserted that it is what comes out of a man, not what goes in, that makes him unclean (Mark 7:14–23). The same revelation came to Peter, with revolutionary consequences for his attitude to Gentiles, during a vision on a housetop in the seaside town of Joppa (Acts 10). The early Christians subsequently came to abandon all the exclusivity laws whose intention was to mark Israel off from other nations. Presumably it was the concern for separation of types, which we now understand as playing only a temporary part in God's purposes, which underlies regulations about different kinds of clothing material.

St Paul distinguishes between different aspects of the Law when he writes 'For neither circumcision counts for anything nor uncircumcision, but keeping the commandments of God' (1 Corinthians 7:19). Although circumcision was a command from God, Paul contrasts it with those commandments which are of lasting validity. The book of Hebrews is at pains to emphasise that the sacrificial system has had its day. Jesus on the cross provided the one perfect sacrifice which renders further offerings of animals and birds unnecessary.

To some extent, this process of discriminating between different layers of material in the Law starts within the pages of the Old Testament. The eighth-century BC Israelites against whom the prophets Hosea and Amos fulminate appear to have been regular in performing the required sacrifices, but God was singularly unimpressed. He is much more concerned with their obedience to the *moral* requirements of the Law. This does not simply consist of the Ten Commandments, though there appears to be an echo of the second half of the Decalogue in Hosea's complaint that 'there is swearing, lying, killing, stealing, and committing adultery; they break all bounds and murder follows murder' (Hosea 4:2). Such offences were highly instrumental in the breakdown of social order and the Israelites' estrangement from God. But there are other laws about whose violation the prophets seem particularly concerned. Neglect of the widow and orphan; dishonesty in commercial transactions; bribery affecting the dispensation of justice – all these come under regular critical scrutiny. We can be absolutely confident in saying that such actions are as wrong now as they were then. They offend against that basic God-given moral awareness to which another prophet, Micah, appeals:

He has showed you, O man, what is good;
   and what does the Lord require of you
but to do justice, and to love kindness,
   and to walk humbly with your God? (Micah 6:8)

The third category of law, *civil* law, is much the most
difficult for Christians to know how to interpret and
apply today. The phrase is used to refer to that body of
legal material which is concerned with social, economic
and political arrangements. As such it possesses a strong
ethical character, so the distinction between it and moral
law is not clearcut. The regulations concerning the jubilee
and sabbath years in Leviticus 25 come into this third
category. Concern for the dignity and well-being of each
individual family runs through this passage, but is the
scheme for redirecting land to its original owners really
meant to be universal in scope, either with regard to the
detail or the basic principle involved?

The view of the Reformers was that though Christians
seeking to shape and influence the society of their day
are likely to find helpful guidance through reflection
upon the civil law, they need not feel obliged to follow
these regulations. I believe this is correct. In applying
this material we need to be sensitive to the promptings
of the Holy Spirit, and to the lessons taught by history.
A passage written by the Anglican House of Bishops in
a report addressing issues of sexual ethics is equally
relevant in this context:

At any given time we ... feed into this Spirit-fed
dialogue our own world view and our awareness of
new circumstances. The result may be one of two
things or a mixture of both. In some cases the
message of Scripture will judge our contemporary
views, showing up their superficiality or wrong-
headedness. But where new factors or new under-
standings make our situation significantly different
from that of the biblical writers, Scripture may guide
us more by stimulating new perceptions in us than

by giving direction that can be applied as it stands. *(Issues in Human Sexuality*, Statement by the House of Bishops, p. 14)

Charging interest – right or wrong?

To give an example of applying the Bible afresh, in such a way that we draw on the lessons of history, let us take the question of charging interest on loans. It is a practice which has become a bedrock of our modern economic system. But it was opposed for many centuries by the church, and the distress caused by the practice of credit in parts of the world today is leading some to ask whether the church was mistaken in changing its traditional stance of disapproval.

Israel was unique among ancient Middle Eastern countries in prohibiting the charging of interest. This prohibition occurs frequently:

> If you lend money to any of my people with you who is poor, you shall not be to him as a creditor, and you shall not exact interest from him. If ever you take your neighbour's garment in pledge, you shall restore it to him before the sun goes down; for that is his only covering, it is his mantle for his body; in what else shall he sleep? And if he cries to me, I will hear, for I am compassionate. (Exodus 22:25–27)

> And if your brother becomes poor, and cannot maintain himself with you, you shall maintain him; as a stranger and a sojourner he shall live with you. Take no interest from him or increase, but fear your God; that your brother may live beside you. You shall not lend him your money at interest, nor give him your food for profit. (Leviticus 25:35–37)

> You shall not lend upon interest to your brother, interest on money, interest on victuals, interest on

anything that is lent for interest. To a foreigner you
may lend upon interest, but to your brother you
shall not lend upon interest; that the Lord your
God may bless you in all that you undertake in
the land which you are entering to take possession
of it. (Deuteronomy 23:19–20)

Faced by these strong-worded Old Testament pronounce-
ments, the early Church Fathers roundly condemned the
charging of interest, which they called *usury*. (It was
only in modern times that the word 'usury' changed so
that it came to mean an excessive charging of interest.)
The early Church Fathers, men such as St Ambrose
and St Chrysostom, believed the practice ran contrary
to Christian obligations of love and mercy. Some even
followed Aristotle, who held that money was essentially
barren, in regarding interest as contrary to the law of
nature. Church councils embodied such disapproval in
their canons from AD 306 onwards.

This ban on interest was maintained by the church for
the next thousand years, though enforcement was always
less than complete. However, some of the Scholastic
theologians started to make exceptions in the Middle
Ages. Interest was allowed, first, on the grounds of
damnum emergens, to compensate the lender for the
anticipated monetary loss incurred. More controversial,
though a logical extension, was interest on the grounds
of *lucrum cessans*, to compensate for the loss of gain
which could have been anticipated if the loan had not
been made. Relaxation of the ban on interest therefore
predated the time of the Reformation, though the leading
Reformers certainly opened the gates wider. Both Calvin
and Luther (in his later years) allowed interest in a
limited way, though they stipulated that it should not
infringe the principles of charity and equity. Calvin saw
the Israelite ban on interest as part of their political
constitution, and thought that in his own day it was
permissible to 'make concession to the common utility'.
But his carefully qualified approval of interest in certain
circumstances was eagerly endorsed in the practices of

the bankers and merchants who were at the heart of Europe's expanding economy.

Certainly, from the sixteenth century onwards, acceptance of interest became widespread. An English Act of Parliament of 1571 accepted interest in principle but made charges of over 10 per cent illegal. In the seventeenth century, the group of moral theologians known as the Carolines (bishops who served during the reigns of the two Kings Charles, such as Joseph Hall and Robert Sanderson) continued to wrestle with the issue. They distinguished between legitimate lending of money (why, for instance, should a rich person borrowing money make a profit at others' expense?) and usury which represented an idle way to make a living. The Roman Catholic Church, which maintained an implacable stance for many centuries, eventually dropped its opposition to charging interest in 1854.

In assessing the church's record on this issue, there appears to be reason for saying that during its first millennium, Christians were mistaken in their total opposition to the charging of interest, whereas in more recent centuries, they have tended to become indifferent to dangers which are inherent in the practice. Whether or not one agrees with that judgement is related to what sense one makes of the key Old Testament passages.

Beware the exploitation of the poor

When we engage with these passages which spell out civil law, it is vital to identify the principle which is embodied in any particular prescription. Sometimes we are left guessing; neither the text nor the context makes it clear. But the passages on interest do not leave us in any reasonable doubt. Exodus 22 and Leviticus 25 show explicit concern for the position of the poor man. In banning interest, they seek to prevent his vulnerable position being exploited. The generosity which God has shown to the Israelites requires that they show similar kindness to the individual who has fallen upon hard times and that, far from adding to his burdens, they should support him in his plight.

This is a different scenario from that involved in most

commercial situations. When a company borrows money
from a bank to finance expansion, the one need not
be exploiting the other. The company gains from the
infusion of needed capital, the bank gains from the return
of interest on the loan. Presumably this is a type of
situation closer to that where the Israelites were allowed
to lend at interest, namely, in trading with foreigners.
This was not the stranger living in their midst (whom
they were commanded to treat like one of their own) but
the stranger who lived in a foreign nation, with whom
close-knit community ties did not exist. Here, levying
interest on loans represented a sensible minimisation
of risk, and meant that Israel could take its place as
an equal partner on the commercial playing-ground of
the ancient Middle East.

In the light of this distinction, the case for some sort of
credit provision in sophisticated modern economies is difficult to deny. Credit makes money available to those who
lack capital at present but who display wealth-creating
potential in the eyes of the lender. Essentially, it is the
price of lending money over time, with market forces
serving to determine the rate of interest, just as they do
in relation to prices generally. From the saver's point of
view, interest represents a way of maintaining the value
of capital in an age of inflation. Shrewd investment is a
means of putting one's savings to productive use at the
same time as providing for oneself in the days of one's
retirement.

But there is another side to the story. It should not be
assumed that, just because the Old Testament passages
have loans to individuals in view, they therefore have no
relevance to a commercial setting. The key principle, that
lending money should not be a cloak for exploiting the
poor, must be kept firmly in view. As I have said, this
is not a criticism which can be levied at most forms of
credit in the modern world. But is it true of some? That is
a challenge which all Christians involved in the financial
services industry need to take very seriously.

Heavily marketed credit cards are one form of credit
which the Jubilee Centre has rightly brought under

the ethical microscope. Although the customer who discharges his debts promptly at the end of the month has no need to pay any interest, it is precisely the person or family who find it difficult to make ends meet who are likely to end up doing so. When people start using individual store cards as well as bankers' cards, problems are liable to escalate. Too often there is an irresponsible attitude in the issuing of cards, the creditworthiness of the customers concerned not being properly checked. Where they are used wisely, credit cards represent an enhancement in the quality of life because of their easy convenience. But it is hard to avoid the impression that they also entail making money at the expense of the poorer sections of society.

A more serious issue still is that of Third World debt. The loans which were made by oil-producing countries during the period 1975–82 have proved crippling burdens for many countries struggling with problems of severe malnutrition, famine and disease. Governments which undertook these borrowings cannot be spared some of the blame because money has too often been squandered or not spent on the most pressing needs. But the combination of debt plus the interest on the debt is a millstone which hangs heavy upon the prospects of most Third World countries. The governments and banks of the West should not allow it to stay there. There is a corollary between the discomfort of children dying in the poorest countries of the world and the comfort of investors profiting in the richest countries of the world.

Admittedly, the issue is more complex than those who picket the entrances to banks often recognise. A wholesale cancelling of debts hurts the debtor as well as the creditor. It means that the likelihood of the debtor country receiving further loans (even loans on more generous terms) is drastically reduced. What is needed is some mutually agreed solution which enshrines, in a balanced way, the principles of justice (i.e., the borrowing institution makes some attempt to discharge its obligations), mercy (so that a significant portion of the debt is actually written off) and hope (working out new arrangements which hold more promise for the future).

The Old Testament supports the idea of a periodic release from debt:

> At the end of every seven years you shall grant a release. And this is the manner of the release: every creditor shall release what he has lent to his neighbour; he shall not exact it of his neighbour, his brother, because the Lord's release has been proclaimed. (Deuteronomy 15:1–2)

We cannot expect a modern society to implement a law like this in a literal way. Indeed, the lack of reference to the Jubilee provisions in the history and prophetic books of the Old Testament provokes scepticism as to whether they were ever put into operation in Israel. If debts are released too frequently, there is obvious scope for a form of inverted abuse, that of debtors exploiting the good will of creditors! What this material bears witness to, however, is a recognition that credit can create a vicious circle of debt, devoid of hope, unless decisive measures are taken periodically to cut through it. Clearly this is more difficult to practise where institutions, not just individuals, are concerned. One can only go along with the hope expressed by Bishop Richard Harries that Christians who are in a position of knowledge and influence to address issues like Third World debt will have the creative energy and depth of concern to do so. (See chapter 11 of his book *Is there a Gospel for the rich?*.)

The Law as paradigm

Although I offered critical observations earlier in this chapter about the approach to the Old Testament adopted by Michael Schluter and Roy Clements, the gap between our respective positions is not a huge one. Like them, I want to draw on the legal material in the Old Testament as a valuable resource. I hesitate, however, to suggest that the first five books of the Bible provide us with something so complete as the *model* they describe. I am more conscious of the factors which have changed, many of them irreversibly, over the last two and a half thousand years. It is not irreverent to say that the Bible contains a certain number of dead ends, roads down which an ancient people travelled and it would be unhelpful to try to travel again. Who would want to recreate a society where women were considered unclean for a lengthy period after childbirth, twice as long in the case of a daughter as a son (Leviticus 12:1–5)?

What is far more striking, however, are the many fruitful lines of enquiry which the Bible opens up. The civil law of the Old Testament includes many regulations (like those on charging interest) which are rightly taken as *paradigms* – a word I prefer to 'model'. Paradigms are examples of a principle in action. We must take the principle to heart and seek to apply it, but the form in which we do that in our modern society will probably differ from the way in which it is articulated in the Bible.

The example of slavery is instructive, because here we find biblical material which at the same time strikes us as remote from modern concerns and yet is highly relevant. Slavery was a prominent feature of Old Testament society, and a consistent application of the 'normative model' approach would lead to the conclusion: if it was permissible then, why not now? But twentieth-century Christians universally resist such thinking. When we read in Exodus 21:21 that if a man strikes a slave, and the slave survives a day or two, the master is not to be punished, 'for the slave is his money', we are very conscious of the gulf in cultural attitudes between Mosaic and modern times. The reason why slavery is considered anathema today, that it is thought belittling to human dignity for one person to be the *possession* of another, is not articulated by the biblical writers.

At the same time, we ought to take note of numerous legal regulations which served to humanise and reduce the harshness of slavery in Old Testament Israel. These conditions compare very favourably with those in surrounding countries. Effectively, slaves were residential domestic workers, supplementing the labour of free members of the household. The law stipulated that they should be guaranteed their sabbath rest, share in the religious festivals, and be released (though usually this would mean becoming a slave in someone else's household) at the end of six years. A master could be punished for certain physical misdemeanours inflicted on a slave (Exodus 21:20, 26–27). There is a sense of the unnaturalness of the institution, especially among a people whom God has delivered from slavery – a fact often used to urge compassionate treatment of slaves (e.g., Leviticus 25:39–46). In the context of the rebuilding of Jerusalem, Nehemiah rails against those Jews who exploited the impoverished circumstances of their compatriots and made slaves of them (Nehemiah 5:1–13). The most remarkable law relating to slavery, and one which was potentially subversive of the whole institution, is that allowing the right of asylum to a runaway slave (Deuteronomy 23:15–16). Finally, there is a striking passage in Job which is very much in tune with modern concerns, because it witnesses to a fundamental human equality:

> If I ever rejected the plea of my slave or slave-girl
> when they brought a complaint against me,
> what shall I do if God appears?
> What shall I answer if he intervenes?
> Did not he who made me in the belly make them?
> Did not the same God create us in the womb?
> (Job 31:13–15, REB)

It is important, therefore, to note the *direction* in which Scripture is moving. We do not have to dig very far below the surface of the biblical material on slavery to find sentiments and convictions which raise radical questions about the fundamental legitimacy of slavery. The following-through of these questions to their logical conclusion only took place many centuries after Scripture was complete. The lesson is that we should take our lead, not so much from where the biblical writers end up, but from that to which their underlying concerns point.

The material on slavery still has paradigmatic relevance. As Christopher Wright observes:

> There are still vast areas of the developing world where the nature of human labour has changed little from the ancient patterns such as are found in biblical times. And there are societies where the conditions of allegedly 'free' employees are pitiably more harsh and oppressive than those of slaves in Israel. (*Living as the People of God: The relevance of Old Testament ethics*, pp. 79–80)

In both types of society, there is a moral obligation on the part of those in power to provide statutory rest days and holidays, clear terms and conditions of employment, protection from infringement of personal rights and physical dignity, and the prompt payment of fair wages – all stipulations which are found in Old Testament law.

CHAPTER 8

BRINGING WISDOM DOWN TO EARTH

The Word Made Flesh

In seeking to persuade people how to behave, the Bible offers a variety of approaches. Law is one. The writings which have come to be known as the Wisdom literature provide another. Only rarely in books like Proverbs and Ecclesiastes does one hear the imperative voice: the phrase 'thus says the Lord' is notable by its absence. Indeed, the book of Proverbs draws freely on the wisdom of foreigners, the teaching of the queen mother of the Arab kingdom of Massa being a particularly interesting example of the latter (chapter 31). The overall theological context is still that of faith in the Israelite God, but unlike the law and the prophets, there is no appeal to God's saving acts in Jewish history. The focus is on God as creator.

What the book of Proverbs expresses is a practical wisdom about what makes for a good life. This is based on observation about life's experience, reflections on what works for the best and what doesn't. Moral points are made through a series of contrasting, sometimes comical pictures: the worker and the sluggard, the just man and the crook, the wise man and the fool. Set in the memorable form of proverbs, this is the type of distilled wisdom which is passed on from generation to generation on a mother's knee.

Many of these sayings are relevant to the world of business. Proverbs has much to impart about the conduct of human *relationships,* teaching such virtues as keeping confidences, honest admonition and moral consistency:

He who goes about as a talebearer reveals secrets,
but he who is trustworthy in spirit keeps a thing
hidden. (11:13)

Faithful are the wounds of a friend; profuse are the
kisses of an enemy. (27:6)

He who walks in integrity walks securely, but he
who perverts his ways will be found out. (10:9)

It is quite clear about the benefits which come from
hard *work*:

He who tills his land will have plenty of bread, but
he who follows worthless pursuits has no sense.
(12:11)

In all toil there is profit, but mere talk tends only to
want. (14:23)

Prosperity is seen as the natural sequel to industrious
endeavour. But on the subject of wealth and poverty,
Proverbs shows a subtle mixture of realism, generosity
and recognition that both states carry their temptations:

A rich man's wealth is his strong city; the poverty
of the poor is their ruin. (10:15)

He who oppresses a poor man insults his Maker, but
he who is kind to the needy honours him. (14:31)

Remove far from me falsehood and lying; give me
neither poverty nor riches; feed me with the food
that is needful for me, lest I be full, and deny thee,
and say, 'Who is the Lord?' or lest I be poor, and
steal, and profane the name of my God. (30:8–9)

Experience is a great teacher. One of the problems in
industry at present is that companies are making many

able people redundant at fifty, and subsequently ruing the loss of experience this represents. Experience matters both with regard to the technical aspects of doing a job, and with regard to wisdom in forming corporate strategy and handling difficult relationships. Nor do secular wisdom and Christian thinking have to be at variance with each other. True, the Holy Spirit is present in a special way in the Christian community, but he is also at work in the wider world. Christians in business should not despise the wisdom displayed by their non-believing colleagues.

The book of Proverbs represents an attempt to set down on paper that wisdom which is the fruit of experience. It does so, moreover, in a form that is readily accessible to everyone. Companies today are increasingly going down the same track. They are trying to bring wisdom down to earth.

Implementing a moral code: one company's experience

ARCO Chemical is an intermediate chemical company which has experienced explosive growth since it was founded in the USA in 1967. It has a strong presence in Europe, with a head office in Maidenhead and factories in or near Rotterdam, Marseille and Ghent. ARCO Chemical is the world's leading manufacturer of propylene oxide (PO), one of the most versatile of all chemicals. Products as diverse as cushions, car bumpers, cosmetics and drinking cups all contain PO. One derivative product is methyl tertiary butyl ether (MTBE). This is used as an additive to petrol, enhancing octane and thus providing an excellent alternative to lead. ARCO Chemical has also developed a non-toxic anti-freeze.

ARCO Chemical has a statement of business principles. They are as follows:

* We will operate with the highest ethical standards and integrity, as individuals and as a company.
* We will operate in a safe and environmentally sound manner.

* We will work to achieve superior profit perfor-
mance.
* We will operate our manufacturing plants as effi-
ciently and cost-effectively as possible.
* We will strive for complete customer satisfaction.
* We will encourage innovation and creativity in
all work.
* We will encourage and reward personal initiative
and team effort.
* We will encourage career development and indi-
vidual growth.
* We will comply with all laws and regulations
governing our business.
* We will treat all vendors fairly and equally.

In itself, this is not an exceptional statement of business
principles. Many other companies have something comparable. It is very easy for such statements to be no
more than a public relations front, and for employees
to treat them with indifference or contempt when the
crunch really comes. Nevertheless, they have a very
important role to play. At their best, these statements
represent expressions of corporate wisdom. Experience
has shown that these are the ideals which need to be
embodied in a company's actions if it is to prove a
successful, well-motivated company which thrives on
an excellent reputation. Such experience is embodied
in statements articulated by a whole industry as well as
by individual companies. ARCO Chemical is committed
to the guiding principles for Responsible Care which
have been published by the Chemical Manufacturers
Association.

ARCO Chemical's ethical stance is notable in two
respects. First, in an industry which uses processes which
are potentially dangerous and has had its share of horrific
accidents, ARCO Chemical puts an impressive premium
on safety. Its code of ethics (a more detailed expansion of
the statement of principles) makes this clear:

In all cases, profit performance is secondary to

operating safely in an ethical and environmentally responsible fashion and observing all laws and regulations. Profit performance must never compromise the fundamental principles under which we operate. We do not want employees risking violation of laws or circumventing the company's policies and procedures. (Cited in *Because We Care*, ARCO Chemical Europe, p. 5)

ARCO Chemical shows every evidence of environmental concern, and its products are 'greener' than those made by many other chemical companies. But environmental considerations too are subordinated to safety:

Safety and environmental protection usually go hand in hand: a safe practice is also likely to have environmental advantages. However, this may not always be the case; on rare occasions, the desirability of environmental conservation may have to be weighed against the necessity of avoiding danger to human life. In such situations, priority would always be given to the safety of our employees and the public at large. (*Because We Care*, p. 18)

This clear prioritisation is both helpful and unusual. Most companies these days speak of the breadth of corporate responsibility and of the various different groups to which they recognise an obligation. ARCO Chemical is bold enough to say that, though profit performance and environmental protection come high on its list of priorities, considerations of safety take precedence over all others.

Second, ARCO Chemical's statement of principles is fleshed out through a series of detailed, demanding standards. There are fifty-five of these in all. Virtually everyone in the organisation is responsible for ensuring that the section of work in which he or she is involved attains these standards. Employees who may be unmoved by expressions of general moral exhortation are therefore held to account for their compliance with regulations which seek to apply the basic principles.

The smell of failure

The books of the Old Testament reveal the same finding that has been made by modern companies: that high-flown moral sentiments, however well-expressed, cannot in themselves guarantee good behaviour. The residue of the fall is a twisted streak in human character which leads people to spurn accumulated wisdom. The book of Ecclesiastes strikes a much more pessimistic note than that of Proverbs. Its author is well aware that a hierarchical bureaucracy can produce injustice, and the desire for money an unsatisfying obsession with material possessions:

> If you see the poor oppressed in a district, and justice and rights denied, do not be surprised at such things; for one official is eyed by a higher one, and over them both are others higher still. The increase from the land is taken by all; the king himself profits from the fields.

> Whoever loves money never has money enough;
>   whoever loves wealth is never satisfied with his
>   income.
>   This too is meaningless.
> As goods increase, so do those who consume them.
> And what benefit are they to the owner except to
>   feast his eyes on them?
> (Ecclesiastes 5:8–11, NIV)

The Old Testament prophets observed the same social evils as Ecclesiastes. But as Christopher Wright has commented, 'They responded not with the shrug of pessimism, but with the shout of anger' (*Living as the People of God: The relevance of Old Testament ethics*, p. 145). There is no mincing of words in such passages as:

I hate, I despise your feasts,
  and I take no delight in your solemn assemblies.
Even though you offer me your burnt offerings and
    cereal offerings,
  I will not accept them,
and the peace offerings of your fatted beasts
  I will not look upon.
Take away from me the noise of your songs;
  to the melody of your harps I will not listen.
But let justice roll down like waters,
  and righteousness like an everflowing stream.
(Amos 5:21–24)

Hear this, you heads of the house of Jacob
  and rulers of the house of Israel,
who abhor justice and pervert all equity,
who build Zion with blood
  and Jerusalem with wrong.
Its heads give judgment for a bribe,
  its priests teach for hire,
  its prophets divine for money;
yet they lean upon the Lord and say,
  'Is not the Lord in the midst of us?
  No evil shall come upon us.'
Therefore because of you
  Zion shall be ploughed as a field;
Jerusalem shall become a heap of ruins,
  and the mountain of the house a wooded height.
(Micah 3:9–12)

Through the prophets God sought to recall his chosen
people to the just and faithful lifestyle spelt out in his
covenant with Moses. They had failed, and he called them
to change their ways decisively. Some of the prophets
made a temporary impact but on the whole they met
with a frosty reception. In the end God went one stage
further. As the writer to the Hebrews puts it:

In many and various ways God spoke of old to our
fathers by the prophets; but in these last days he

has spoken to us by a Son, whom he appointed the
heir of all things, through whom also he created the
world. (Hebrews 1:1–2)

In a nutshell, the business which God had created was
in a mess. Drastic situations require drastic solutions.
Jesus Christ was God's highly original answer.

A second prototype

By becoming man in the person of Jesus, God brought
wisdom down to earth in a very special way. Jesus was
not simply one more prophet through whom God tried to
drag his people back to their senses. Jesus had been with
God in the business of creating life and imparting order
from the very beginning. This was not something that his
earthly contemporaries realised straightaway. It was a
truth which dawned when they came to evaluate Jesus
in the light of his whole career. Thus John, for example,
came to understand Jesus as the *Word*, who was with God
and actually was God; as the *true light* that enlightens
everyone; and, most powerfully of all, as the Word *made
flesh*, who came to dwell amongst the human race, full of
grace and truth (John 1:1–2, 9, 14).

In Jesus we see God pulling off the wraps and revealing
a new prototype. The first model, Adam, had proved a
disappointing failure. A revolution in design was called
for. St Paul makes the contrast between the first man
Adam who was from the earth, a man of dust, and the
second man Christ who is from heaven (1 Corinthians
15:47). But though the origins of Jesus may have been
different, though he had a pre-incarnate existence which
is true of nobody else, his life on earth was one in which
he entered into our full humanity. He experienced the
blood, toil, sweat and tears which is the common lot
of human beings, from sheet-metal workers to money
market managers.

He was a second model who was tested under the most
rigorous of conditions. Unlike the first, he passed with
flying colours. But new products are not automatically

acknowledged as the answer to the market's demands. Similarly, Jesus had to endure a great many hard knocks and a good deal of scepticism along the way.

New and old treasure

Jesus embodied God's wisdom in various respects. First of all, he *taught* it. In many ways Jesus stands solidly in the tradition of the Jewish teachers of wisdom. He shares with them a liking for witty aphorisms which encapsulate profound moral truths in a concise and easily memorable form. Much of the actual content of Jesus' teaching finds parallels in contemporary rabbinic literature. The so-called Golden Rule in Matthew 7:12 ('So whatever you wish that men would do to you, do so to them') is a case in point.

But Jesus refuses to be cast neatly into any conventional mould. He stresses the elements both of continuity and of change with those who had gone before him. In the Sermon on the Mount he says he has come not to abolish but to fulfil the law and the prophets. But he then makes a series of contrasts between what 'You have heard that it was said' and what 'I say unto you' (Matthew 5:17–48). In Mark chapter 2 he emphasises the aspect of novelty which his coming represents. 'No one sews a piece of unshrunk cloth on an old garment'; 'no one puts new wine into old wineskins' (2:21–22). The wine which he produces to forestall an embarrassing social situation at the wedding in Cana is a sign of the new departure from Jewish traditions that he represents. At the heart of those traditions stood writings he recognised as the word of God, but Jesus reserved the authority to interpret them in daring and unconventional ways. He did so, moreover, without feeling the need to justify his intepretation by quoting the opinions of learned commentators: this explains the crowds' astonishment at his teaching, 'for he taught them as one who had authority, and not as the scribes' (Mark 1:22).

Jesus articulated this dual emphasis on continuity and

change in a saying with which he concludes some lengthy
teaching in parables:

> 'Have you understood all this?' They said to him,
> 'Yes.' And he said to them, 'Therefore every scribe
> who has been trained for the kingdom of heaven is
> like a householder who brings out of his treasure
> what is new and what is old.' (Matthew 13:51–52)

Jesus' teaching embraces a discerning conservatism combined with radical innovation. A.E. Harvey has observed
that the saying 'No one can serve two masters' (Matthew
6:24) was probably a conventional maxim, applied both
to political and social life. 'It was Jesus' application of
it to God and money that was arresting' (*Strenuous
Commands: The Ethic of Jesus*, p. 155). Jesus agreed
with a legal expert of his day in seeing love of God and love
of neighbour as the key to understanding the Law. But he
then gives him a rude surprise with the story of the Good
Samaritan. This will have caused consternation in two
ways: first by radically expanding the idea of neighbour
to include even the person traditionally thought of as
the enemy, and secondly by picturing the Jew in the
story as the object, rather than the agent, of love. The
self-satisfied lawyer is being told that sometimes we have
to accept a lesson in caring and compassion from the least
expected people.

In chapter 4 I suggested that the combination of respect
for tried and tested wisdom and openness to radical
new ideas is a vital requirement in business today.
Such an attitude is fully in tune with the teaching of
Jesus. He was a topsy-turvy sort of teacher, sometimes
content to rework conventional teaching (though often
with a characteristic twist), at other times boldly standing
traditional wisdom on its head. Many in his day found
him hard to take; the combination was understandably
mind-blowing. For example, it was difficult to reconcile
his social lifestyle with that of John the Baptist, with
whom he claimed a close affinity. The nitpickers found

fault with them both, but the discerning few could see
that both had an important part to play in God's purposes.
So Jesus comments:

> 'For John the Baptist came neither eating bread nor
> drinking wine, and you say, "He has a demon." The
> Son of Man came eating and drinking, and you say,
> "Here is a glutton and a drunkard, a friend of tax
> collectors and 'sinners'." But wisdom is proved right
> by all her children.' (Luke 7:33–35 NIV)

Similar qualities of discernment are needed by Christians
who work in business. Management literature abounds
with novel techniques from the latest psychometric test
on the one hand to budding New Age philosophy on
the other. Too much of this writing is ephemeral and
superficial in character. But mixed in amongst it are a
few writers (Charles Handy being a notable example)
who have a genuine prophetic quality – shrewdly identifying future trends in the context of present events,
and articulating the need for truly creative management.
In sampling the latest wisdom on offer, we need to be
able to distinguish the gold from the dross. We need
humble, teachable but discriminating spirits, the type of
demeanour which can spot the connection between John
the Baptist and Jesus, and not be offended by either.

Short-term and long-term

A second way in which Jesus radiated God's wisdom
was in his capacity as *leader*. Where Jesus led, people
followed. Three different circles can be distinguished: an
inner band of twelve disciples, a larger group of at least
seventy (see Luke 10:1), who were more loosely associated
with him and helped provide financial support, and the
crowds who were constantly milling around, enthralled
by his spectacular healings and his provocative teaching. When Jesus entered Jerusalem riding on a donkey
the crowds went wild. Here was a man with immense
magnetism of personality, a truly charismatic leader the

like of which politics or business throws up relatively
seldom.

Yet it also has to be said that Jesus' record as a
leader was curiously chequered. He appears to have
spent a lot of time not getting very far with his disciples.
They were a well-meaning, devoted group of men, but
– especially as portrayed in Mark's Gospel – singularly
slow to grasp Jesus' intentions and objectives. They get
into a boat after Jesus has performed a miraculous
feeding, and start worrying about the fact they have
no bread (Mark 8:14–21). Parents bring little children
to Jesus to be blessed by him, but the disciples turn
them away – the very opposite of what Jesus wanted
(Mark 10:13–16). Jesus tells the disciples again and again
that he is destined to suffer and die, but the penny just
does not drop (Mark 9:30–32). Even after his death and
resurrection, they are still mistakenly harbouring the
idea that he might lead a nationalist rebellion: 'Lord, will
you at this time restore the kingdom to Israel?' (Acts 1:6)
During the time of his earthly ministry at least, this elite
inner circle of management was more often a hindrance
than a help.

Similarly, for all the apparent devotion of the crowds,
Jesus' hold on them proved fatally fickle when his moment
of crisis came. The cries of 'Hosanna!' on Palm Sunday
were replaced by 'Crucify him!' on Good Friday. When
Jesus was confronted with arrest and the threat of
execution, all three circles of his followers were notable
largely by their absence.

Yet Jesus' leadership achievement needs to be evaluated in the long term, not the short. His starting line-up
was an unpromising group of twelve, and there was no
way they could be knocked into shape overnight, but
Jesus knew that they had potential. In a particularly
volatile subordinate, Simon, he saw a rock on whom
he would later build his church. And wider even than
the church he had a vision of the kingdom of God,
expanding like a mustard seed from the smallest of
beginnings to the greatest of all shrubs (Mark 4:30–33).
But his was a realistic vision; it was no naive fancy of

smooth, uninterrupted progress. He knew that the way
would often be hard, and he warned of setbacks and
suffering along the way. But Jesus was a man possessed
by a vision – a vision of human beings restored to their
rightful relationship with God and with each other – and
it was his own self-giving initiative which enabled that
vision to come about.

To judge any enterprise correctly, it is important to take
a long-term perspective. Too much of the comment in our
financial press is weighed by purely short-term considerations. With so much buying and selling of shares depending on the appearance of company quarterly results,
companies which curtail profits to make substantial
investments in the future are put at unfair disadvantage.
A chief executive who is adept at cost-cutting or creative
accounting may keep the City happy in the short-term.
To build a solid achievement for the future, he or she
needs supporters willing to back the investing of money in
research and development or suitably tailored training.

Management by wandering around

To suggest that Jesus Christ might offer a valuable model
for management appears trite to many people. For others
the idea is simply laughable. Brought up on the Sunday
School idea of 'gentle Jesus, meek and mild', they cannot
believe that a man who taught the practice of 'turning
the other cheek' has anything to teach the tough world
of business. But to dismiss his significance so summarily
would be wrong. There are at least three ways in which
Jesus' style of leadership offers something to emulate.

Firstly, there is Jesus' *accessibility*. This does not mean
he was necessarily a natural extrovert. Clearly he liked to
withdraw from time to time, treasuring the opportunity
to be on his own with God in prayer (Mark 1:35). But the
interest his actions had stirred up made this difficult.
On two occasions in Mark's Gospel we read of Jesus'
trying to get away from the crowds but then abandoning
this plan of action when confronted by the needs of
desperate people who pursued him: the Galilean crowd,

whom he saw as 'sheep without a shepherd' (6:31–34), and the Syrophoenician woman with the sick daughter (7:24–30). Indeed, the woman's pluck and wit may well have played an important role in broadening Jesus' own understanding of his ministry to include Gentiles as well as Jews.

The Gospels include numerous vignettes of Jesus interacting with other people, whether as individuals or in groups. What is striking is the fullness of attention he gives to each person. Even when he is in a hurry to meet one engagement, he is prepared to break off to attend to someone in an obvious state of need: consider his compassionate treatment of the woman with the blood condition who touched him *en route* to the sickbed of Jairus' daughter (Mark 5:21–34). There is a lesson here for busy managers who feel that they are forever being sidetracked by individuals' unsolicited requests. It is tempting to retreat behind a desk or a secretary and make ourselves inaccessible to the world outside the office, so long is the list of tasks that we desperately want to get done today. Of course this is a measure we may have to resort to occasionally, in order to clear major backlogs of work. But the main image we need to project is one of accessibility. A manager is in the business of handling people, and people need to know that he or she is ready and available to oil troubled relationships, discuss technical problems, or firefight unforeseen emergencies. If employees can never get through to the manager or if they sense that his mind is half elsewhere when they do, they will soon stop trying – with potentially disastrous consequences for staff cohesion and morale.

Hewlett Packard is a highly successful multi-national company which makes electronic instruments and computers. Throughout its history it has enjoyed an excellent track record in employee relations. A key factor in this is the emphasis put on leaders' accessibility. The lay-out of Hewlett Packard's factories is very much open plan, and the company has made 'Management By Wandering Around' a major strategem in its statement of corporate values, the HP Way. The standard approach of one of

HP's founder owners to any formal sort of approach
was 'Don't call me Mr Packard. I'm Dave.' Hewlett
Packard encourages managers to keep up-to-date with
individuals and activities in the plant through informal,
as much as structured, communication. A good deal of
important discussion therefore takes place in hallways,
by the coffee machine and over lunch. Alongside the
stress on wandering around runs what is known as an
'Open Door Policy'. Staff are assured that no adverse
consequences will result from responsibly raising issues
with management or personnel. Managers' doors should
be considered open for the sharing of feelings and frustrations, to put forward proposals for alternative courses
of action, and to discuss career options, difficulties in
business conduct, and breakdowns in communication.
The English side of Hewlett Packard is not quite as
informal in character as the plants in America (where the
company originated), but it has a distinctive, generally
very positive, atmosphere.

Evidence for the fact that Hewlett Packard is a good
company to work for is shown by the length of time staff
tend to stay. It produces people with a strong corporate
loyalty. When the company experienced a lean year
during the downturn in the computer market in 1985,
everyone from the top downwards took a salary cut to
avoid any employee being made redundant. However in
recent years – in response to more long-term changes in
market conditions – there has been some slimming down
of the workforce, with individuals being offered voluntary
severance packages on generous terms.

Knowing what makes people tick

Secondly, there is Jesus' *empathy*. Jesus displays a sympathetic understanding of what is going on inside people.
He immediately grasps the social isolation and genuine
searching of the crooked tax collector Zacchaeus. He takes
a bold initiative in inviting himself to the little man's
house for lunch, and secures a reformation in the man's
business practice without the need for any further words

said (Luke 19:1–10). With another rich man, the young ruler who aspired after eternal life, he was apparently less successful, but he shows both deep affection and cutting perception as he issues the challenge the man found too hard to accept:

> And Jesus looking upon him loved him, and said to him, 'You lack one thing; go, sell what you have, and give to the poor, and you will have treasure in heaven; and come, follow me.' (Mark 10:21)

James and John, two of his leading henchmen, could easily have driven him to distraction when, immediately after his predicting the circumstances of his death, they approach him requesting the best seats in the kingdom to come. But Jesus responds with great patience, making clear that those who sit with him in his glory must first be prepared to experience the dregs of his suffering (Mark 10:35–40; see also Luke 22:28–30). When Jesus shrewdly throws the disciples in at the deep end and sends them out on a mission, they come back pleased as punch with what they've managed to do ('Lord, even the demons are subject to us in your name!'), and Jesus' response is to celebrate joyfully with them (Luke 10:1–24). His prayer of thanks for the special revelation God has given to the disciples must have been a great encouragement to them.

The same qualities of sympathetically understanding people and warmly encouraging them are no less important in business. It is vital to know what makes different individuals tick and what will encourage them to perform better. Some people are strongly motivated by the lure of a bonus or a move to another position. Others are over the moon when the boss simply has the graciousness to say the simple words 'Thank you' or 'Well done'. I know of a hard-nosed manager in the car industry who once surprised a team who had successfully seen a difficult project through to its conclusion by breaking down in tears and saying that he loved them. British people's initial response may be one of embarrassment, but deep down most of us are moved and inspired by the open expression of such feeling.

Gentle Jesus, meek and mild?

Thirdly, there is Jesus' *capacity to challenge.* He knew that there is a time to rebuke as well as a time to build up. Jesus does not spare the disciples some sharp words at times. He openly expresses his disappointment when they prove unequal to the task of coping with the boy suffering from a fit (Mark 9:19: 'O faithless generation ... How long am I to bear with you?'). Simon Peter experiences in quick succession the joy of being called blessed and the horror of being called Satan – when he comes up with the insight that Jesus is the Christ and then thinks he knows better than Jesus what the destiny of this Christ will be (Matthew 16:13–23). There are times when Jesus' handling of people might actually strike us as a bit harsh, when we wish he were a little more the 'gentle Jesus' that so many hard-bitten business people have rejected. But Jesus' plain speaking had at heart the best interests of individuals and he spoke within a relationship of acceptance and love.

Again, the lessons for business practice are clear to be seen. Love for those under the leader's authority is not to be confused with sentimentality. Love is a disposition which delights in other people and wills the best for them. Willing the best includes willing that they give of their best. The manager is therefore right to stretch staff and to expect work of high quality. When an individual or group are letting the company down, they need to be told so.

Robert Greenleaf is a Canadian management consultant who has developed the concept of servant leadership (a phrase, incidentally, which is increasingly coming into vogue). Greenleaf says that 'The servant leader always empathises, always accepts the person but sometimes refuses to accept the person's effort or performance as good enough' (quoted in Graham Tucker's *The Faith-Work Connection,* p. 63). These are precisely the characteristics seen in the person of Jesus. Despite the fact that he and they were often pulling in different directions, Jesus stuck by his motley crew of twelve. Throughout his ministry he was training them – sometimes by teaching, sometimes by personal example, sometimes by sending them off on group exercises – and eventually, after he had physically left them, the training paid off. There is a lot to be learnt in the market place from the leadership style of Jesus.

The right man for the right time

The key to business success often lies in matters of *timing*. Products, processes and investment-drives all need to be launched when market conditions are most apposite and those whom one is trying to persuade most receptive. Marketing directors and corporate strategists show their mettle by decisions they make in this area.

Another aspect of the incarnation which is well worth contemplation is the propitiousness of when it happened. In his letter to the Galatians, Paul expresses this thought of Christ coming at the appropriate time:

> But when the time had fully come, God sent forth his Son, born of woman, born under the law, to redeem those who were under the law, so that we might receive adoption as sons. (Galatians 4:4–5)

Paul's thought here is that the law had run its course. The experience of the people of Israel showed that it was incapable of putting or keeping human beings in a right relationship with God. The highest role that law could perform was that of custodian (3:24). God now intended to fulfil his promise to Abraham with something better.

From a historical perspective, it is also possible to see that the place, the timing and the demographic factors were propitious for the planting of a new religious movement. Jerusalem had links that went to the four points of the compass. The temple, with its three major festivals every year, was the natural centre of gravitation for the $3^1/2$ million Jews trading throughout the Roman

Empire. The account of events on the day of Pentecost in
Acts 2 reveal that the Jews had become an extraordinarily
cosmopolitan group of people. The mass conversion which
took place on that day ensured that the new Christian faith began to spread very quickly. The Romans'
achievement in building roads and imposing order on
the countries of the Middle East also helped the work
of missionaries like Paul. Christianity did not remain a
tiny sect confined to some long-forgotten corner of the
world, because God put secular historical developments
to his purpose.

Nevertheless, it has to be said that Jesus was born into
a highly explosive situation. He grew up in a political
tinder-box. The Romans' rule over the Jews was highly
unpopular; they kept control by a combination of conces-
sions and cruelty, and through the age-old tactic of divid-
ing the opposition against each other. The Sadducees
were ready to collaborate but the Pharisees were not.
Some Jews were in the business of collecting taxes,
while others favoured the revolutionary option. Tension
was unmistakably in the air.

Jesus was a confusing figure in his time because he
sided with none of the established groups. He cut his
own furrow. But in doing so he threatened the security
of others. His hold on the masses worried both the Roman
soldiers and religious leaders, for different reasons. Yet
God's plan for Jesus deliberately included the prospect of
his courting a violent death. He chose a time when the
embodiment of God's wisdom on earth was bound to be
caught in the crossfire between warring factions.

This brings us to the third important way in which
Jesus embodied this wisdom. In AD 33 he was the wisdom
of God on the streets, not just in the way that he taught,
nor in the style with which he led. Nothing expresses the
wisdom of God more than the manner and meaning of
his death.

CHAPTER 9

SNATCHING VICTORY
FROM DEFEAT

The Triumph of the Cross

Those of us who follow the fortunes of the English cricket team may well remember that the 1990/1 tour of Australia was a very painful experience. It was not for lack of self-sacrificial effort on our part! With the devotion of fanatics we set our alarms, plugged in our earphones and tuned in to the dulcit tones of Christopher Martin-Jenkins (the BBC's cricket correspondent) at four o'clock in the morning. But the news we became accustomed to hearing was far from good. On some mornings, it was the news that the English team was sliding towards a crushing defeat, and in due course this likelihood was confirmed; England suffered crushing defeat. But on other mornings there was the prospect that England might actually win. Yet what happened? The team's fragile middle-order batting collapsed again, and another crushing defeat was recorded. Come half-past seven, we stumbled out onto the streets with shadows under our eyes and sorrow in our hearts. We realised that we were supporters of a team that had become expert at one thing: at snatching defeat from the jaws of victory.

What Jesus did on the cross was the precise opposite of this distressing habit of England's cricketers. Jesus is the one, not who snatched defeat from the jaws of victory, but who snatched victory from the jaws of defeat. Before we can savour the wonder of that victory, we must first reckon with the imminence of the defeat. When Jesus was nailed to the cross, it looked to all appearances

like a triumph for the forces of evil. Never have these
forces been rampant in so ugly a style as in the way
they connived at and gloated over Jesus' death. It is
worth reflecting, for a moment, on the way in which
those forces were manifest.

The first evil force which pinned Jesus to the cross
was the power of *legalism*. The Jews said to Pilate: 'We
have a law, and by that law he ought to die, because
he has made himself the Son of God' (John 19:7). Jesus
infuriated the religious establishment of his day because
they saw him as a lawbreaker. His free reinterpretation
of the law about the sabbath, his willingness to spend
time eating with notorious sinners, the claims he made
directly and indirectly about his own person – not all
these actions constituted a technical breaking of the law,
but to those determined to find fault that was the overall
image he conveyed. They could not appreciate and refused
to praise God for the new work he was doing in Jesus of
Nazareth. They were legalists. That represented a very
real bondage to the power of evil, as Paul's letter to the
Galatians makes clear.

The second evil force we see at work in the events
of Good Friday is a vicious, malevolent spirit of *envy*.
The far-from-blameless procurator Pontius Pilate saw
that: 'For he perceived that it was out of envy that
the chief priests had delivered him up' (Mark 15:10).
The religious leaders were furious with Jesus, not just
because they disagreed with his understanding of the
law, but because he was popular with the people. The
crowds listened to him and hung on his every word; they
went to him with their ailments and they had given him
a royal reception on his arrival in Jerusalem. In short,
Jesus had displaced the religious leaders from the centre
of popular esteem. We should not underestimate the
element of bitter personal jealousy in the events which
led to Jesus' crucifixion.

A third evil force which showed its ugly face, as the
crucified Jesus hung dying, was the spirit of *cynicism*.
Consider those mocking words which rang cruelly in
Jesus' ears: 'Aha! You who would destroy the temple

and build it in three days, save yourself, and come down from the cross!' 'He saved others; he cannot save himself. Let the Christ, the King of Israel, come down now from the cross, that we may see and believe' (Mark 15:29–30; 31–32). This is the ultimate in snide talk. Jesus' onlookers and opponents here display that cynicism which is essentially a love of exposing human weakness and revelling in it.

So these three evil forces, legalism, envy and cynicism, temptations to which human beings have always been prone and always will be, enjoyed a field day. The legalists could be satisfied because Jesus hung on a tree, a sure sign that he was cursed by the law (Galatians 3:13). The envious could be satisfied because, in the end, the crowds deserted Jesus: the spell of his hold on popular affection was broken. The cynics could be satisfied because there was no sign of God vindicating Jesus by coming to his rescue – on the contrary, he died complaining that God had forsaken him (Mark 15:34). A crushing victory for the forces of sin and evil? It certainly looked that way.

A knock-out blow

But the truth of the matter (a truth which was mostly hidden that Friday, but the truth nonetheless) was completely different. Jesus actually delivered a knock-out blow to the forces of legalism, envy and cynicism. This is how he did it.

First, legalism. In Colossians 2:14 Paul says that God 'cancelled the bond which stood against us with its legal demands'. The Greek word for bond means an IOU, the acknowledgement of a debt to be paid. Human sin represents one vast mountain of *bankruptcy*. 'Forgive us our sins' meant originally 'forgive us our debts'; the Germans have kept the link more closely because their one word *Schuld* means both guilt and debt. 'This he set aside, nailing it to the cross' (Colossians 2:14). Here we have a vivid picture of the IOU, comprising the debts of the whole human race being hammered into the cross on which Jesus died. Jesus takes upon himself the full

weight of our sins, sins that loom large and sins that
seem small, sins of commission and sins of omission. He
satisfies the demands of the law, and by doing that breaks
the power of legalism, once and for all. Legalism appeared
to have triumphed when Jesus went through the terrible
experience of knowing God's curse, an experience hinted
at in those heart-rending words: 'My God, my God, why
hast thou forsaken me?' Yet the truth of the matter is
that Jesus having experienced that curse once and for
all, the curse then lost its sting. Legalism becomes a
spent force.

Second, envy. Yes, Jesus' hold over the crowds was
badly shaken when he died on the cross. Many of his
closest followers deserted him. But even then, the spell
was not entirely broken. A few women, so often the most
loyal of friends, stayed huddled around the cross. For
one pagan Roman centurion witnessing the whole event,
it was absolutely clear that this was no commonplace
execution: 'Truly this man was the Son of God!', he finds
himself marvelling (Mark 15:39). Those words contained
a hint that the high priests had not heard the last of
Jesus. History since has provided many examples of
a leader's violent death providing fresh impetus and
inspiration for a struggling movement. Jesus' death is
the example which dwarfs all others.

Third, cynicism. The passers-by and the chief priests
scoffed at the idea of Jesus being vindicated – the accused
man being shown to be right after all. But that is exactly
what God did reveal in the event of the resurrection.
Jesus' death did not mean that his Father had abandoned
him for ever. God was simply biding his time. But there
was a striking demonstration of God's power even on
Good Friday. 'The curtain of the temple was torn in two,
from top to bottom' (Mark 15:38). There was sufficient
evidence in that symbolic event that the cynics were being
put to rout.

In the previously cited passage from Colossians 2 Paul
uses another striking image about what God was up to
on the cross. Behind the forces of sin and evil he sees the
work of spiritual powers and authorities, using the phrase

here in a thoroughly negative sense (see my comments on pp. 33–34).

> And having disarmed the powers and authorities, he made a public spectacle of them, triumphing over them by the cross. (Colossians 2:15, NIV)

The sense of this verse is that far from being defeated by the powers and authorities, God actually made a fool of them. The image is one of a Roman general humiliating his captives, by parading them through the streets in a procession at the end of a foreign campaign. That is the total nature of Jesus' victory. We can therefore see why Paul says in 1 Corinthians 2:8 that if the 'rulers of this age' had understood all this, 'they would not have crucified the Lord of glory'.

The relevance of redemption

Christians down the ages have unpacked the nature of Jesus' triumph on the cross in terms of a doctrine of *redemption*. A redeemer is one who effects others' freedom through delivering a payment. Jesus buys back the freedom of the human race by paying for their sin in his death. It may well be asked what on earth this has to do with the tough world of business. The answer is: if we think carefully, a great deal.

First, the redeemer is somebody who is content to play a *servant* role. The focus of his actions is the wellbeing of others. Jesus Christ is one who 'was in the form of God' but 'emptied himself, taking the form of a servant' and 'humbled himself and became obedient unto death, even death on a cross' (Philippians 2:7–8). Christians are called to be emulators of a Master who said 'I am among you as one who serves' (Luke 22:27). As we have seen, this is not a concept which is alien to business: the phrase 'serving the customer' is one which passes a businessman's lips often enough. But they are empty words when the customer becomes an object of scorn, manipulation or indifference, as can happen all too easily. The Christian businessperson should have a solid commitment to a genuine ideal of service.

Second, taking the life and ministry of Christ seriously sets before us the possibilities of a *new start*. Redemption signifies deliverance from the power of evil, passing from darkness into light, a new beginning: all the metaphors used in the New Testament about the salvation God has achieved in Christ have a stark, radical quality. True, life on earth will always partake of the character of the fall, but redemption gives us hope that some at least of the unsatisfactory aspects of business can be changed.

Third, we are faced by the sobering fact that, for the world to be saved, Jesus had to die. Radical transformation of a situation is rarely possible without *cost*. Individuals and groups have to be ready for change, including self-sacrificial change, if business is to be run in the way that God desires. And radical change is likely to be resisted by all who stand to gain from maintenance of the *status quo*, the way things are run at present.

What all this amounts to is that there are actions in business which have a *quasi-redemptive* character. They show the marks of costly Christlikeness. What sort of actions might these be? Here are some possible examples.

Taking the blame

Every organisation, however fine its record of service, is bound to come under critical fire from time to time. The nature of people's jobs is such that some are much more in the public eye than others. They may have to steel themselves to take the blame on behalf of the organisation as a whole. Think of the technical service engineer who in the course of carrying out routine maintenance work receives a mouthful from a customer complaining of faulty goods or a late delivery. He could easily say, with a jerk of the thumb: 'It wasn't me, it was them back at the works', because others in his company are responsible for mistakes which have been made. But it is actually much more constructive, and he is much more likely to reconcile the customer, if he finds the grace to say 'I'm sorry' on behalf of the organisation. In a sense, the engineer who does that redeems the situation by taking the blame vicariously.

Being caught in this situation can involve very real suffering, especially if it happens repeatedly. I have every sympathy for those who work in complaints departments so that apologising to the customer becomes, as it were, part of their job description. If the individuals concerned have a living relationship with Christ and can look to his example, they are more likely to find the resources to be sustained in this uncomfortable scapegoat role.

Risking a loss of reputation

Derek is the Managing Director of a food company which has a £500m. annual turnover. Four months ago the company launched a new brand of yoghurt, which was thoroughly tested beforehand. It soon acquired popularity and already accounts for 12 per cent of the company's sales. However, an epidemic of food poisoning has now broken out in the London area; 350 people have been reported ill with similar symptoms. When their recent food consumption habits were analysed, it was discovered that all but five had eaten yoghurt within twenty-four hours of the onset of illness. One elderly person has since died. Derek is disturbed to discover that his company's new brand of yoghurt is implicated in 75 per cent of the poisoning cases, including the fatality. His team of scientists examine the production system and the products currently being manufactured but are unable to identify a specific cause or connection. However, public concern is escalating fast and the new brand has been blamed in the media. Derek and his Board of Directors meet to discuss how they should respond to a potentially disastrous scenario.

After calling in the company's Chief Scientist for his frank assessment of the situation, the Board feels reassured that there is nothing wrong with the product.

They suspect that the problem may lie at the transport or retail end; the Production Director is firmly of the opinion that the yoghurts have been tampered with after leaving the factory. The police, on the other hand, are adamant that there is no sign of the miscreant yoghurts having been opened and are sceptical that tampering could take place on such a large scale. The Board is not convinced by this. There is a defiant air among the directors and they incline to the view that the company should refuse to take the brand off the market until the link between the yoghurt and the food poisoning has been proven scientifically.

Before they come to a definite decision, however, Derek is called away by his secretary to take a phone call. It is a reporter from a national newspaper relaying him the information that another of the individuals suffering from food poisoning has taken a drastic turn for the worse. She is now fighting for her life in the intensive care unit of a London hospital. The reporter asks Derek how many people are going to have to die before his company remove their lethal product from the supermarket shelves.

Derek returns to the board meeting with his mind made up. He tells the directors that whether or not their brand is to blame, the company does not have any option. They must act responsibly to ease public anxiety, and do so at once. The yoghurt should be removed from all retail outlets forthwith. Some directors favour a compromise solution, suggesting that they keep the yoghurt in the shops but attach warning labels saying there may be a small element of risk involved. Derek laughs that idea out of court: it would increase rather than allay public anxiety, and make the company the object of ridicule. He insists that there is no alternative to a decisive act of damage limitation, and the Board eventually agrees.

Derek bitterly regrets the demise of the company's best-selling yoghurt, not least because he is still inclined to believe the report of his Chief Scientist. But he knows that events have now reached the stage where withdrawal of the product from the market is in the best interests both of the public and the company. There is a saying of Jesus

which could be adapted here, that those who are willing
to lose their life will save it (Mark 8:35). Companies
which are willing to lose their reputation will save it –
or at any rate are more likely to do so than companies
which fight a protracted, defensive rearguard action in
the teeth of mounting evidence against them. Derek
has no intention of admitting corporate responsibility
for the cases of food poisoning. But by withdrawing the
yoghurt he is acknowledging there may be a possible
link, so he is putting the company's reputation on the
line. Nevertheless, he is confident that, in the long run,
this will be offset by the reputation which will be gained
for acting responsibly, with the welfare of the public
at heart.

Letting go

Another board meeting which featured in chapter 4 was
that involving Martin, chairman of the hi-tech company
which has hit troubled waters. The directors want Martin
to resign, believing that Norman (whom Martin had
appointed as managing director) should become chief
executive with the company continuing to draw on
Martin's scientific expertise as an outside consultant.
Faced with this bombshell, Martin has the options of
agreeing to resign, refusing to do so and thereby forcing
the Board to sack him, or making a concerted attempt to
persuade the directors that his continued employment in
a full-time role is crucial to the good of the company.

It will be very difficult for Martin to make a sensible,
rational decision on the spur of the moment. The attitude
of the Board has taken him by surprise. If the directors
are willing to let him, the best immediate course of action
may be to ask the Board for time to think about their
request so that he can consider his options carefully. It
is desirable that he takes advice from those who know
him well.

Having done so, it could be that Martin will be confirmed in his gut belief that the company really needs
him. After all, his name is associated with the original

technology which made the company's reputation. Maybe
his and Norman's roles need redefining, but the company
would be foolish to jettison the advantages he brings it as
its figurehead. He may feel that the Board has misjudged
his skills in thinking that they lie only in the area of
technology. After all, in the early years of its existence he
was instrumental in forging a close-knit, caring company
where the level of staff cooperation was unusually high.

Alternatively, Martin's soul-searching might point in
an opposite direction. Difficult though it is to admit, the
Board has seen something hitherto hidden to Martin. He
is a businessman whose talent lies in launching companies with exciting innovative ideas. He is an entrepreneur, not a consolidator. He is not devoid of interpersonal
skills (especially when he is radiating enthusiasm with a
new idea) but his abilities rest much more in the technical
area. Martin and Norman are both strong characters and
there is no longer room for both of them in senior positions. The Board's judgement that Norman's all-round
management skills are more important to the company's
next stage of development is essentially correct.

Even if Martin acknowledges this in his head, it will not
be easy for him to do so in his heart. He has an enormous
amount of emotional energy invested in a company which
he set up. But close friends who are more impartial may
be able to show him that, crucial though his contribution
has been, he has largely outlived his usefulness to the
company. It is time to let go and make way for others.
Martin's undoubted talents would be better put to work
in some new enterprise.

'Greater love has no man than this, that a man lay
down his life for his friends' (John 15:13). The comparison
is deliberately overdrawn. The call to Martin to give up
his own company is not of the same order as Jesus' to lay
down his life. But the measure of self-sacrificial giving
involved in what Martin is about to do cannot be denied.
To go back to the Board of Directors and accede to their
request will certainly feel like death to Martin. Yet it
could just be that out of that death will spring a glorious
new life – for the company, for Martin, or for both.

On a less dramatic level, there can be a self-sacrificial element of letting go in daily acts of conscious delegation. It is often difficult to delegate, especially when we know a job will be done much better if we undertake it, rather than an employee who is attempting it for the first or second time. But we ourselves, the staff to whom tasks are delegated and the organisation as a whole, may all be served much better in the long run if we are prepared to pass certain responsibilities on to others. The more kudos is put on individual achievement in a company, of course, the stronger will be the temptation *not* to delegate.

Resigning on a matter of principle

There is another type of resignation which has quite a different feel to it. This is when an individual decides to leave a company because he or she has moral objections to what is going on. Another example provides scope for exploring the issues involved.

Liz is the thirty-eight-year-old head of a clinical trials unit which is the subsidiary of a contract research company. She has extensive experience of the pharmaceutical industry and was instrumental in developing the unit into one of the most respected in the area of clinical research. She works extremely hard, often sixty hours or more a week. Unfortunately her marriage has broken up and she is now a single parent with three young children to whom she longs to give more attention. Recognising her difficult situation, the Board of the parent company has agreed that, from the coming autumn, Liz should come home at 3 p.m. to spend time with her children during the late afternoon and early evening, and then devote the latter part of the evening to further work.

Liz is happy to have secured the Board's agreement to this arrangement, but is increasingly worried about the way things are going in the company generally. She has always prided herself on the high quality of the research which comes the way of her unit. However, the drug industry has its share of controversial research, in particular research which lacks a serious scientific basis

and is more a marketing exercise than a clinical trial.
The parent company has hitherto supported the selective
stand she has taken but now, with the company facing
increasing competition, Liz is coming under pressure to
be more compromising and to 'cut corners'. She is unwilling to jeopardise her unit's high quality reputation.

Symptomatic of the change in the parent company's
attitude is its appointment of a new marketing manager,
a man with no previous experience of the industry and
an undiscriminating attitude to drug development. He
returns from a visit to the Continent with proposals for
trials which do not even make clear the disease the drug
is meant to be treating. Liz asks for more information,
but is told to submit a quotation, an instruction she finds
not only unreasonable, but potentially dangerous for the
company. Then she starts coming under pressure to cut
costs by reducing the size of the samples she uses in trials.
She finds this objectionable because she has no wish at
all to see evidence supplied by her being used to support
medical claims which cannot be justified.

Liz's increasing unhappiness with the parent company
comes to a head during the process of negotiating a
contract with a respectable client who has a dilatory
legal department. Liz's practice is never to start trials
with patients before the contract has been finalised. The
Board of Directors, anxious to keep work moving as fast
as possible, tell her to make an exception. Liz objects,
appealing to the Managing Director with whom she has
previously had an agreeable relationship. 'You will do as
you are told' is his frosty response over the telephone.

In early summer, Liz goes on a sailing holiday to
consider her situation. A keen Christian, she asks God
to guide her clearly one way or the other. Two words
imprint themselves on her mind, so powerfully that she
is convinced they are a message from God. The words
are: Only Love. At first she is disconcerted by this. Who
is she to love and how is she meant to love them? God
gives her no discernible answer. But over the next few
days the words have a soothing effect, seeping deep into
her consciousness, so that by the end of the holiday her

jangled nerves have been replaced by a feeling of calm serenity.

A week later, Liz sees the Managing Director. The meeting was at her request but he hardly gives her the chance to speak. He tells her that the parent company is in trouble, her scruples are a luxury that her colleagues cannot afford, and 'You will do as you are told!'. Liz hears these words resounding in her ears again and again. Usually she is quite a fiery character who is prepared to give as good as she gets. She knows the criticisms are unjustified: it is her standards which have attracted business and prestige to the company, and the unit itself is financially sound. But on this occasion she sits patiently through the tirade. She recalls St Peter's comment about the suffering Christ: 'When he was reviled, he did not revile in return; when he suffered, he did not threaten; but he trusted to him who judges justly' (1 Peter 2:23). She realises that her relationship with the Managing Director has irretrievably broken down, that there will indeed have to be a parting of the ways, but she feels curiously peaceful about it. Although the Managing Director is giving her hell, the emotions which stir within her are those of love and sorrow, not hatred and anger. God's message of 'Only Love' is proving its relevance.

When the interview ends, the Managing Director thinks that he has won Liz round. He could not be more wrong. When Liz is invited to the meeting of the next Board of Directors, his manner is very different: all smiles and conciliation. He is visibly shocked when she hands in her notice. He tries to dissuade her: 'This is a disaster,' he says. But Liz refuses to change her decision.

Why does Liz resign? Ostensibly, the factors she cites seem slight. Obscure trial proposals, reducing the size of a sample, proceeding with a clinical trial without legal protection – are these really matters on which to take a heroic stand? But Liz correctly detects that such episodes are symptomatic of the way the company is going. Her interview with the Managing Director confirms her view that there has been a genuine change in management

style. There is a clash between the pragmatic outlook
of the Board of Directors and her own commitment to
high professional standards; she can no longer work for
the company with integrity.

It is a costly decision for Liz. Most of her savings and ten
years of work have been invested in her unit. She believes
she may be able to make a living as an independent
consultant, but that represents a very uncertain future.
She rules out seeking another job, since it is highly
unlikely that she would be able to secure agreement to
the time she has committed herself to spending with her
children. She feels very vulnerable. But as she works out
her notice, the words 'Only Love' continue to sustain her.
She tries to avoid further conflict with the company and
to ensure that the unit's activities are left in as tidy a
state for her successor as she can. Further attempts are
made to persuade her to stay but she resists, convinced
that the decision she has made is the right one.

It is difficult to give generalised advice about when it
is and isn't appropriate to resign. Clearly, it is a decision
which requires the most careful thought. For most people,
if they do it at all, resigning on a matter of principle will
be a once-in-a-lifetime decision; those who make a habit
of it are in danger of making themselves unemployable!
In the majority of situations, the appropriate response
for a Christian faced by dubious demands at work will
be to stick it out, argue the case for a different way of
proceeding and be patient. Christians in business are
sometimes pleasantly surprised to discover that when
they stand up for their convictions, others actually respect
them for it. Colleagues may even be grateful for someone
willing to take a moral lead, and they may then be
prepared to follow.

The circumstances in which resignation becomes a serious prospect are when the company seems irreversibly set
on a downward moral trend. As long as the organisation
offers hope that changes can be made for the better, the
morally sensitive person has a crucial role to play in
reinforcing and bolstering forces in that direction. But
a company which hounds and isolates employees who

represent its own better self (essentially, its conscience) is one where it is difficult to keep such hope alive. In Liz's case, the arrival of the Marketing Manager and the shift of policy on the part of the Managing Director and the Board convince her that the company has abandoned the professional values she treasures so highly. Like Jesus, she takes a costly stand in going it alone.

Making a clean sweep

Taking the blame, risking loss of reputation, letting go and resigning on principle are all examples of quasi-redemptive action in business. They are all actions which involve considerable cost to individual or company. But in certain situations they represent the right course of action, and through them (painful though they are at the time) much good may come. Yet it is important that we do not understand the relevance of redemption in a distorted or one-sided way, so that we glorify a weak or passive attitude in business.

The truth is that to act self-sacrificially is a very bold and courageous thing to do. The individual involved is not simply submitting to the ebb and flow of events, but is exercising some control over them and seeking to influence them. Jesus went to the cross voluntarily. He made this point to the people who arrested him:

> 'Do you think that I cannot appeal to my Father, and he will at once send me more than twelve legions of angels? But how then should the scriptures be fulfilled, that it must be so?' (Matthew 26:53–54)

In Luke's Gospel, this element of control is vividly expressed at the point of death:

> Then Jesus, crying with a loud voice, said, 'Father, into thy hands I commit my spirit!' And having said this he breathed his last. (Luke 23:46)

In acting as they did, Derek, Martin and Liz are not

meekly submitting to defeat, though in the superficial
judgement of the world it may look that way. Each, in
their different ways, is snatching some sort of victory
from the jaws of defeat.

But there is one more example of redemptive activity
in business we need to consider. Let us return to the
unfortunate engineer who is repeatedly put in the position of having to apologise on behalf of his organisation.
The fact is that taking responsibility for the mistakes
of others is not something anyone should have to put
up with indefinitely. A good organisation has a fairly
low tolerance level of mistakes, because it is genuinely
concerned to serve its customers better. So a managing
director may have a quasi-redemptive role to play in
sweeping out of the system the evil represented by complacency with low standards and indifference to customer
needs. In critical situations he may need to take very
radical steps, removing people, reforming practices, and
replacing products. Effectively, he makes a clean sweep.

It may well be asked what is redemptive about such
a course of action. Doesn't this call to mind, not the
image of Jesus on the cross, but Jesus expelling the
money-changers from the temple (though that incident in
itself may suggest there is a valid place for such action)?
Doesn't it conform much more to a conventional macho
image of management? Of course, it may be carried out
in precisely that mould. But not necessarily. There can
well be considerable cost involved for the wielder of the
new broom. The action he takes will almost certainly be
to the customer's benefit, but it is still likely to provoke
considerable resistance from within the company. People
do not like being stirred out of their cosy little ruts.
The managing director will experience resentment and
receive flak. Jesus certainly did when he evacuated the
temple.

A business leader who is modelling his or her life on
Christ need not be inhibited about leading from the front.
Jesus did this, literally, even as he set out on that fateful
journey to Jerusalem, which ended with the cross. Mark
records a telling piece of detail about the disciples' sense

of awe as they observed the purposeful way in which
Jesus strode out ahead, fully aware of the suffering which
lay in store:

> And they were on the road, going up to Jerusalem,
> and Jesus was walking ahead of them; and they
> were amazed, and those who followed were afraid.
> And taking the twelve again, he began to tell them
> what was to happen to him, saying, 'Behold, we are
> going up to Jerusalem; and the Son of man will be
> delivered to the chief priests and the scribes, and
> they will condemn him to death, and deliver him to
> the Gentiles; and they will mock him, and spit upon
> him, and scourge him, and kill him; and after three
> days he will rise. (Mark 10:32–34)

CHAPTER 10

BOUNCING BACK TO GOOD EFFECT

Resurrection Power At Work

The difficulty which Jesus' disciples had in com-
prehending the fact that his destiny was a violent
death extended also to the predictions he made about his
resurrection. When Jesus died on the cross, they were a
shattered, despondent group of men. Their dreams and
aspirations for a liberated Israel lay in ruins. Nothing is clearer from the Gospel accounts than the fact
that the resurrection of Jesus took them by complete
surprise.

This is especially evident in one of the best loved Easter
stories, the account of the two lesser-known disciples
walking home to the village of Emmaus (Luke 24:13–35).
Cleopas and his partner (quite possibly his wife) are
absorbed in melancholy discussion about the tragic fate
which has befallen their leader. Their heads are down,
their spirits at rock bottom. Even when the risen Jesus
joins them, talks with them and explains the Scriptures to
them, they do not recognise him. True, a profound experience is taking place. The couple express this later by
saying 'Did not our hearts burn within us while he talked
to us on the road, while he opened to us the scriptures?'
(24:32). The phrase 'hearts burn' is open to a variety
of interpretations: a gradually dawning understanding?
the first subconscious hints of recognition? a warmth
blossoming into love for the mysterious interpreter? But
it is only after they have invited him into their house
and during Jesus' characteristic act of breaking the
bread that the penny drops. Cleopas and his partner
realise who Jesus is. The surprise is immense, and
the effect electrifying. Forgetting the weariness of their

seven-mile walk, they leap from their chairs and hurry back to Jerusalem to tell the core group of disciples.

A resilient God

The resurrection of Jesus was an amazing event. It took the disciples by surprise, energising and enabling them in turn to take the world by storm. Of all the miracles which the Bible reports, it stands head and shoulders above the rest in terms of importance. But there is a sense in which it is not such a surprising event after all. John Polkinghorne has described a miracle as the expected consequence of an unprecedented circumstance. The point is that if God was uniquely present in Jesus Christ, the unexpected was indeed to be expected. Even if you nail him to the cross, you cannot keep a good God down that easily. A God who is not only good but great bounces back – to dramatic effect.

Gradually the New Testament church came to discern that the resurrection possessed its own inner logic. It was no one-off wonder, but an event pregnant with meaning. There are three main aspects to this.

First, Jesus' rising from the dead gives us a sure hope that there is life beyond the grave. It is a decisive demonstration that our present existence is not the sum total of things. St Paul argues thus:

> If for this life only we have hoped in Christ, we are of all men most to be pitied. But in fact Christ has been raised from the dead, the first fruits of those who have fallen asleep. For as by a man came death, by a man has come also the resurrection of the dead. For as in Adam all die, so also in Christ shall all be made alive. But each in his own order: Christ the first fruits, then at his coming those who belong to Christ. (1 Corinthians 15:19–23)

Peter makes a similar point in his first letter:

Blessed be the God and Father of our Lord Jesus

Christ! By his great mercy we have been born anew
to a living hope through the resurrection of Jesus
Christ from the dead, and to an inheritance which
is imperishable, undefiled, and unfading, kept in
heaven for you, who by God's power are guarded
through faith for a salvation ready to be revealed
in the last time. (1 Peter 1:3–5)

The New Testament links Jesus' resurrection and our
resurrection very closely together. The one is an antici-
pation and assurance of the other.

Second, Jesus' rising from the dead was God's way
of confirming his unique identity. Otherwise we would
have no reason for according Jesus anything more than
a very minor footnote in history, as an eccentric, itinerant
Jewish rabbi who came to a sadly sticky end. The resurrection gives solid ground for endorsing the centurion's
confession: 'Truly this man was the Son of God'. Paul
makes this point in the course of explaining the nature
of his gospel right at the beginning of the letter to the
Romans:

... the gospel concerning his Son, who was de-
scended from David according to the flesh and des-
ignated Son of God in power according to the Spirit
of holiness by his resurrection from the dead, Jesus
Christ our Lord ... (Romans 1:3–4)

The question of Jesus' true identity aroused persistent
controversy throughout his career. By raising him from
the dead, God provided the answer. The breathtaking
power inherent in the act was his way of proclaiming
that Jesus was indeed part of his very being, a man who
could rightly be called *Son of God*.

Third, Jesus' rising from the dead is the vindication of
the man who was crucified. It is God's stamp of approval,
not just on the person of Jesus, but on the mission he came
to perform. It gives us cause for regarding the crucifixion
not as a tragedy (though it contained a tragic dimension),
but as an integral part of God's plan for saving the

world. Jesus' death and resurrection belong indissolubly together:

> He was delivered over to death for our sins and was raised to life for our justification. (Romans 4:25, NIV)

The distinction made in this verse should not be interpreted in a wooden manner: the meaning of the latter phrase is 'raised to life to guarantee our justification'. If it were not for God's great act of raising Jesus from the tomb, we would have no sensible reason for imagining that our sins could be forgiven through his death.

Surprising on one level, the resurrection therefore has a remorseless logic on another. The New Testament verse which states this most clearly occurs in Peter's speech on the Day of Pentecost:

> But God raised him up, having loosed the pangs of death, because it was not possible for him to be held by it. (Acts 2:24)

A premature death could not contain the God who was present and active in Jesus. He was far too resilient for that. Although he made himself genuinely weak and vulnerable, so that he died on the cross looking an abject failure, this was not the end of the story. God bounced back.

Fishing – the heights and the depths

Few people go through a career in business without experiencing some sharp shocks along the way. There are the episodes which look like failures and the episodes which constitute genuine failures. There is the blunder which costs the company serious money, the close working relationship which sadly deteriorates, the ghastly interview which tells you your services are no longer required. There is no point in kidding ourselves otherwise: failure in the place of work can be absolutely miserable and personally demoralising. But it can be very difficult to admit this frankly to other people.

A prominent Christian who has spoken in public with admirable honesty about success and failure is Lady Judith Wilcox, Chairman of the National Consumer Council. Most of her working career has been spent in the fishing industry. She pinpoints two critical episodes in her life where things she was involved with went disastrously wrong. The first happened when she was running a family business of high street shops in the south-west of England. Trading in shellfish gave her the idea of purchasing two fishing trawlers as a sideline. But owning and running a trawler proved very different from running shops. The crew 'share fished', the price of oil soared, the costs of running the boat escalated, and Cornish women were losing enthusiasm for going down to the quay and buying unfilleted fish. The business sank to the point where its owner suffered the shame of watching a writ being nailed to the mast of her ship and the heartbreak of the MAM GOZ being registered as a wreck.

But Judith is nothing if not a resilient person. It took her three years to recoup the losses made financially in this venture (they included the sale of three shops), but the experience had very constructive effects in terms of focusing the mind. She learnt lessons about herself, realising she should concentrate on her strengths – namely cost and management accounting on the one hand, and the organisation of people and buildings ashore on the other.

She also learnt lessons about the way the fishing industry was going. Seeing that the future lay with those who added value to the basic product of fish, by making it easier to cook and tastier to eat, she moved into the processing industry, setting up Channel Foods, a company which specialised in smoking fish. The move was a success. By the mid-1980s Channel Foods was employing 350 people and had a £10m. turnover.

Like many up-and-coming companies, the time came when it was propitious to sell the business to a large multi-national. The new owners rapidly found a fresh challenge for Judith. Another of their recent acquisitions was a canning factory in Boulogne, Pêcheries De La Morinie (P.D.L.M.), a business imperilled by years of no investment, massive overmanning, restrictive working practices and outdated technical procedures. Judith was appointed President Directeur-Général of the factory with the task of streamlining the business and slimming it down, ready for the challenge of 1992.

True to her character, she threw herself into this challenge with gusto. Monsieur Dupont, the trade union leader who turned out to be a devout Communist, a dapper man who looked like Hercules Poirot without the moustache, was certainly a formidable opponent. But gradually Judith convinced even him of the necessity for change. She shared the financial gravity of the factory's situation openly with Dupont and the local managers, and took some of them over to Channel Foods (in which she maintained a financial stake) in order to show them a modern smoking factory and give them a glimpse of what P.D.L.M. might become. She submitted to head office a proposal for the transformation of the business and promised the union that she would stay and see the changes through. All was progressing well: Judith had built her team and gained their trust.

Meanwhile, back at head office, the multi-national had come under severe financial pressure and was going through a necessary rationalisation. Sacrifices and hard decisions had to be made. A letter duly arrived in Boulogne. It said that for the wellbeing of the company as a whole, the investment strategy for P.D.L.M. had to be halted. Judith found herself having to pass on the unpalatable information that the business had to be reduced to a skeleton staff which would serve as the basis for recruitment and expansion when the company was in a position to resume investment in upgrading the facilities.

The lesson Judith learnt from this second episode was that she had confused responsibility with power. She had previously directed business as an owner, but now she was in a position of middle management. The ultimate

decisions were no longer hers to take. She had failed
to recognise that a worst case scenario could happen
elsewhere in the company, with serious knock-on effects
for her own sphere of responsibility. The result was that
she had made undertakings to Monsieur Dupont that she
was unable to guarantee could be kept.

Again, however, Judith's resilience stood her in good
stead. She did not simply deliver the bad news and run.
Establishing a fish farm and a property development
company in the Boulogne vicinity, she was able to employ
some of the people who had been made redundant. She
showed that she still cared about and was committed to
the area, and she remains so to this day.

Failing forward

I am grateful to Lady Wilcox for allowing me to share
something of her experience. Her story, along with that
of many others, shows that failure need not be totally
destructive. Initially, its effect may be so numbing that
'shattered' is the only word fit for self-description. But as
the dust settles, there are almost always practical lessons
to be learnt, if only we have eyes to see them. The fact is
that there is often a thin line between success and failure,
and in the ashes of many a failure lie the seeds of a future
success. The business world needs to take seriously the
concept of *failing forward*.

Those who put their faith in Jesus Christ should
be particularly alive to this possibility. The one who
bounced back from death can help us to recover from
setbacks in the work-place. Admittedly, the analogy has
its limitations: Jesus went to his death in obedience to
God's will, whereas we often (not always) encounter
failure through deviating from his will. Yet the central
point at issue is the same. Whatever the reason for
failure, it need not be the last word. A resilient God
equips us with the same capacity for bouncing back. On
one level, he helps us to learn practical lessons from what
went wrong, so that we do not make the same mistakes
again. On another level, he sustains us with a love which

is not conditional on our standing in the eyes of the world. No passage states this more memorably than the final verses of Romans 8:

> We know that in everything God works for good with those who love him, who are called according to his purpose ... What then shall we say to this? If God is for us, who is against us? He who did not spare his own Son but gave him up for us all, will he not also give us all things with him? Who shall bring any charge against God's elect? It is God who justifies; who is to condemn? Is it Christ Jesus, who died, yes, who was raised from the dead, who is at the right hand of God, who indeed intercedes for us? Who shall separate us from the love of Christ? ... No, in all these things we are more than conquerors through him who loved us. (Romans 8:28, 31–35, 37)

A memorable breakfast

One of the resurrection stories is very much about the difference which the risen Lord makes to a situation at work. Sadly, this fact often goes unobserved by commentators and preachers. It is the story which describes an amazing incident in the same industry with which Lady Wilcox is so familiar – that of fish.

> Afterwards Jesus appeared again to his disciples, by the Sea of Tiberias. It happened this way: Simon Peter, Thomas (called Didymus), Nathanael from Cana in Galilee, the sons of Zebedee, and two other disciples were together. 'I'm going out to fish,' Simon Peter told them, and they said, 'We'll go with you.' So they went out and got into the boat, but that night they caught nothing.
> Early in the morning, Jesus stood on the shore, but the disciples did not realise that it was Jesus. He called out to them, 'Friends, haven't you any fish?' 'No,' they answered. He said, 'Throw your

net on the right side of the boat and you will find
some.' When they did, they were unable to haul the
net in because of the large number of fish. Then the
disciple whom Jesus loved said to Peter, 'It is the
Lord!' As soon as Simon Peter heard him say, 'It is
the Lord,' he wrapped his outer garment around him
(for he had taken it off) and jumped into the water.
The other disciples followed in the boat, towing the
net full of fish, for they were not far from shore, about
a hundred yards.

When they landed, they saw a fire of burning coals
there with fish on it, and some bread. Jesus said to
them, 'Bring some of the fish you have just caught.'
Simon Peter climbed aboard and dragged the net
ashore. It was full of large fish, 153, but even with
so many the net was not torn. Jesus said to them,
'Come and have breakfast.' None of the disciples
dared ask him, 'Who are you?' They knew it was
the Lord. Jesus came, took the bread and gave it to
them, and did the same with the fish. This was now
the third time Jesus appeared to his disciples after
he was raised from the dead. (John 21:1–14, NIV)

It may well have been a sense of anti-climax which
prompted Peter to decide he was going fishing. Certainly,
he'd experienced the excitement of Easter Sunday, he had
seen the risen Lord, but where was all that excitement
leading? Jesus himself had disappeared as suddenly and
mysteriously as he had appeared. Peter and the other
disciples may well have had a feeling of being left in
the lurch. With Peter in particular, there may have been
a sense of unfinished business, of reconciliation as yet
unmade, after the awful matter of denying Jesus. What
were the disciples meant to do now? For three years
they had been Jesus' near constant companions. Now
there was a gaping hole in their lives, and they were
left wondering how to fill it.

Peter, always a man who liked practical action, comes
up with a very obvious solution: *back to work*. Back to
the practice and the trade he and the others knew so well,

that of fishing. I have come across one commentator who describes this as an act of apostasy, an abandonment of discipleship. That is a very harsh judgement. It is entirely understandable that the disciples wanted to fill their time doing something positive. They may well have needed to do so for financial reasons.

These fishermen were real professionals. They knew what they were doing when it came to fish. That was why they went out at night: experience had taught them this was the most productive time. But on this occasion they fished with a singular lack of success. When morning came, their nets were as empty as when they'd begun. We can imagine their feelings: tired, frustrated, tetchy, baffled, hungry.

That simple phrase 'they caught nothing' is profoundly evocative. It calls to mind all the occasions when we work extremely hard over something and achieve nothing. There is the house that a housewife spends all day tidying up which is systematically untidied by the small child who trails round after her. There is the contract which the project manager has worked so hard to secure only for it to be awarded at the last minute to somebody else. There is the report which the secretary has lovingly transcribed on to the word processor and is lost when the disc develops signs of terminal damage. There is the employee with the alcohol problem who seems to be responding to the treatment for which his company has paid, and then all the progress is undone in an evening of wild drinking.

What we experience at times like these is the futility of work. A sense of time, money and energy having been wasted: in the words of Ecclesiastes, 'a striving after wind ... What has a man from all the toil and strain with which he toils beneath the sun?' (Ecclesiastes 2:17, 22). Like Peter and his colleagues, we catch nothing, and find it difficult to understand where we've gone wrong.

So exasperated were the disciples, so completely at their wits' end, that they are ready to act on the advice of a complete stranger, even though this must have been a serious blow to their pride. Who was this clever fellow on the shore who asked the painful question: 'Friends, haven't you any fish?' Never mind, from his vantage point he might be able to see something they couldn't. They cast their net in to the right, and this time they really do catch something. The realisation that it is the risen Jesus who is the mysterious stranger rapidly follows.

Christians who work in business should take encouragement from the fact that the glorified Lord makes himself known to the disciples in their doing of a secular job. Jesus does *not* criticise the disciples for going back to their old occupation. They may have had an inflated sense of their self-sufficiency, but the actual work they sought to do was not wrong. What Jesus does is to bring success to their working endeavours, to lead their night out fishing to a marvellous conclusion.

This story raises the question of whether we expect, look for and long for the resurrection power of Jesus to be evident in our places of work. Do we believe he can transform our mundane, complex and often difficult situations just as he filled those fishing nets to bursting point? Just as there are episodes of depressing futility at work, so there are also moments of exciting transformation. It could be a dreaded interview with a member of staff, which turns out much better than expected: a hostile relationship turned into a friendly one, with real reconciliation taking place. It might be the breakthrough in a research programme when months of painstaking investigation and experiments suddenly come to fruition. It may be a sudden influx of customer orders after a period of deep recession and constant cutbacks.

There is a delicate theological balance to observe here. Jesus' metaphorical presence with us on the shore does not guarantee that everything in the place of work will go wonderfully smoothly. The Christian faith is not that sort of insurance policy. Frustrations and setbacks, crossed lines and empty nets will continue to afflict us from time to time. But in Jesus Christ there is a scope for transformation, which is relevant to working life as well as to church life. In this particular story, change is effected through listening to a word of advice: 'Throw

your net on the right side of the boat.' Christians need
to be on the alert for similar words of wisdom. If they
are living in a state of close relationship with their risen
Lord, they may be surprised at the flashes of inspiration
which sometimes come their way.

   In this story there is a fine sense of Jesus and the
disciples being co-workers. Admittedly, Jesus provides
the decisive piece of information, but the disciples have to
haul the fish ashore, and quite a weight it was too. When
they reach the beach they find Jesus has already been
busying himself cooking a breakfast, apparently having
access to some private fish supply of his own. Putting all
their food together, they concoct what must have been
a marvellous meal: a barbecue to beat all barbecues,
a breakfast party in a class of its own. No doubt the
disciples forgot their tiredness, the crossness about the
long hours wasted catching nothing, and marvelled at
the transformation which had taken place – all because
of the risen Jesus who was in their midst.

After Japan

The modern business world has its share of turnaround
stories, companies which have come back from a state
of decline or potentially fatal slumber. One of the most
interesting is Ford Motor Co.

   In the mid-1970s the British side of Ford's operations
presented a curiously mixed picture. Ford cars were
selling well, and the company appeared to hold sway in
Britain's largely captive market. But this apparent state
of wellbeing was deceptive. The management style was
authoritarian, the union style militant. Efficiency levels
were poor, and strikes, real or threatened, were a regular
feature of the company's annual round of pay bargaining.
Ford was not the only car company where there were such
problems, but they were symptomatic of a dangerous
state of complacency in the face of emerging competition from Japanese manufacturers who were starting to
import cars into Europe.

   In 1978 Bill Hayden, Vice-President of Manufacturing

for Ford of Europe, visited Japan to gauge for himself
the nature and extent of the coming competition. The
experience dealt him a severe shock. He realised that
Japanese companies like Toyota and Nissan were years
ahead of Ford in terms both of technology and the levels
of commitment and co-operation they were able to con-
jure from the work-force. If Ford failed to change its
production methods, keep abreast of the latest technology
and break its destructive mould of internecine strife, he
believed that it was doomed. The company needed to
discover a new competitive edge. This visit proved a
turning-point in Ford's history. The message which Bill
Hayden brought back was communicated effectively to
the whole of the work-force. The company could not afford
to slumber in a state of complacency.

The results were impressive. Industrial relations were
not transformed overnight, but gradually bridges of confidence were built and the barriers of mutual suspicion
and distrust broken down. A particularly notable aspect
of the Ford experience is the way that management and
unions discovered habits of relating to each other in a non-
confrontational way through co-operation in schemes outside the main manufacturing activity. In the mid-1980s,
Ford started an Employee Development and Assistance
Programme (EDAP). This is a programme, funded by
the company, which pays for study classes chosen by
the employee as part of his or her personal development. These classes involve anything from Chinese brush
painting to bicycle maintenance or learning Spanish; they
even include degree courses. Most have nothing to do with
making cars. This programme has been hugely popular
and the current employee take-up stands at 45 per cent.

In reorganising its methods of production, Ford drew
upon the example of Japanese companies, as Western
companies have in many other sectors of industry. But
while there is much to learn from Japan's formidable
economic achievement, it is important to recognise cultural differences when it comes to making appropriate
changes. Western workers are not going to follow the
habit practised in some Japanese companies of starting

the working day by singing a song enshrining the corporate values. In contrast, 'Quality Circles' and 'Just In Time' are well established practices in Japan which have caught on to some extent in the West. What management at Ford discovered was that employees and their trade unions were suspicious of any new technique which was presented with capital letters. To them it inferred a threat to the established order of doing things. Ford therefore abandoned the phrase 'Quality Circle' and found its own way of conveying the message which the phrase implies, namely small groups owning responsibility for the efficiency of the process and the quality of the product with which they are involved.

In the late 1980s, systems of car assembly were changed so that individual workers experienced more variety of tasks operating within a team. The time taken to assemble a car from start to finish was systematically reduced. Cars like the Fiesta and Sierra sold solidly during the 1980s and Ford improved its competitive position. So striking was the overall change that people who work at Ford describe their recent history in terms of what happened 'Before' and 'After Japan' – the latter even being referred to as AJ!

In her book *The Change Masters*, Rosabeth Moss Kanter identifies a crisis or *galvanising event* as one of the major building blocks in bringing about constructive corporate change. Ford's After Japan experience certainly bears this out. The company, along with the rest of the motor industry in Britain, still faces a very challenging future. Having given a rival like Toyota so many years start, it is difficult ever to catch up. But the change in style and transformation of ambience which have been effected since 1978 represent a very considerable achievement.

Sharing the success

Another remarkable success story of recent years raises wider questions about company ownership. It is well described in the autobiography of Sir Peter Thompson, *Sharing the Success: The Story of NFC*.

During the 1970s the National Freight Corporation
consisted of a state-owned assortment of mainly loss-
making transport and distribution companies, including
BRS, Pickfords and National Carriers. When the Con-
servatives came to power in 1979 they were determined
to privatise it, but NFC's fortunes had sunk so low that
an advisory team of merchant bankers said there was no
hope of a successful stock flotation. The Chief Executive
of NFC was Peter Thompson, a man who entered the
public sector with high hopes but who gradually became
disillusioned with the workings of nationalised industry.
Faced with the verdict of the City experts, his mind
turned to the possibility of a management buy-out. But
as he relates:

> At the same time, all my socialist instincts of yester-
> year came to the fore. Why not make it an employee
> buy-out and include the whole of the workforce? But
> the company we wanted to create had to be different
> from a consensus co-operative which cannot take dif-
> ficult decisions; different from a normal capitalistic
> company where the emphasis is too much upon the
> satisfaction of the needs of the shareholders; differ-
> ent from a nationalised industry where the concept
> of ownership-in-common had failed to motivate. Our
> 'different' company finally emerged in concept and
> vision as a new form of employee capitalism. The
> company would be owned by the employees who
> would *buy* rather than be given the shares. They
> would have a role to play in the policy-making of the
> business, but the managers would have the mandate
> to manage. All employees would share in the wealth
> that they created. (*Sharing the Success*, p. 75)

Thompson soon won the support of his fellow-directors,
and indeed of the then Transport Secretary, Norman
Fowler, who saw it as a novel way of stealing the Labour
Party's political clothes. But he still faced formidable
obstacles before his ideal could be realised. He had difficulty persuading the senior management of Pickfords,

whose commitment lay with Pickfords rather than NFC and were initially unenthusiastic about putting their money into the conglomerate business. The privatisation scheme was actively opposed by the major union involved, the Transport and General Workers. They argued that workers holding shares could produce 'serious conflict of interest and damaging division of loyalties', the argument being that workers' principal loyalty was to their union, not the company. In the event, many members defied the union stance and bought shares, but management and employees could only raise £7m. of the required £53.5m. In order to complete the purchase, NFC were beneficiaries of an unsecured loan from their backers, Barclays Merchant Bank – the only way to get round Section 54 of the Companies Act, 'Thou shalt not pledge the assets of the company you are seeking to buy in order to raise the money to buy it'. Finally, however, the deal did go through.

The privatisation of NFC was the prelude to a spectacular revival of fortunes. In the next six years it achieved compound growth in pre-tax profits of over 40 per cent per annum, and growth in earnings per share of over 30 per cent. Curiously, the recession of 1981–3 worked in NFC's favour. Companies which were feeling the pinch cut the cost of operating their own transport and distribution systems, and contracted the business out to NFC. The Corporation penetrated the international removals market in a big way. Meanwhile, radical changes in corporate style were taking place. Managers worked on their communication skills and became far more consultative. The workforce became better motivated, more productive, and – especially those who had invested in shares – markedly more prosperous.

A different debate

At the present time, it is fair to say that the century-long debate over the merits of capitalism and socialism has run its course. Whatever the excellence of socialism's egalitarian ideal, practical expressions of it which were

tried proved ineffective in creating wealth. The market
system has established its superiority in that respect.
But there still remains plenty of scope for debate about
what type of capitalism, and more precisely, what type of
corporate ownership, is desirable. The model adopted by
the National Freight Corporation provides an interesting
variant on the standard formula of the public limited
company.

The Companies Act of 1862 which established the
principle of limited liability was a key event in British economic history. Although it was instrumental in
generating the flow of capital necessary to maintain
a process of rapid industrialisation, it has not passed
without criticism. The nub of the problem was well
expressed by the distinguished social historian Sir Arthur
Bryant when he said 'A limited liability company has
no conscience' (*English Saga 1840–1940*, p. 329). His
concerns have been taken up in recent years by two
senior Christian businessmen with radical ideas, George
Goyder and John Davis.

First of all, it is argued that the limited liability
company tends to separate ownership from stewardship.
John Davis expresses concern that such companies

> ... enable shareholders to accumulate unlimited
> wealth without any participation in the wealth-
> creating activity, but with the power to buy or sell
> such companies like any other piece of property.
> Consequently those whose working lives are devoted
> to the well-being of the Company – employee direc-
> tors, managers and the rest of the work-force – are
> legitimately bought and sold at the whim of owners
> and for their personal gain. (John Davis, *Greening
> Business*, p. 128)

In *Sharing the Success*, Peter Thompson makes the point
that in a PLC directors and shareholders should regard
each other as partners, but all too often this is not
the case:

... AGMs in the main have not been successful in securing shareholder involvement. This is primarily as a result of the average shareholder's indifference to the way a company is managed. Many boards have not welcomed shareholder involvement, and many company chairmen take pride in their ability to complete an AGM in the least possible time. The record probably stands at well under three minutes. Only when things are going wrong do the shareholders turn up in force to question the board. But this makes the shareholder the equivalent of an absentee landlord. He owns a piece of the company and, so long as he is getting his annual 'rent' in the form of dividends and capital growth, he really does not need to visit the 'farm'. This is even more the case when the 'owner' of the shares is not an individual but a financial institution which 'owns' the shares on behalf of its clients, whether pensioners or insured persons. (*Sharing the Success*, p. 114)

The power without responsibility enshrined in limited liability also has serious consequences for the situation where a company is forced into liquidation. Is it right that shareholders bear no responsibility for the debts incurred by the company? In this situation the people who are left holding the short straw are the suppliers and others who are owed money by the bankrupt company.

Christians believe in a resurrection power which delights in the creation of new things. Alternative forms of ownership which engender a strong sense of corporate loyalty, and encourage greater accountability all round, have much to commend them. The National Freight Corporation had some notable precursors: the John Lewis Partnership, whose shares have been held in trust for the firm's employees since 1929, and the Scott Bader Company whose employees were given the company by its founder, Ernest Bader, in 1957. Despite its success, NFC has not as yet had any emulators. The incidence of employees holding shares in their own company, or companies operating profit-share schemes, is increasing, but usually these fall well short of the reality of managers and employees together owning the company.

The fact is, of course, that there are practical financial constraints which make this difficult. NFC itself has modified its original concept with the passage of time. It was unable to finance continued expansion from its own internal market in shares. In 1988 it was successfully floated on the Stock Exchange. But NFC took special measures to ensure that it became no ordinary public limited company. First, in advance of the public quotation of shares, existing shareholders were allowed to buy new shares at a cheaper price. Second, employee shareholders have double voting rights in the circumstance of the company being faced by the prospect of a takeover. Peter Thompson in his book is confident that NFC will retain its special character and not abandon its values lightly.

Employee ownership is a laudable objective, but it should not be seen as the panacea for all problems. Some people will always buy shares for purely financial reasons; interest in or loyalty to a company are considerations which pass them by. Additional finance from external sources is a necessity for all organisations which aspire to flourish in a world market: the pressure for large-scale operations is very strong. The claim that Christian theology points irresistibly towards any particular form of corporate ownership is difficult to sustain. The conventional PLC appears set to continue for some time to come. But it is encouraging that variants upon it are being tried. It is to be hoped that debate on these structural issues will continue, and that Christians will play their part, both by way of theoretical contributions and – where they are in a position of influence to effect this – by practical experiments in alternative forms of ownership.

CHAPTER 11

DRAWING ON THE SPIRIT

The Neglected Source of Creative Energy

During the last half-century the worldwide Christian church has witnessed a great revival of interest in the doctrine and person of the Holy Spirit. The most obvious manifestation of this is the rapid expansion of churches with a strong pentecostal or charismatic emphasis. Gifts of the Spirit such as prophecy and speaking in tongues, which earlier generations of Christians largely assumed had died out with the passing of the New Testament era, have been rediscovered in a spectacular way. But there is also a fresh emphasis on the Holy Spirit in many churches which do not belong to the pentecostal wing, and tend to look upon these gifts with caution or suspicion. Whether the focus of the Spirit's activity is seen in terms of supernatural power or whether it is seen in a quieter mode of refreshing dry souls and reconciling warring factions, Christians are waking up to two facts: first, that they desperately need the active presence of God in their lives, and second, that this is something they really can experience through the renewing person of the Holy Spirit.

This has been a welcome rediscovery on the church's part, even if it has sometimes been accompanied by extreme and eccentric fringe activities. Charismatic churches can be places of disorder and breeders of confusion, but they are generally lively places where members worship God whole-heartedly and genuinely seek the Spirit's help in changing their lives and attracting other people to Christ.

The chief danger in all this, however, is that Christians' focus becomes unduly domesticated. The Holy Spirit is not just relevant to the sphere of the church, to the work of reviving the committed and sending them out into the local community to win new converts – important though that is. The Spirit is concerned with renewing the whole of God's creation. This obviously includes the world of work.

In this chapter I shall outline several qualities which are part and parcel of the Spirit's activity, and have special relevance for men and women involved in business.

Two unsung heroes

And Moses said to the people of Israel, 'See, the Lord has called by name Bezalel the son of Uri, son of Hur, of the tribe of Judah; and he has filled him with the Spirit of God, with ability, with intelligence, with knowledge, and with all craftsmanship, to devise artistic designs, to work in gold and silver and bronze, in cutting stones for setting, and in carving wood, for work in every skilled craft. And he has inspired him to teach, both him and Oholiab the son of Ahisamach of the tribe of Dan. He has filled them with ability to do every sort of work done by a craftsman or by a designer or by an embroiderer in blue and purple and scarlet stuff and fine twined linen, or by a weaver – by any sort of workman or skilled designer. Bezalel and Oholiab and every able man in whom the Lord has put ability and intelligence to know how to do any work in the construction of the sanctuary shall work in accordance with all that the Lord has commanded. (Exodus 35:30–36:1; see also Exodus 31:1–11)

Bezalel and Oholiab are two of the unsung heroes of the Old Testament. Nobody teaches about them in Sunday School, yet the practical contribution they made to the life of the pilgrim people of God was immense. The full extent of their work is described in detail in Exodus chapters 36–39. Bezalel was a skilled carpenter, metalsmith and engraver. He led the work on the tabernacle and its precious cargo, the ark of the covenant. Oholiab was his able assistant, specialising in the skills of design, weaving and embroidery. This passage offers some fascinating insights about them.

First, it is notable how the biblical writer describes Bezalel and Oholiab as being *filled with the Spirit of God*. This is a phrase used sparingly in the Old Testament. Usually it is reserved for specific individuals occupying the roles of prophet, priest or king, but here we find it used about the skills of the craftsman. By implication, we can see evidence of the Spirit's activity in 'every able man in whom the Lord has put ability and intelligence to know how to do any work . . .' (36:1).

Second, God's gifts to Bezalel and Oholiab include the knack of passing their knowledge on. These two men could not do all the work by themselves. They were given inspiration to *teach* (35:34). Whether it is done on a one-to-one basis, the apprentice learning by observation of the master craftsman at work, or whether it happens in a more didactic way, the expert imparting knowledge to pupils in a group, the gift of teaching is one of priceless value.

Third, the emphasis on artistic design (35:32, 35) appears to put a strong premium on *creativity*. These men did not work to stereotyped formulae. The Spirit of God released their imaginations to create something powerful in its originality. They used a great variety of colours, materials and forms in the making of the tabernacle and all it contained.

Modern counterparts

These passages from Exodus should serve as a tonic and encouragement to Christians working in business. The specialist skills which we are privileged to possess and paid to practice are abilities given by the Holy Spirit. Bezalel and Oholiab have a great profusion of modern counterparts. Two objects I have in the room where I work remind me of this. One is a vivid poster depicting the latest tractor made by JCB Landpower. It was sent to

me by a project manager who designed the suspension, a
revolutionary new design which helps enable the vehicle
to travel at the unlikely speed for tractors of 45 mph.
Another is a paper on 'Personal mobile communications
– a vision of the future'. It was written by a research
engineer who works for British Telecommunications and
outlines recent developments in radiopaging, cordless
telephony and cellular radio. Both these friends are
established experts in their fields.

The fact that different individuals are equipped with
varying skills in the spheres of craftsmanship and technology has long been recognised. Much more recent is the
appreciation that there is also a range of specialist skills
to be drawn upon in the workings of a management team.
Meredith Belbin, the distinguished Cambridge theorist,
has usefully analysed these skills in terms of eight
main types:

* *The Chairman* (a role which does not necessarily
correspond to actual function), who has a keen sense
of each individual's strengths and is good at co-
ordinating the activities of the group.

* *The Shaper*, who likes to take initiatives and
imposes direction on the activities of the group.

* *The Plant*, who has an original, creative mind and
is forever coming up with new ideas for tackling the
activities of the group.

* *The Monitor Evaluator*, who is good at analysing
problems, and is keen to measure and assess what
is being achieved.

* *The Company Worker*, who likes to know what
needs to be done and to get on and implement it.

* *The Team Worker*, who is good at encouraging others and lubricating relationships within the
team.

* *The Resource Investigator*, who has a good range of
contacts and knows how to tap valuable resources.

* Last but not least, the *Completer Finisher*, who
ensures that something is produced at the end of it
all!

Belbin has devised a questionnaire which enables individuals to ascertain which of these they are and what is the
balance of their different skills. The question: 'What is a
desirable mix?' is one which warrants a different answer
from person to person. Some managers, especially those
working in very small organisations, require a broad
range of skills; they cannot afford to be very weak
in any department. Others, especially those working
in large organisations where there is a wide range of
skills, are best advised not to spread themselves too
thinly. It is better that they play up to their particular
strength, confident in the knowledge that colleagues are
demonstrating theirs. Ideally, a team of eight comprises
eight individuals who are strong in these different areas.
The reality is that teams rarely work out that neatly,
so if there is a shortage of skills in one particular area,
those who reveal most potential in that area should be
encouraged to develop the appropriate skills, in order to
fulfil the aim of a well-balanced team.

Being on a high

Bezalel and Oholiab provide one Old Testament picture
of what it means to be filled with the Spirit. They applied
their God-given, practical intelligence in a sober and
aesthetically beautiful way. The experience of the prophet
Ezekiel was very different. The operation of the Spirit in
his life is described thus:

And he said to me, 'Son of man, stand upon your
feet, and I will speak with you.' And when he spoke
to me, the Spirit entered into me and set me upon
my feet; and I heard him speaking to me . . .

Then the Spirit lifted me up, and as the glory of the

> Lord arose from its place, I heard behind me the
> sound of a great earthquake . . .
>
> And the Spirit lifted me up and brought me in
> the vision by the Spirit of God into Chaldea, to
> the exiles.
>
> (Ezekiel 2:1–2; 3:12; 11:24)

This is the language of possession and ecstatic experience.
Ezekiel, we might say, is 'on a high'. Literally or meta-
phorically, the Spirit carries him away, on journeys over
which he has no control and into experiences he would
rather have done without.

It is much more difficult to apply this sort of experience
of the Spirit to business, and the point of comparison
is limited. But there are individuals who embark on a
business enterprise with a burning sense of mission.
Whether they are filled with enthusiasm for an exciting
new product, or determined to put into operation a
distinctive style of organisation, they behave at times
like men and women who are possessed. They are people
of vision, striding out along the mountain-tops, hurdling
over the obstacles, and often rather allergic to the detailed
running of the organisation. Such individuals may be
driven only by the force of their own ego, and if things
go wrong, they have the capacity to bring an awful lot
of employees tumbling down with them. But this bold
entrepreneurial spirit can be something that is genuinely
inspired by God and by a concern for human wellbeing.
There is a very real place for the business visionary.

Studies which have been done on the subject of leadership are showing an increasing recognition of the vital
quality of *enthusiasm*. Subordinates respond to a person
who is really excited about what the organisation is
doing. Americans have always been less inhibited than
the British about appearing enthusiastic; there are some
welcome signs now that people on this side of the Atlantic
may be discarding their suspicions of the person who
attacks his job with gusto. Enthusiasm at best is an

infectious sort of quality, improving staff morale as much as it quickens productivity. It is not to be sniffed at.

An improbable transaction

In Ezekiel's case, being caught up by the Holy Spirit was not a particularly happy experience. This was because the message he was commanded to convey to the Jewish people was one of judgement and doom. Very much the same is true of the prophet Jeremiah. He predicted the imminent fall of the city of Jerusalem, and made himself highly unpopular with the kings of Judah because of it. Yet there is one striking incident where Jeremiah performed an improbable business transaction as a pledge of his confidence in the future. It is found in Jeremiah 32.

The year is 588 BC, with the armies of Babylon hammering at the gates of Jerusalem and Jeremiah under arrest in the court of King Zedekiah. For the Jewish inhabitants of the city, the writing lies plainly upon the wall. Hanamel, Jeremiah's cousin, decides it is time to be cutting his losses and selling the family property. Surprisingly, since no-one was more convinced that the Babylonians would take the city than Jeremiah, he accepts Hanamel's offer to purchase the field. The transaction is described in graphic detail:

> And I bought the field at Anathoth from Hanamel my cousin, and weighed out the money to him, seventeen shekels of silver. I signed the deed, sealed it, got witnesses, and weighed the money on scales. Then I took the sealed deed of purchase, containing the terms and conditions, and the open copy; and I gave the deed of purchase to Baruch the son of Neriah son of Mahseiah, in the presence of Hanamel my cousin, in the presence of the witnesses who signed the deed of purchase, and in the presence of all the Jews who were sitting in the court of the guard. I charged Baruch in their presence, saying, 'Thus says the Lord of hosts, the God of Israel: Take these deeds, both this sealed deed of purchase and this

open deed, and put them in an earthenware vessel,
that they may last for a long time. For thus says the
Lord of hosts, the God of Israel: Houses and fields
and vineyards shall again be bought in this land.'
(Jeremiah 32:9–15)

Jeremiah is a very human character. He believed that
God had told him to buy the field, but after doing so he
has second thoughts about the wisdom of his action. He
takes his worry to God in prayer (32:16–25). He receives
a reassuring word from God that though Jerusalem will
indeed fall into the hands of the Babylonians – justly so,
because of the nation's many failings – God still has a
positive future in store for them. Fields will again be
bought, and deeds of property signed, in a city whose
immediate destiny is desolation (32:42–44).

The purchase of the field at Anathoth is therefore no
ordinary business transaction. Jeremiah himself never
benefited from it. After the fall of Jerusalem, some Jewish
refugees fled to Egypt, Jeremiah being an unwilling member of this group. As far as we know, he never returned.
His action was not a serious commercial transaction, but
a powerful prophetic gesture. He did what he did, not
on his own behalf, but in the name of the Lord and
as an expression of hope for the future of his younger
compatriots.

Recently I attended a conference for Christian business
people on the theme of recession and recovery. Someone
raised the question of whether Jeremiah's land-purchase
represented a model for bold adventurous action in the
midst of dire economic circumstances. Precisely because
this was a prophetic rather than commercial transaction,
we must beware of jumping to any hasty conclusions.
Most Christians who buy property during an economic
downturn will have exactly the same experience as their
secular counterparts: they will lose money on the deal,
and that will be all there is to be said about it.

Nevertheless, economic downturns have a habit of
levelling out sooner or later. The property developer who
picks up a large plot of land dirt-cheap at the bottom of

the market could be on to something very lucrative. So it is that the defiant spirit who flouts conventional business wisdom sometimes comes up trumps. It is not outside the bounds of possibility that the Holy Spirit might be the one inciting such acts of *adventure*.

The irony of the situation is, of course, that if more people were prepared to take acts expressing confidence in market conditions together, general recovery would take place much quicker. But once a trend has been established, it is very difficult to reverse it. Every company understandably fights for its own survival, and in making economies and clinging on hard to its cash makes life difficult for lots of others. The way out of recession actually lies in collective action – but that would amount to a colossal defiance of conventional wisdom.

Making connections

Basic ability, allied to enthusiasm and a spirit of adventure are important requisites in business, especially for those who aspire to be business innovators. But these qualities on their own are not enough. Enthusiasm can be misdirected; adventures may turn out to be blind alleys. The crucial attribute of *discernment* is also needed.

Discernment too is a gift of the Holy Spirit. Again there are lessons to be learnt from the Old Testament prophets. They read the signs of the times accurately, unlike their all too complacent contemporaries. In particular, they displayed a capacity for making creative connections. Amos 8 provides an interesting example of this:

> Thus the Lord God showed me: behold, a basket of summer fruit. And he said, 'Amos, what do you see?' And I said, 'A basket of summer fruit.' Then the Lord said to me,
> 'The end has come upon my people Israel;
> I will never again pass by them.' (Amos 8:1–2)

The sequence of thought here tends to be lost on those

who do not know any Hebrew! The word for 'summer' (*qayits*) sounds very similar to that for 'end' (*qets*). Seeing a basket of fruit leads Amos to think of the judgement he already knew God had in store for Israel. Effectively what he coins is a prophetic pun. A similar occurrence is found in Jeremiah 1:11–12 where there is a play on the words 'almond' (Hebrew *shaqed*) and 'watching' (Hebrew *shoqed*). Making connections between things that, on the surface, have little or nothing to do with each other is a phenomenon central to the process of innovation. Many a useful invention has occurred by accident. Alexander Graham Bell was trying to design a hearing aid in 1876 when he invented the telephone. The person who had the idea for an anglepoise table-lamp did so through observing the flexible mechanism of the human arm. The notion of cellophane drinking straws came to Otto Dietenbach when he was idly twisting the outer wrap from a cigarette packet round a thin steel rod. It is a pattern which has been repeated again and again.

Girlies on the wall

Another area where discernment is required relates to the extent one is willing to delegate responsibility for the making of important decisions. Consider this intriguing scenario.

Terry is the Managing Director of a small engineering company employing 180 people. Most of his work-force pride themselves on being red-blooded males who enjoy having calendars portraying very scantily clad females at their place of work. Terry doesn't really like this, but he has not made any serious objection hitherto. However, he has recently appointed two able women, Karen and Sheila, to his management team, Karen as Finance Director and Sheila in charge of Personnel. They are adamant that they will not tolerate the calendars, which they regard as sexist and demeaning to women. When Terry explains their objection to Len, the workers' shop steward, he says there is no way that the men will consent to having the calendars removed. Dark hints about strike action are muttered. When Terry reports this to the women managers Karen, whose financial skills have already proved very valuable to the company, starts talking about looking for another job. Suddenly Terry finds that an issue which to begin with appeared trivial is in danger of blowing up into a crisis.

There seem to be three options which are open to Terry.

1. On the central issue of whether the calendars are offensive, Terry's instinct is to side with Karen and Sheila. Although he had got used to the calendars so that he scarcely noticed them any more, he had always vaguely disapproved of them, and sometimes been embarrassed when showing distinguished visitors round the factory. It is within his power simply to call the workers' bluff and remove the calendars, perhaps after they have gone home from work or before they arrive one morning.

2. On the other hand, Terry has some sympathy with a point made by Len, that the display of the calendars predated the arrival of the two women managers. They were shown round the factory when they came for their interviews, and they did not voice any unhappiness then. Len says that the workers simply regard the pictures as a 'bit of fun'; they do not intend to show any disrespect to women in general, least of all Karen and Sheila in particular. Terry sees considerable force in this argument and is strongly tempted to tell the women managers that they are getting the whole thing out of proportion, and that they ought to respect the workers' freedom of action.

3. Terry may decide that this is an issue where it would be inappropriate for him to arbitrate. He could tell Karen and Sheila that they should get together with Len (and perhaps one or two of the more experienced and level-headed engineers), and see if they can work out a mutually agreeable solution. Although emotions have run high and there seems little scope for compromise at the moment, it may be that when the two sides have sat down and listened to each other's point of view, something

tolerable to both may emerge. For instance, the places
in which calendars are displayed might be restricted, so
that they are less exposed to public view, or Karen and
Sheila could be invited to identify calendars they find
more tasteful and less offensive.

Which of these three options should Terry go for?

The argument in favour of either of the first two is that
a clear decision is made, the issue is not fudged, and Terry
shows that he is not afraid to exercise responsibility. As I
have already argued on p. 150, there is a very real place
for leaders who are prepared to lead from the front. When
it comes to deciding on corporate strategy, taking drastic
measures to clear a deficit, or attempting to transform the
company's values, a chief executive has no business leaving
the task to others. But the gift of discernment suggests that
this is not such a situation. The moral case is not clear-cut.
Terry sees strong arguments on both sides, and if he was
to take decisive steps either on Len's side or on Karen's, he
could not live easily with such action. It would be a denial of
something valid in the other's point of view. Also, he would
be likely to precipitate either industrial action on the one
hand or Karen's departure on the other.

Superficially, the third option may look like an abdica-
tion of responsibility on Terry's part. It might not work:
the two sides may fail to reach agreement, and this could
deepen the impasse. But on balance, it seems to represent
the most constructive option. Essentially, Terry will be
saying to the different parties: I believe you have got
this issue out of perspective. You are adult people, and
the onus is on you to find a solution which is mutually
acceptable. But there may still be a positive role for Terry
to play in terms of preparing the ground for the encounter.
He could stress to the engineers that they need to take
seriously the fact that the business world is changing,
that women are playing an increasingly significant role
and that their sensitivities must be respected; and to
the women managers that much as he shares their
dislike of pornography, they cannot expect to transform
deeply entrenched cultural attitudes overnight. If Terry
expresses such sentiments clearly before the different

individuals come together, then he is not actually abdicating responsibility at all, and it is likely that agreement will be reached, Karen will stay in her job, and production can continue uninterrupted.

Effective communication

The incidence of references to the Holy Spirit increases greatly when we come to the New Testament. It is the descent of the Spirit at Jesus' baptism which sets him up for his teaching and healing ministry. Jesus attributed his ability to deliver people from powers of evil to the work of the Spirit of God, and as evidence that the kingdom of God had dawned (Matthew 12:28). He promised his disciples that after his departure, the Holy Spirit would come to them:

> 'These things I have spoken to you, while I am still with you. But the Counsellor, the Holy Spirit, whom the Father will send in my name, he will teach you all things, and bring to your remembrance all that I have said to you.' (John 14:25–26)

Jesus underlines the crucial role of the Spirit in *communication* a little later on:

> 'When the Spirit of truth comes, he will guide you into all the truth; for he will not speak on his own authority, but whatever he hears he will speak, and he will declare to you the things that are to come.' (John 16:13)

Even with this warning, however, the disciples must have been amazed just how effectively the Spirit helped them to communicate when he arrived on the day of Pentecost. There are two striking aspects to this.

First, the Spirit releases them from the fear which had confined them to the upper room since Jesus left them. They went out boldly to proclaim the good news about Jesus of Nazareth in public. Before long they were in trouble with the religious authorities, but Peter, 'filled

with the Holy Spirit', surprises the high priest and his
entourage with a splendidly lucid speech (Acts 4:8–13).
In this we can see fulfilment of a promise made by Jesus,
namely:

> 'When they deliver you up, do not be anxious how
> you are to speak or what you are to say; for what
> you are to say will be given to you in that hour; for
> it is not you who speak, but the Spirit of your Father
> speaking through you.' (Matthew 10:19–20)

Second, the Spirit's gift on the Day of Pentecost included
a miraculous ability to speak in other languages. This
enabled the apostles to communicate 'the mighty acts
of God' (Acts 2:11) in the native tongues of the Jewish
pilgrims who were in Jerusalem. The Spirit helped them
to overcome linguistic barriers. An even more formidable
hurdle, arguably, were the cultural barriers which stood
in the way of spreading the new Christian message
into Gentile society. But here too the Spirit of God
was at work, preparing Gentile hearts, bringing about
a gradual revolution in the mindset of Jewish believers,
and demonstrating his favour by giving to the Gentile
converts similar experience and gifts (see especially Acts
10 and 15). So Peter could say at that important strategic
appraisal, the Council of Jerusalem:

> 'Brethren, you know that in the early days God made
> choice among you, that by my mouth the Gentiles
> should hear the word of the gospel and believe. And
> God who knows the heart bore witness to them,
> giving them the Holy Spirit just as he did to us;
> and he made no distinction between us and them,
> but cleansed their hearts by faith.' (Acts 15:7–9)

Paul saw the dismantling of the barrier between Jew
and Greek as lying at the very heart of the gospel: he
describes it as his insight into the mystery of Christ,
revealed in the present time by the Spirit (Ephesians
3:4–5; see also 2:11–22).

The fact was, however, that it was not easy to keep everyone in the New Testament church thinking that way. Paul fought a hard battle (not, it seems, definitively settled by the Council of Jerusalem) to convince the Jewish Christians that Gentile believers did not need to be circumcised. In time, the success of his Gentile mission eclipsed that of work among the Jews, so that the Christian church developed into a largely non-Jewish phenomenon. In modern times, the church has repeatedly set up new forms of spiritual apartheid – whether this consists of the policy of the South African Dutch Reformed Church, which for many years supported the political programme of that name, or the argument posed by sections of the Church Growth Movement, that it is better for individual churches to be culturally homogeneous, because like is more effective in attracting like. But what does a church gain in increasing numbers if in doing so it denies an essential tenet of the gospel?

Doing business across different cultures

Issues of culture and the obstacles to crossing culture are just as relevant to the conduct of business. They matter when it comes to winning contracts in other countries. They matter when it comes to holding together a multi-national company which has employees from many different nationalities. They matter when it comes to merging the operations of two or more companies each of which has a distinct culture.

One organisation which dispenses a great deal of wisdom in this area is The Centre for International Briefing, based at Farnham Castle in Surrey. It runs courses for businesspeople, politicians, diplomats and any others wishing to acquaint themselves with particular cultures. There is indeed much to be learnt if one is to avoid needless offence and embarrassment to people of other countries. For instance, it is important when dealing with the Japanese to be careful with one's physical movements. To lounge back in a soft chair and reveal the soles of one's feet is not the done thing. The Japanese put great store by balance and calm, and they are disconcerted by sudden movements. Because they themselves do not wish to offend, they are apt to conceal information which the listener is likely to find disagreeable – a trait which to Western eyes looks hypocritical but is really only a desire to be polite.

The need to tread warily is, curiously, even greater when mixing with people whose culture one assumes to be similar to one's own. Americans and British share (for the most part!) a common language, but they say and do things differently. I know a British manager with Shell, operating in the States, who was seriously offended when his American boss described his work as 'quite good'. The boss used the word 'quite' to mean 'very'; my friend misinterpreted his comment to mean 'moderate'. If an American says that he agrees to doing something in principle, that implies a much greater level of commitment than it does in a British setting, where what is desirable in principle is often deemed unattainable in practice. When negotiations run into trouble, Americans, having a history of using the law to define boundaries, are much readier to appeal to the institutions of justice. The British resort to courts of law much later in the pursuit of an argument.

All these, of course, are generalisations. There are individuals within these national groupings who provide exceptions to them. It is useful to have knowledge about general cultural tendencies as a starting-point, but dangerous if we then mould everyone we meet into stereotypes. Sometimes half-baked knowledge is more dangerous than no knowledge at all. The wise businessman operating across cultures proceeds cautiously, avoiding the arrogant presumption that everyone else's culture is a deviation from his own, and not assuming either that every German or Arab or Korean he meets is a typecast representative of their own culture. The best policy, according to the late Richard Hobbs, former Director of The Centre for International Briefing, is to be sensitive, but to be yourself. It is important to enter sympathetically into the perceptions of a person from another culture, but it is no good pretending that we will ever be one of them: doing business across cultures does not mean being a pseudo-national.

The problems are formidable, but they are not insurmountable. There are many successful multi-national companies which show that it is possible both to wield employees drawn from different races into close-knit teams, working to commonly recognised objectives, and to win the confidence of diverse peoples among whom they operate. The task demands considerable skills in communication, ranging from fluency in languages to understanding of physical cues. This is very much the province of the Holy Spirit, and Christians who work in such contexts can be grateful that they have hidden resources on which to draw. Breaking down the misunderstandings which are bound up with history, geography and colour is not just a crucial business requirement. It is a central part of the Spirit's concern.

In mint condition?

When one company takes over another company, the issue of crossing cultures appears in another form. In many such cases, the takeover would not be taking place unless something was deemed to be defective in the performance of the target company. The new owners will almost certainly want to make changes. But does a successful acquisition give them licence to ride roughshod over all that has gone before? How can one eradicate the worst and bring out the best in a corporate culture? The case of Trebor Bassett provides an instructive example.

Trebor (as it used to be called) is a firm based in the south-east of England which has made various types of confectionery since 1906. For nearly three decades it was run by two brothers, John and Ian Marks. In the course of building Trebor up to a point where it claimed 14 per cent of the UK sugar confectionery market, they developed a highly distinctive corporate culture. This was especially pronounced at a new, specially designed factory which was opened at Colchester in 1981; there Refreshers and various types of mints are made. The Marks brothers put great emphasis on Trebor being a pleasant place to work, in which individuals would experience personal fulfilment. The organisation had a very flat management structure, with the work groups who were churning out the sweets exercising a high degree of autonomy. The factory prided itself on its involvement and reputation in the community.

Although Trebor's turnover grew steadily throughout the Marks' stay at the helm, profits began to slacken during the mid and late 1980s. Having resisted offers to sell for twenty years, they finally accepted a bid in excess of £100m. from Cadbury Schweppes in 1989. Around the same time Cadbury bought another confectionery firm, Bassetts, and in March 1990 it merged the two acquisitions to form a new subsidiary company – Trebor Bassett.

When the takeover news was announced at the Colchester factory, there was considerable consternation. The Marks brothers softened the blow by making generous distributions among the workforce from the company sale. But there was a fear that acquisition by a large public limited company would spell the end of Trebor's special character. Speculation abounded that the Colchester plant would close, causing big redundancies.

Cadbury Schweppes itself is a company with an interesting history. Its origins are strongly Quaker, George Cadbury being one of the great paternalist employers who wielded much influence around 1900. He built a garden village for his employees in Bournville, Birmingham. In the century since, the distinctive ethos he promoted has inevitably become somewhat diluted. The present breed of Cadbury Schweppes managers pride themselves on their professionalism. Having emerged in the mid-1980s from a takeover threat themselves, they have a highly developed focus on profitability and margin enhancement. For them, the key word which was missing from Trebor's vocabulary was that of *accountability*. Workers needed to be made more accountable for what they did; managers needed to be made more accountable to shareholders. The changes brought about by Cadbury Schweppes in Trebor Bassett have been principally concerned with instilling this key attribute into operations.

The improvements made in financial performance have been striking. Trebor Bassett increased its trading profit by 28 per cent in the first full year after the merger, and enhanced its trading margin from 9.8 per cent to 11.3 per cent. The response from the City, which at the time of acquisition could only be described as muted, has become markedly more enthusiastic.

The changes necessary to make such improvements have not been altogether popular at the factory level, as they have involved the alteration of a number of lax working practices which had developed in the wake of the Trebor culture. But it would be a mistake to suggest that Cadbury's policy towards what they found in Trebor has simply been to criticise and to dismantle. They have recognised positive aspects in the Trebor culture which they have tried to reinforce. The factory had a strong social network, with employees displaying a high degree of commitment to each other. An improved communications system has built upon this. Pay settlements also take an interesting form: essentially the senior managers negotiate with the whole of the work-force, each of twenty different groups being called in to hear management's view of past performance and future plans, and then to consider their pay offer. The response to this form of negotiation has been largely positive. Here is seen most clearly the emergence of a hybrid culture, a system which reflects something of both the Cadbury and the Trebor way of doing things. This can only be described as an interim report, but so far there is evidence both of firmness and sensitivity in the way this large company has proceeded after taking over a smaller one.

Spiritual treasure in clay pots

A final comment about the relevance of the Holy Spirit to business is to note that the claims made in the New Testament about the transforming power of the Spirit are

breathtaking. In 2 Corinthians 3:18 Paul says that 'we
all, with unveiled face, beholding the glory of the Lord,
are being changed into his likeness from one degree of
glory to another'. Where does this change come from?
Paul gives the answer straightaway: 'from the Lord who
is the Spirit'.

Yet Paul was no starry-eyed optimist. In the very next
chapter he shows how frail he feels his mortal nature to
be. Talking about the demanding task of preaching the
Gospel, he writes thus:

> But we have this treasure in earthen vessels, to show
> that the transcendent power belongs to God and not
> to us. We are afflicted in every way, but not crushed;
> perplexed, but not driven to despair; persecuted, but
> not forsaken; struck down, but not destroyed; always
> carrying in the body the death of Jesus, so that the
> life of Jesus may also be manifested in our bodies.
> (2 Corinthians 4:7–10)

This description of the experience of the first missionaries
is one that is familiar to many a Christian in business,
especially those who feel a strong vocational element
about what they are doing. They experience their share of
affliction, perplexity, even persecution. Friendly gestures
are misunderstood, suppliers of a critical order produce
substandard work, Sod's Law seems to be operating
overtime. It is all too easy to feel drained of creative
energy, particularly when family and church are making
major demands to add to those of work. We do indeed
feel like earthen vessels, or, as the Good News Bible
puts it, 'clay pots'. One of the most important lessons
in the Christian life is to learn, at such points of need, to
draw – consciously and deliberately – on the sustaining
power of the Holy Spirit. The Spirit is a great source of
creative energy. When we are drained, he can revive.
Not the least of the Spirit's gifts to his people is the
nitty-gritty attribute of *perseverance*.

CHAPTER 12

LOOKING FOR A BETTER COUNTRY

The End Time as Inspiration and Warning

Jürgen Moltmann is one of the best-known among contemporary German theologians. The book with which he established his reputation is *Theology of Hope*, first published in English in 1967. It starts with a criticism of the way Christian eschatology, the doctrine of the 'last things' or 'end', has traditionally been sidelined. He argues that the relegating of events like the return of Christ and the judgement of the world to a last day beyond history has robbed them of their directive, uplifting and critical significance for all the days which are spent here, this side of the end, in history. Moltmann thinks that eschatology has therefore tended to lead a peculiarly barren existence at the end of Christian dogmatics: a loosely attached appendix wandering off into obscure irrelevancies.

Moltmann proposes instead a quite different view:

In actual fact, however, eschatology means the doctrine of the Christian hope, which embraces both the object hoped for and also the hope inspired by it. From first to last, and not merely in the epilogue, Christianity is eschatology, is hope, forward looking and forward moving, and therefore also revolutionising and transforming the present. The eschatological is not one element *of* Christianity, but it is the medium of Christian faith as such, the key in which everything in it is set, the glow that suffuses everything here in the dawn of an expected new day. For Christian faith lives from the raising of the crucified Christ, and strains after the promises of the universal future of Christ. (*Theology of Hope,* p. 16)

In essence, Moltmann is correct. Eschatology is a doctrine too often relegated to the category of the obscure, and its relevance needs to be demonstrated in a fresh way. Yet there is a delicate theological balance to be observed. The Christian doctrine of our future hope embraces both the present world and a world beyond it. It is a hope which inspires us to work for something better in the here and now, but also alerts us to the reality of divine judgement on the last day.

Hebrews 11 contains some very poignant remarks about Christian hope. The writer is talking about some of the heroes and heroines of faith in the Old Testament:

> These all died in faith, not having received what was promised, but having seen it and greeted it from afar, and having acknowledged that they were strangers and exiles on the earth. For people who speak thus make it clear that they are seeking a homeland. If they had been thinking of that land from which they had gone out, they would have had opportunity to return. But as it is, they desire a better country, that is, a heavenly one. Therefore God is not ashamed to be called their God, for he has prepared for them a city. (Hebrews 11:13–16)

It is clear that what the writer to the Hebrews has in mind here is an existence beyond this world. The Old Testament heroes saw this only in fleeting glimpses. Christians, taking assurance from the resurrection of Jesus, have much more solid grounds for hope. As they bear the brunt of widespread indifference and hostility to the things of God, they frequently know what it means to be 'strangers and exiles on the earth'. They are comforted by the belief that the full experience of salvation, the coming to completion of the kingdom of God, will take place the other side of the grave. They are looking and longing for 'a better country, that is, a heavenly one'. It is only in 'a new heaven and a new earth' (Revelation 21:1), which comes after the first heaven and earth have passed away, that the effects of the fall will be wholly reversed.

Utopia on earth?

The phrase 'new heaven and new earth' is not found only in the book of Revelation. It also occurs in the last two chapters of the prophet Isaiah (65:17; 66:22). The first of these passages is well worth considering at length:

> 'For behold, I create new heavens and a new earth;
> and the former things shall not be remembered
>   or come into mind.
> But be glad and rejoice for ever in that which I
>   create;
> for behold, I create Jerusalem a rejoicing,
>   and her people a joy.
> I will rejoice in Jerusalem,
>   and be glad in my people;
> no more shall be heard in it the sound of weeping
>   and the cry of distress.
> No more shall there be in it
>   an infant that lives but a few days,
>   or an old man who does not fill out his days,
> for the child shall die a hundred years old,
>   and the sinner a hundred years old shall be
>   accursed.
> They shall build houses and inhabit them;
>   they shall plant vineyards and eat their fruit.
> They shall not build and another inhabit;
>   they shall not plant and another eat;
> for like the days of a tree shall the days of my
>   people be,
>   and my chosen shall long enjoy the work of their
>   hands.
> They shall not labour in vain,
>   or bear children for calamity;

for they shall be the offspring of the blessed of
   the Lord,
  and their children with them.
Before they call I will answer,
  while they are yet speaking I will hear.
The wolf and the lamb shall feed together,
  the lion shall eat straw like the ox;
  and dust shall be the serpent's food.
They shall not hurt or destroy
  in all my holy mountain,
                      says the Lord.' (Isaiah 65:17–25)

This too is future hope, but the prophet's expectation
of a Golden Age lies squarely within the confines of
earthly history. He sees Jerusalem as the focus of this
transformed existence. He is still thinking in terms of
human mortality, even though everyone is now guaranteed of living to a good old age. But the extent of the
transformation is so great, the vision of life so Utopian,
that it is difficult from our perspective to believe that
this will ever be realised within history. An end to all
conflict in the animal kingdom? No more expropriation of
people's property (one is tempted to substitute the phrase
'hostile takeovers')? We do not seem to be any closer to
such idealised conditions than the Jews were at the time
of the prophet's writing.

A similarly blissful state of affairs is evoked in Psalm
85. The psalmist begins by giving thanks for a great
deliverance (vv.1–3). This probably refers to the Jews'
return from exile in Babylon. He then pleads to God
to revive and restore his people again (vv.4–7). This
may reflect the fact that conditions when they returned
were much harsher than the Jews expected. But then
the psalmist strikes a note of unbounded confidence:

I will listen to what God the Lord will say;
  he promises peace to his people, his saints –
  but let them not return to folly.
Surely his salvation is near those who fear him,
  that his glory may dwell in our land.

> Love and faithfulness meet together;
>   righteousness and peace kiss each other.
> Faithfulness springs forth from the earth,
>   and righteousness looks down from heaven.
> The Lord will indeed give what is good,
>   and our land will yield its harvest.
> Righteousness goes before him
>   and prepares the way for his steps.
> (Psalm 85:8–13, NIV)

Here is a picture of heaven and earth in perfect partnership. It is plausible to see love and righteousness as divine attributes, with faithfulness and peace as appropriate human attributes in response. When God and human beings act together in harmony, a rich harvest of material provision will be the result. So sure is the psalmist that this state of concord and prosperity will take place, that he writes as if it is already happening. The vision is breathtaking, but we are still left wondering when to expect its fulfilment.

The fact is that we live in an age when snakes still bite, young lives are tragically cut short in their prime and the little guy easily gets trampled on by the corporation with industrial muscle. Hope is often at odds with current experience. St Paul recognised this when he wrote:

> Now hope that is seen is not hope. For who hopes for what he sees? But if we hope for what we do not see, we wait for it with patience. (Romans 8:24–25)

Nevertheless, the quality of patience should not be confused with passivity. Moltmann is right. The hope we have as Christians ought to excite us so much, we should be embracing it with so eager a desire, that we do in fact allow it to revolutionise and transform our present existence. Although we may not realise it, this is essentially what we are asking every time we pray the Lord's Prayer. What does it mean to request that God's kingdom will come? The very next phrase in the prayer supplies the answer: that God's will should be done on earth, as perfectly as it already is in heaven. In making this request, we open ourselves up to the possibility that it may indeed be granted. We are in the business of doing God's will. By simple acts of obedient discipleship, we can play a part in bringing the present world more into conformity with that glorious future age of which the biblical passages speak.

In the world of business we may only get glimpses of this, but there are moments worth savouring. Examples might include:

* The glow of satisfaction over a finished product, one which has taken a lot of money, time and effort to achieve, but produces a sense of exhilaration because of the benefits we know it will bring to those who buy it.

* The unravelling of manipulative accounting practice, so that confusion and corruption are brushed away and the true state of financial affairs is clearly revealed.

* The clicking together of individuals in a close-knit team, with every member being respected for the particular gifts they have to offer on a project assignment.

* The breakdown of hierarchical structures which have impeded progress, and the establishment of confidence and goodwill between those previously dubbed blue and white collar workers.

All these and other things are well worth striving for. They are not irrelevant to the fulfilment of the psalmist's delightful image of justice and peace locked in embrace. It is right to be excited when substantial progress is made in the direction of any one of them.

There is no doubt that the eschatological passages in the Bible present a hermeneutical challenge. It is not always easy to know which dimension of future existence they refer to. This is partly because there is a shift of perspective as one moves from Old Testament to New, and partly because it is difficult to talk about the geography and topography of heaven except in very 'this-earthly' language. What images are we to use if not those such as banquets and wine (Isaiah 25:6), or gold and precious jewels (Revelation 21:15–21)? But in a way this blurring of the distinction between heaven and earth is salutary. These two dimensions of human existence are not meant to be kept worlds apart. The point is that the vision of the one should be an inspiration for change in the life of the other.

A rude shock

When the Bible speaks of the 'end time', however, it is certainly not all hunky-dory. The solemn theme of judgement cannot be ignored. Paul asserts that 'we shall all stand before the judgment seat of God' (Romans 14:10); Peter even speaks of judgement beginning with the household of God (1 Peter 4:17). True, this should not be a matter of alarm for Christians. It would be if we were relying on our own efforts, but that should not be the case. On the day of judgement there is only one way in which we can stand before God justified – restored to a right relationship with him – and that is through his grace. However hard we try, we can never justify ourselves.

Nevertheless, God's grace is not cheap. If we misinterpret his forgiving love as a pretext for self-satisfaction and living like the rest of the world, it is seriously questionable whether we are recipients of his grace at all. God does care, passionately, about the way in which we conduct our lives. In Romans 14 Paul goes on to explain the reality of judgement in terms of each of us giving account of himself to God (14:12). There will – to use a piece of current jargon – be something akin to a *personal audit*, when we will be called to account for what we have done with the abilities, opportunities and savings he has put at our disposal. Hopefully we will then be able to hear the words 'Well done, good and faithful servant . . . enter into the joy of your master' (Matthew 25:21). Alternatively, if we have deluded ourselves that we really are in the business of his service, we could be in for a rude shock.

A New Testament passage which speaks very powerfully of judgment in a business context is Revelation 18. It describes the fall of the city of Rome, here called Babylon (the sins of the one being associated with the sins of the other) and pictured in terms of a harlot. As such she had allured a number of different groups of people by her glamour and her wiles. They then mourn her demise:

> And the kings of the earth, who committed fornication and were wanton with her, will weep and wail over her when they see the smoke of her burning; they will stand far off, in fear of her torment, and say,

> 'Alas! alas! thou great city,
> thou mighty city, Babylon!
> In one hour has thy judgment come.'

> And the merchants of the earth weep and mourn for her, since no one buys their cargo any more, cargo of gold, silver, jewels and pearls, fine linen, purple, silk and scarlet, all kinds of scented wood, all articles of ivory, all articles of costly wood, bronze, iron and marble, cinnamon, spice, incense, myrrh, frankincense, wine, oil, fine flour and wheat, cattle and sheep, horses and chariots, and slaves, that is, human souls.

> 'The fruit for which thy soul longed has gone from thee,
> and all thy dainties and thy splendour are lost to thee, never to be found again!'

> The merchants of these wares, who gained wealth from her, will stand far off, in fear of her torment, weeping and mourning aloud,

'Alas, alas, for the great city
that was clothed in fine linen, in purple and scarlet,
bedecked with gold, with jewels, and with pearls!
In one hour all this wealth has been laid waste.'

And all shipmasters and seafaring men, sailors and
all whose trade is on the sea, stood far off and cried
out as they saw the smoke of her burning,

'What city was like the great city?'

And they threw dust on their heads, as they wept
and mourned, crying out,

'Alas, alas, for the great city
where all who had ships at sea grew rich by her
        wealth!
In one hour she has been laid waste.
Rejoice over her, O heaven,
O saints and apostles and prophets,
for God has given judgment for you against her!'

Then a mighty angel took up a stone like a great
millstone and threw it into the sea, saying,

'So shall Babylon the great city be thrown down with
        violence,
    and shall be found no more;
and the sound of harpers and minstrels, of flute
        players and trumpeters,
    shall be heard in thee no more;
and a craftsman of any craft
    shall be found in thee no more;
and the light of a lamp
    shall shine in thee no more;
and the voice of bridegroom and bride
    shall be heard in thee no more;
for thy merchants were the great men of the earth,
    and all nations were deceived by thy sorcery.
And in her was found the blood of prophets and of
        saints,
    and of all who have been slain on earth.'
(Revelation 18:9-24)

Rulers, merchants and mariners are the three groups
who had profited most from their involvement in Rome's
commercial activity. Now they see the city going up in
smoke, and their own fortunes with it. It is a time for
sober reflection.

The question raised by this passage is: what is it about
the people and practice of Rome which provokes God's
wrath? Why is the livelihood of these three classes of
people destroyed? Presumably not because they indulged
in the practice of trade as such. It is the way in which they
participated in trade which God finds objectionable, and
the passage affords some clues about this.

Trade's unacceptable face

First, there is a hint of *human exploitation*. Richard
Bauckham, author of an interesting treatment of this
chapter in his book *The Bible in Politics*, makes rather
more of this than is strictly justified by the passage. He
argues that Rome is a harlot because she exploits her
association with the subject peoples of the empire for
her own economic benefit. 'For the favours of Rome –
the security and prosperity of the *Pax Romana* – her
lovers pay a high price' (*The Bible in Politics*, p. 90). This
may be in the mind of John the seer, but the evidence is
rather scanty. Nevertheless, there is an unmistakeably
sinister note in the phrase at the end of verse 13. The
cargo whose loss the merchants mourn includes 'slaves,
that is, human souls'. The constant flow of slaves from
the rest of the empire to the city of Rome was indeed a
moral disgrace. Human souls should not be bought and
sold as chattels. Interestingly, this is the closest the New
Testament comes to an attack on trading in slaves as an
affront to human dignity.

Second, there is a critique of *ostentatious lifestyle*.
Verse 14 speaks of 'all thy dainties and thy splendour';
Bauckham suggests the neat translation 'all your luxu-
ries and your glittering prizes'. Nearly all the goods in
the merchants' list are luxury items, pandering to the
opulent, decadent lifestyle of the Roman upper classes.

The extravagant use of commodities like gold, ivory and marble is well documented in the secular writers of the period like the satirist Juvenal. Meanwhile, the not-inconsiderable poor population of Rome had to make do with monthly hand-outs of corn – wheat being the one modest item we find in the lengthy list of cargoes. The commercial activity of the kings, the merchants and the shipmasters comes under judgement because it has an unhealthy bias towards the wants of those who already have. It is neglectful of the needs of those who possess very little.

Third, there is an underlying attitude of *self-congratulatory pride*. To appreciate this, it is important to realise that Revelation 18 is full of allusions to various passages in the Old Testament prophets proclaiming judgement on the cities of Babylon and Tyre. Relevant chapters include Jeremiah 50–51, Isaiah 47 and Ezekiel 26–28. For instance, the proud boast of harlot Rome in Revelation 18:7 ('A queen I sit, I am no widow, mourning I shall never see') is a precise echo of attitudes attributed to the city of Babylon in Isaiah 47:8. The list of precious cargoes, on the other hand, bears comparison with the trading activity of Tyre, the great Mediterranean port, as described in Ezekiel 27. Ezekiel depicts God as holding Tyre and its king in very high favour: 'You were the signet of perfection, full of wisdom and perfect in beauty' (Ezekiel 28:12). But Tyre evokes his displeasure for the following reason:

'Because your heart is proud,
    and you have said, "I am a god,
I sit in the seat of the gods,
    in the heart of the seas,"
yet you are but a man, and no god,
    though you consider yourself as wise as a god . . .
    (Ezekiel 28:2)

God discerns the same overweening arrogance on the quaysides and in the luxury homes of the people of

Rome. They thought they had it made. They were indeed enjoying a rich reward, but the revelation God gives to John is that one day they will get their comeuppance.

Not just the problem of others

For Christians in the West today, not just those involved in business, but all who are caught up in the present materialist culture, it is vital to take seriously the challenge of Revelation 18. Do the marks of exploitation, ostentation and pride characterise the nature of our involvement? It is tempting to delude ourselves that such attitudes are reserved for secular humanists, and that we escape uncontaminated. These are features which were far from absent from City life in the mid-1980s, when a spate of takeovers, mergers and new share offers raised temperatures in the City to fever-pitch, and a number of illegal actions took place. Sadly, there were sincere Christians who got caught up in this, but far from pointing the finger at them, we should have the humility to say: 'there but for the grace of God go I'.

Certainly we are not allowed the luxury of dismissing Revelation 18 as off-beat rambles which are untypical of the Bible as a whole. Two of the minor epistles give similar warnings in a different style. The letter of James condemns the rich for exploiting workers and living ostentatiously:

> Your gold and silver have rusted, and their rust will be evidence against you and will eat your flesh like fire. You have laid up treasure for the last days. Behold, the wages of the labourers who mowed your fields, which you kept back by fraud, cry out; and the cries of the harvesters have reached the ears of the Lord of hosts. You have lived on the earth in luxury and in pleasure; you have fattened your hearts in a day of slaughter. (James 5:3–5)

The fact is that we can all too easily be seduced by 'the lust of the flesh and the lust of the eyes and the pride of life' (1 John 2:16). It is crucial to remember what John goes on to say: 'The world passes away, and the lust of it; but he who does the will of God abides for ever' (2:17).

There are other passages in the New Testament, however, which raise even more of a challenge. Those which I have been considering so far refer to behaviour which is clearly, in one way or the other, *excessive*: to a selfish revelling in the pleasures of the world with scant consideration for one's fellow human beings. But what of certain all too familiar sayings of Jesus, which seem to strike more fundamentally at the affluent businessperson's peace of mind? Obvious examples are 'You cannot serve God and mammon' (Matthew 6:24) or 'It is easier for a camel to go through the eye of a needle than for a rich man to enter the kingdom of God' (Matthew 19:24).

Many Christians who work in business, including most at the levels of middle and senior management, find themselves preoccupied for much of the time with questions of mammon (money) and are often recipients of substantial salaries (certainly in the top income tax bracket). Does that put them beyond the pale as far as Jesus is concerned? It is not a question to be taken lightly.

Four different attitudes

The subject which occupies the rest of this chapter is one to which I have devoted greater space in a Grove Booklet, *Living with Affluence*. Owing to a recognition that affluence is a condition which brings problems as well as privileges, which sits uneasily on the shoulders of not a few Christian businesspeople, I decided to do some research on the subject. This research included detailed interviews with a sample of twenty individuals who were ready (some reluctantly) to admit to the description 'affluent'. Affluence is a word which is extremely difficult to define satisfactorily, but I believe the definition I settled on, 'A state of plenty, in which the amount of money coming in comfortably exceeds the outlay required to satisfy occupational, personal and family needs', is as good as any.

In the course of my interviews I discovered four main attitudes to affluence. Some co-existed within the same person. I shall here attribute them to some of the characters already introduced in this book.

Blessed
This is how Martin, chairman of the hi-tech company which experienced rapid growth but is now faced by problems which threaten Martin's own position (see pp. 57–59 and pp. 143–145), describes his state of affluence. The success of the company, allied to the fact that Martin possesses substantial shares in it, has led to his becoming a wealthy man in his mid-thirties – a fact which will remain true even if he now leaves the company. Martin recognises that the application of his God-given talent has played a major part in this coming about. But he also has a sense of totally undeserved good fortune. Often during the years of success he has risen in the morning echoing the words of the psalmist: 'O taste and see that the Lord is good! ... those who seek the Lord lack no good thing' (Psalm 34:8–10). When he was asked to leave the company he had been instrumental in building up, this certainly unsettled his confidence for a while, but he is actually coming to a deeper faith through it. He is coming to see that, just as God can raise people up and cause them to prosper, so he can cast them down and lead them through troubled times. He believes he is learning the knack of which Paul spoke:

> I know how to be abased, and I know how to abound; in any and all circumstances I have learned the secret of facing plenty and hunger, abundance and want. (Philippians 4:12)

Uneasy
We have already seen how Fiona, the tax accountant who is wondering whether she should leave her job (see pp. 9–11 and pp. 41–42), is uneasy about the fact that she is becoming so affluent. She is worried that her handsome salary and the agreeable lifestyle

it generates may be isolating her from the 'real world' populated by the vast majority of people. She has already found that affluence is a distancing factor when it comes to relating both to members of her congregation who live in the more modest end of the parish, and to friends from childhood and university days who haven't prospered in a comparable way. Although Fiona gives away a generous proportion of her income to good causes, she also feels acutely uncomfortable when confronted – whether on the television screen or in real life – by people in situations of acute poverty. Her route to work takes her regularly past the homeless, unkempt men who occupy London's 'Cardboard City'. Fiona is challenged by the passage in Job 31, where that unfortunate but unbowed man insists that he had never 'withheld anything that the poor desired', 'eaten my morsel alone', or 'seen any one perish for lack of clothing' (31:16, 17, 19). She knows she cannot claim the same herself. 'Sell your possessions, and give alms', said Jesus to the disciples (Luke 12:33). Fiona does not see how this makes any practical sense, but she feels uneasy nonetheless.

Free
Such concerns are very far from the mind of Barry, the builder who has left a big company to set up on his own and now feels customers are exploiting his good will (pp. 5–8). Barry comes from a working-class background; his father was often out of work and the family experienced real hardship as Barry grew up. Barry is not yet affluent but he has come a long way in financial terms during the fourteen years of his working life. He desires to be comfortably off, not because he aspires after a plush BMW or a house with every sort of modern convenience, but in order to provide his family with a security he never knew. Barry sees affluence as the route to freedom from the nagging anxiety of struggling to make ends meet. He does not want to be a drain on other people's resources (including the resources of the state) but longs to stand on his own two feet. Right now Barry has encountered difficulties in the running of his business. He wishes he

had already attained more in the way of affluence so that he felt less constrained about the way he tackled them.

As a young Christian, Barry's thinking about money has not yet been greatly effected by his new-found faith. But he is motivated by a simple trust that if he works hard, puts God first in his life and conducts his working life with integrity, God will give him everything he and his family need. He will find the freedom he is looking for.

Guilty

Miles, the unconventional company director whose views are discussed on pp. 11–14 and p. 93–94, shares much of the unease about affluence felt by Fiona. For him, however, the feelings go deeper. They have hardened into a profound sense of guilt about his condition. This finds expression in three key convictions. First, Miles believes it cannot be right to be rich in a world where so many are so poor. He is blowed if he can see how giving up his worldly wealth will make much difference to alleviating the poverty of a world whose injustices are structural and political, but he still feels that by continuing in a condition of affluence he is collaborating in the present evil state of affairs. Second, Miles is convinced that what people are paid bears little relation to the value of their jobs. Sometimes he has fantasies of radically revising the whole salary system of his company along the lines of 'many that are first will be last, and the last first' (Matthew 19:30). Third, Miles grew up in a prosperous family, and feels it is unfair that he has been the beneficiary of so much privilege. The advantages of financial security, a private education and an excellent network of family contacts gave him a head start in making a success of his career. He is all too aware that most people are nothing like as fortunate.

Living with affluence

Readers may identify closely with one or other of these characters, or they may indeed empathise with all four.

None of the four attitudes represented here is obviously wrong. In a sense Martin, Fiona, Barry and Miles are all voicing sentiments which are appropriate to their situations. Although it might seem hard to reconcile these four responses to the reality or the prospect of affluence, taken together they embody a *tension* which is entirely fitting as a Christian response. The challenge which Christians face is to try to make this tension creative and not destructive.

I have already argued on pp. 73–75 that wealth creation, understood in terms of adding value to resource, is a legitimate goal for people in business. A market economy, which encourages attitudes of enterprise and creativity, provides the most congenial context for that process to take place. In the market system the rate of people's salaries is inevitably determined largely by laws of supply and demand. If you have a rare skill which is in relatively small supply others are willing to pay you a lot for it. Handsome rewards are forthcoming for those who demonstrate the crucial wealth-creating skills, whether this be finding gas fields or bringing sanity to a company's financial affairs.

In these circumstances, there is little reason for Christians in the higher echelons of business to feel guilty simply because they are the recipients of large salaries. The fact that one person commands a large salary and another in the same company is paid a low one does not necessarily mean the latter is being exploited or devalued; it could just be that what the first person does has far greater influence on the company's performance. If Christians are among those who can contribute substantially to the process of wealth creation, which clearly they are, they should not feel inhibited from making that contribution by the prospect of being well paid.

Nevertheless, the solemn warnings of the Bible (both Old Testament and New) about the dangers attached to riches need to be taken seriously. St Luke's Gospel in particular makes uncomfortable reading for the affluent. There are repeated warnings of the snares of wealth. According to the parables of Jesus, rich individuals who

either glory in their own material wellbeing or neglect
the starving beggar at the door find the tables drastically
turned on them at death (Luke 12:16–21; 16:19–31).
There is no mistaking that the state of affluence carries with it a *spiritual health warning*. It is all too
easy to become dangerously comfortable on this present
earth.

What then should the high-earning Christian businessperson do? At least three important areas require attention.

Firstly, one's *position*. Working in a senior position
brings privileges but it also carries responsibilities and
provides opportunities. Miles should rejoice in the fact
that he has been given a place on the Board of a major
company, where he can be a powerful advocate for views
which go against the stream. Certainly, he has to be
careful how he proceeds; he is not going to win every
argument, and he needs to be selective which battles he
considers worth fighting. Issues to do with top people's
pay may well be one of them. Miles is particularly
sensitive to the way in which the market defence of wage
differentials is abused, so that directors vote themselves
perks and bonuses which carry their basic salaries to
quite superfluous levels. If he as a director stands up
and protests about this, his colleagues are likely to give
him a hearing. It is crucial that people like Miles get
into positions of influence, and that they use their power
courageously and responsibly when they do.

Secondly, one's *lifestyle*. Affluent Christians face significant questions as consumers. These include:

* the type of area where they buy a home
* what sort of car they drive
* where they send their children to school
* where they go on holiday
* what kind of leisure pursuit they follow

The reaction of most people who achieve substantial
wealth is to opt for a detached house in suburbia or the
country, a vehicle that is fast and luxurious, private education for their children, holidays in the Mediterranean

sun, a heated swimming pool in the garden, and so on. Are affluent Christians any different? The impression I gleaned from my very limited sample of research is: not as much as they might be. This is not to imply that any of the things I have suggested are wrong in themselves. It is possible to justify and, no doubt, indulge in each of them with a good conscience. But if the totality of a Christian's lifestyle is such that there is little discernible difference between him or her and the rest of the world, there is surely something wrong. 'A man's life does not consist in the abundance of his possessions' (Luke 12:15). To go without some trapping of our modern life which society quickly comes to consider essential (a video-recorder? a dish-washer? add your own example) may seem an irksome act of self-denial, but it could just be a significant dimension of Christian witness. It is not for me to prescribe precisely what affluent Christians should and shouldn't do, but in the lifestyles of all of us there ought to be some element of asceticism, both for our own good and the good of others.

Thirdly, one's *giving*. Christians are, in general, more clearly differentiated from other people by their attitude to giving. Of course, there are some very generous non-Christians, but Christians almost universally see this as an essential obligation – though not in a negative, unwelcome sense. For some, giving away a fixed proportion of their income forms part of a systematic stewardship of resources. They may follow the Old Testament precedent of the tithe (Leviticus 27:30–31), and make use of opportunities for tax reclamation afforded by covenant schemes. Others prefer not to scrutinise their giving so closely, and to give more spontaneously. While they are unlikely to be so carefree that they adhere literally to Jesus' saying 'do not let your left hand know what your right hand is doing' (Matthew 6:3), this is more the spirit in which they give. Either way, there is much to be said for not spreading one's donations too thinly, but ensuring there is at least one object of concern where the level of giving is such that it carries with it real personal commitment. For Fiona, troubled as she is about the plight of homeless

people, this might be the area where she could make a
significant contribution; but clearly this is one among a
myriad of worthy causes which jostle for attention.

Both the models referred to have their biblical justification. They may well be suited to different types
of personal temperament, but ideally, every pattern of
Christian giving should contain elements of both. The
stewardship model helps to ensure consistency and efficiency in giving, while the *spontaneity* model suggests
more openness to immediate and unanticipated need.

The affluent have opportunities not only for Christian
generosity in what they give away, but also in what they
share. A second house in the country might seem like an
unpardonable extravagance, but not if its use is shared
among other people. I am impressed by the growing
numbers of affluent Christians who are opening up rooms
and homes in beautiful places for others to enjoy as places
of refreshment, quiet and retreat. The same principle can
be applied to many other types of material possession.

'You cannot serve God and mammon' is a saying which
brooks no evasion. We must not delude ourselves about
which master we are serving. Nevertheless, money has
a proper part to play in God's purposes. There are very
real opportunities of serving God *through* mammon, if
we have the eye to see them and the determination to
make use of them.

CHAPTER 13

WALKING BETWEEN TWO WORLDS

The Path of Christian Integrity

During the seminar weeks we have run at Ridley Hall on the subject of leadership we have carried out an exercise borrowed from John Adair's helpful book *Effective Leadership*. Adair invites readers to rank twenty-five attributes in order of 'most valuable at the top level of management'. He himself tried this on some top executives. Interestingly, the attribute which they ranked third was *integrity*, behind only 'Ability to take decisions' and 'Capacity to lead people'. When we have used the same exercise with participants on our seminar weeks, the aggregate score has always put integrity first. Whether managers are Christian or not, there is increasing recognition that integrity is a crucial quality in what their job is all about, with our findings (limited statistical sample though they represent) suggesting that this is likely to be prized especially highly by Christians.

But what does the word 'integrity' mean? It is often used in business these days, particularly in the context of company mission statements. But its meaning is rarely unpacked: it needs teasing out.

First of all, integrity suggests a life that is well integrated. There is a coherence between the different parts of it. The value systems professed by the person or company concerned are adhered to in all areas of life, public and private. A company chairman who preaches scrupulous loyalty to one's word in every business transaction shows a lack of integrity if at the same time he is breaking his marriage vows by carrying on an adulterous affair with a colleague's wife.

Following on from this, integrity implies high moral standards. I suggest that it carries specific connotations of honesty, consistency and public defensibility. Each of these three qualities warrant further comment in themselves.

Being honest is an attribute which is widely prized, and equally as often notable by its absence. It sounds an easy enough thing to do, but the reality of experience belies this. The temptation to cover up underhand deals, personal mistakes and unwelcome news in business is frequently a strong one. Honesty can be costly, but it is also a trait which is generally appreciated. Honesty breeds an atmosphere of trust.

The moral requirement to be honest, however, does not mean that one is always required in business to play a fully open hand. There is information which it is right to protect from disclosure for a variety of reasons: in order to preserve confidences, for instance, or to safeguard a competitive position. In the words of Ecclesiastes 3:7, there is 'a time to keep silence, and a time to speak'.

Judgements about when it is right to disclose the truth are linked to our assessment of whether other people are ready to receive the truth – in short, of whether they are in a ripe or mature enough state to do so. This is most obviously the case with regard to dilemmas involving people near either the very end or the very beginning of life. Thus it may not be appropriate to tell a relative who has just been diagnosed as having a fatal illness of the terminal nature of her condition straightaway. People need time to make the shift from thinking of death in abstract and timeless terms (as something that happens to humanity, or will happen on a remote 'one day') to thinking of it in personal and historical terms (as something that will happen to *me*, possibly quite soon). In other words, they may not yet be ready for the truth. But there is an important difference between disclosing the truth *sensitively and gradually* (when the relative shows signs of coming to terms with the gravity of her condition) and blatantly denying it (as might happen if the patient asks the point-blank question: 'Is this cancer going to kill me?'). To say 'no' in defiance of the plain facts is not only clearly dishonest; it is likely to undermine the patient's faith in the trustworthiness of relatives and doctor, damage the state of the relationship, and muddy communication in the future.

Similar issues are involved in the matter of how parents should reply to the very young child's question: 'Where do babies come from?' A detailed explanation of the act of intercourse is an inappropriate answer, not because there is anything shameful about it, but because the idea that human genitals can be put to such uses will be mind-boggling to the child, and the fact that this physical activity takes place in the context of a loving relationship difficult to grasp. A suitable reply would seem to be along the lines of: 'God gives little children to two people when they love each other, and puts them in the mummy's tummy for protection until they are strong enough to come into the world.' When the child is a little older, and asks again, one can move on to talk of 'Mum and Dad's special cuddles'. Responses of this sort tell the young child all that he needs (and probably wants) to know. Crucially – in contrast to silly legends about storks – they do not contradict any further information about the mechanics of child-begetting which will be given to him at a later stage. The content and style of the disclosure have been tailored to the child's particular stage of maturity.

With these considerations in mind, let us examine a business situation which entails, among other things, a dilemma about disclosing the truth.

The politics of downsizing

Walter is the Managing Director of a group of companies in the electronics industry. One of the companies is in telecommunications, with a £25m. turnover and 600 staff. It has returned losses of increasing size for three years and its market share is declining. Efforts to increase sales volume and reduce operating costs have proved unsuccessful in turning the situation round. Walter and his board have decided that the time has come to sell this ailing company. They have entered into secret negotiations with a potential buyer, who has made a satisfactory offer with the proviso that only 200 staff will be retained. Walter is understandably concerned about the fate of the remaining 400 staff.

Walter and the Board of Directors now face a dilemma. They weigh the pros and cons of three different possible courses of action:

1. They could tell the work-force openly what is happening, make 400 staff redundant on good terms (thereby taking upon the company the cost of doing that), and sell the business immediately. It would be important that there should not be a significant delay between the announcement to sell and actually doing so, because in the meantime the share price may drop, important customers close their accounts, and key staff depart, thereby imperilling the sale of the business.

2. They could make the 400 people redundant (on good terms) in two stages, telling the employees at each stage that this downsizing should make the company viable within the parent group, and then finally sell the company without prior warning. In the directors' eyes, this gradual process would have the advantage of 'softening the shock' to the employees.

3. They could sell the company as it is, without making any of the 600 staff redundant themselves. The cost and the hassle of making 400 redundant would therefore fall on the new owner (though this in turn would be reflected in the price he is willing to pay for the company). Walter and his Board know that these redundancies will be on poorer terms than those which they are willing to offer. They would however avoid any mention of people losing their jobs in announcing the move to the employees, talking instead of the bright new future which is promised by the sale of the company.

Both the second and third alternatives are tempting. It

would be possible to carry out the third in a way which does not involve anything directly dishonest. But it is difficult to avoid the impression that this would be a course of action which lacks integrity. The employees are being deceived, and of the three options being considered, this is the one which will have the worst consequences for them.

The second alternative might seem to have the virtue of the gradual style of disclosure which I commended earlier. Yet it makes very little business sense (unless the financial fortunes of the company, and with that the selling price it can command, show some improvement during the interim period). It harks of an indecisive style of management. Although there is an argument that employees are being treated sensitively, because the staged nature of the redundancies enables them to get accustomed to the fact that the company's circumstances are critical, this type of gradual disclosure actually amounts to deceit. Employees are being told something which at a later stage they will discover was untrue. Doing redundancies by halves did not ensure the retention of the company within the parent group. If Walter and his Board opt for this alternative, it is not a course of action which is morally comparable with the cases of gradual disclosure cited earlier, because they will have to go back on statements they have previously made.

People who work for telecommunications companies are grown adults. They are obviously subject to vulnerability and hurt, but in general they are robust enough not to need protecting from uncomfortable truths when their company is in trouble. The first alternative has the virtue of dealing with them straight, without any attempt at subterfuge. Dishonesty which is carried out in the name of 'softening the shock' is all too often an exercise in self-deception. It is rather a means of avoiding the flak which is likely to be experienced by those who announce unpopular news. The irony is that bad news will come out sooner or later, and when its hearers realise that the wool has been pulled over their

eyes, their resentment against the Board of Directors is
likely to be all the greater.

Of course, the details of this case only need to be
changed in slight particulars for judgement upon it to
be rather different. For it could be that in the case of the
second alternative, Walter and his Board decide against
finalising agreement on sale of the company at this point.
They make 200 people redundant in the genuine hope
that such an action will pull the company round, and
make its sale unnecessary. They talk confidently about
'continuing viability', because they think the employees'
belief in that is crucial to their acting in the purposeful
way which will translate conviction into reality. Suppose
such efforts fail, further redundancies are made, and
the company is duly sold? The staff may still feel that
they have been misled by Walter and the Board, but
in this case the charge would be unjust. The tactic
management pursued may have been forlorn, but it was
not dishonest.

Consistency

Being consistent is another key part of what it means
to have integrity. Leaders who are consistent do not
surprise too many people with their moral decisions.
Having set out their stall, they stick by it. They do not
say one thing one day and something radically different
the next. Whereas a leader who makes arbitrary decisions
spreads confusion and even fear among the ranks, the
person who is consistent has a reassuring effect upon his
or her staff.

But consistent does not mean wooden. It does not
mean the leader is lacking in flexibility, nor that there
is a constant resort to the rule-book. The consistent
leader is well prepared to make allowance for life's
complexities. The fact is that when problematical moral
situations are subjected to comparative analysis, they
display a mixture of similar and dissimilar features.
The superficial mind often misses this. It says that if
the international community has approved the use of

force to sort out one of the world's trouble spots, it should be equally ready to do so in another. There *may* be force in this argument, but the case for armed intervention is more clear-cut in a situation where one country has actually invaded another, than in one where two different ethnic groups are involved in a civil war. The person who thinks more deeply is able to discriminate.

Similar distinctions are relevant to the world of business. There are moral rules which generally hold good, and situations when exceptions should be made. But the exceptions should not be decided upon arbitrarily. There should be some consistent pattern to the exceptions. Usually it will be because there is a clash of moral obligations, and a duty which is normally unquestioned has had to make way to a duty which has higher priority. Again an example will serve to illustrate this.

Some multi-national companies are criticised for selling commodities in the Third World which, for reasons of health, safety, or environmental damage, they are no longer legally allowed to sell in the West. Generally speaking this criticism is just, because companies who do this are failing to treat the lives or habitats of people in the Third World with the respect that they deserve. They are being inconsistent. But what about the following situation? An African country is being devastated by a swarm of locusts which is ruining the crops on which the people's survival depends. A multi-national chemicals company has a cheap pesticide available, one that is banned in Europe because it has some toxic side-effects. In fact this pesticide is less harmful in Africa than Europe because it degrades more quickly there. In the desperate conditions induced by the locust swarm, is not the chemicals company justified in making the pesticide available? There is a strong case for arguing that for those Africans in that situation starvation, not pesticide poisoning, is the greater threat. The immediate threat to life demands a moral *prioritisation*. To make an exception in such a case is not inconsistent.

This leads on to a third dimension of integrity, *public*

defensibility. By this I mean that the person or company with integrity is willing and able to defend actions which have been taken without embarrassment in public. Hopefully defence can be made without the spokesperson appearing defens*ive*: perhaps 'explain' would be a better way to describe the positive public presentation I have in mind. Of course, the action in question may well be controversial, so that there is a temptation for the organisation concerned to conceal or deny its involvement in the practice. The tendency of the press to distort and present twisted versions of corporate statements needs to be taken seriously, and weighed against the damage which may result in not making any statement at all. But it is a mark of the leader with integrity that he or she is, generally speaking, prepared to make an open profession. Such a profession may not convince everyone, but the willingness to come forward and present a plausible case, and answer questions from potential critics, is surely laudable.

The position which undoubtedly lacks integrity is where a company's professed stance is palpably at odds with the actual practice of its employees out in the market-place. The disclaimers which companies make about their attitude to special payments (see my discussion on pp. 89–92) do not always coincide with what actually happens. To cite a phrase used by J.K. Galbraith, the American social commentator, this is 'institutional truth which ignores reality'. It is an easy language-game to fall into, and politicians and church leaders can be guilty of it, as well as business leaders. It is salutary to remember that the vice for which Jesus reserved his harshest words was that of hypocrisy. His memorable diatribe against the scribes and Pharisees, found in Matthew 23, shows that all too clearly. Neither as individuals nor as organisations should we be people who fail to practise what we preach.

Why compromise need not be a dirty word

A discussion on integrity cannot avoid consideration of the place of compromise. For many people 'compromise' is a rather perjorative word. It suggests settling on a course of action which is morally tainted: an abandonment of principle for the sake of expediency. Clearly there are many compromises made in business and elsewhere which do bear that character, and are open to criticism because of it.

But there is a much more positive way of viewing compromise. Some compromises are an attempt to do justice to different moral claims, both or all of which are valid. The social market economics which have been generally favoured in the West represent something of a compromise between the claims of freedom and equality. Their proponents are committed to the market system but believe that the government should buttress and to some extent modify this with a social infrastructure which provides a number of services not provided by the market. The balance of the equation varies from country to country, but supporters of the social market are all seeking some sort of mix between the maximisation of efficiency in wealth creation and the redistribution of wealth towards those in greatest need. Few regard that as a compromise in any negative sense of the word.

As has been observed earlier in this book, companies owe and generally acknowledge responsibilities to a range of different groups: shareholders, employees, customers, business partners and 'stakeholders', the word increasingly being used to describe all who may be effected in some way by the activities of the company. Much of the time there is no serious conflict between the interests and expectations felt by these different groups in relation to the company. Sometimes, especially when times are hard, there will be a clash. Faced with the necessity to cut costs, the company may have to choose between reducing the shareholders' dividend, making some staff redundant, and raising prices for its customers. Often it will be appropriate to spread the burden of cost. Compromise here will have the character of seeking to balance the interests (and maintain the confidence) of different groups, rather than completely abandoning one group in favour of another.

There are other compromises which are more clearly a case of making some concession to the fallen realities of this world. Because we are constrained by the forces and the standards which are operative in the world around us, our freedom of action is limited. We have to accept some things which are not satisfactory, which we would like to change but where it is outside our power to do so. We are obliged to temper our idealism. Yet it is neither logical nor helpful to feel terribly guilty about this.

Going back to the suppliers

Consider again the case of Barry, the self-employed builder whose quandary was described in chapter 1. He wants to pay his suppliers promptly but is suffering a severe cash-flow problem because a number of his customers are delaying (possibly evading) payment of their bills to him. Readers will recall that the options Barry is considering are as follows:

1. Asking a solicitor to write letters threatening to take non-paying customers to court.

2. Explaining the nature of the problem to Barry's suppliers and asking them to accept staged payment from him.

3. Continuing to make full payment promptly, in the belief that God will honour him for the stand he has taken.

Ostensibly, the third option looks like the most 'Christian' course of action. But is it? The fact of the matter seems to be, that in the first flush of his new-found faith, Barry has acted in a way which is understandably naive. He knew about the conditions which prevailed in his particular industry, but he started his new company making a rash commitment which effectively defied them. He was over-confident, either about his own capacity to influence the habits of others by the force of his own example, or about God's willingness to overrule the decisions of free human agents, as to whether or not they would pay up on time! Following on from that, it is unreasonable to expect God to rescue us, without any personal discomfort, from pickles which are very much of our own making.

Of the other two alternatives, using a solicitor may have its place, with selected parties whose custom Barry is unlikely to seek again in the future. But in his present predicament he does not want to be running up sizeable legal fees. Going back to his suppliers will undoubtedly be embarrassing, and some may give him a sticky ride, but it has the virtue of being honest. Barry will be facing up to the realities of his business situation. The level and timing of his payment to suppliers must be based on what he actually has in the corporate bank account, as his bank manager will doubtless be at pains to remind him. Perhaps in the future Barry might also consider using a third party, such as a factoring service, to collect the debts owing to him.

Accepting the harsh facts of life does not mean that Barry should abandon all vestiges of moral idealism. It is good and laudable that he wants to see invoices paid more quickly. To pay one's invoices quicker than the industry's norm is possible – within limits. The problem with Barry's policy is not that he has tried to improve on the average wait in paying invoices, but that he has tried to more than halve it. He is attempting too radical a change too quickly, before he is in a position of strength to consider whether or not he can afford it.

It is right and proper then that Barry should compromise. He will probably feel dreadful about this, and will require pastoral help so that his faith either in himself or in God does not receive a severe jolt. But he will not have acted dishonourably in doing so. And by having the humility to swallow his pride, it could just be that he will succeed in saving his business.

Doves and serpents

How should we understand compromise theologically? It is important to take seriously the insights of the last chapter, about the nature of Christian eschatology. The fact is that as Christians we stand in a field of tension between two aeons, the present world which is one day to pass away, and the coming world which will replace it and already makes inroads upon it. Christians are called out of their old lives into a new existence, yet still have to live in a far from perfect world with all the circumscriptions upon action which that brings. They therefore stand in a relationship both of continuity and discontinuity with the conventions and practices of the present world. Helmut Thielicke, who was for many years Professor of Systematic Theology at the University of Hamburg, has spelt out the dynamics of Christian existence like this:

> The theme of ethics is this 'walking between two worlds'. It is in the strict sense the theme of a 'wayfarer's theology', a 'theologia viatorum'. It lives under the law of the 'not yet' but within the peace of the 'I am coming soon' (Revelation 22:20). Theological ethics is eschatological or it is nothing. (Helmut Thielicke, *Theological Ethics* vol. I, p. 47)

If compromise is to be understood in this way, it is important to affirm the element of tension. Where this is lacking, compromise easily degenerates into uncritical conformity, a complacent acceptance of the status quo. The best compromises are those which take the 'promise' part of the word seriously. In other words, they are creative, and hold out hope for something better in the future.

When Jesus sent his disciples out on a missionary journey, he did so with this intriguing message: 'Behold, I send you out as sheep in the midst of wolves; so be wise as serpents and innocent as doves' (Matthew 10:16). These are not just words which are applicable to Christian missionaries. They are very appropriate words for a Christian businessperson also, because they combine that mixture of idealism tempered by realism, principle laced by shrewdness, which are just the attitudes he or she needs. Christians help nobody, least of all themselves, by being naive, but they are called at the same time to maintain a purity of thought, speech and action. It is a testing vocation.

CHAPTER 14

PULLING IT ALL TOGETHER

A Method for Moral Decision-Making

It is time to take stock and recapitulate some of the main ideas this book has sought to express. From the wide range of topics covered, is there anything which amounts to a checklist for action? Is it possible to glean a Christian methodology for moral decision-making? I believe it is. In this chapter I shall retrace some of the ground already covered, but in order to prevent the material becoming repetitive or unduly abstract, I shall 'earth' the methodology by reference to a topical issue, that of Sunday trading. In a highly competitive situation where increasing numbers of retailers (notably the big food retailers) are opening on Sundays, shopowners in Britain often face crises of conscience over whether or not to follow suit. But it is an issue not just for retailers, but for society as a whole. The time is ripe for decision-making, not just about the Sunday trading law we want to see engraved on the statute book, but the Sunday trading law we want to see enforced.

When we are confronted with an ethical problem, many of us respond in a highly *ad hoc* manner. Under pressure, we make a hurried decision: 'thinking on our feet' is the polite way to describe the process. My conviction is that we often need to reflect more thoroughly upon a critical choice than is the typical human response. Certainly decisions – especially in business – have to be made at speed, but that makes it all the more important that we learn to practise mature and well-informed habits of judgement which will stand us in good stead when the pressure is on. Moreover, in relation to many key issues which confront us, e.g., whether it is right to take up a morally questionable job, or what our position is on a controversial issue which lies at the very heart of our job, we do have scope for reflection.

As someone with a decade's experience in teaching ethics, I feel a particular concern to promote some semblance of method as far as moral decision-making is concerned. There are different methodologies espoused by different Christian ethicists, but there are certain elements which tend to be common to them all. I shall here commend a methodology which is essentially very simple.

Stage one: consider the relevant facts

I emphasised the importance of this on pp. 75–78. Discussion which takes place in ignorance of the key facts is both debilitating for the ill-informed and irritating for the well-informed. It is crucial to survey an issue in all its many different dimensions, with reference to all the participants involved. Indeed, to have as full as possible a picture of what is going on, we need to bring together the facts as perceived by those of differing views, because most people are partial in their presentation of certain facts, to the exclusion of others. Of course, the facts which are presented by some individuals or groups may actually be incorrect – but to ascertain this will require careful investigation.

In the world of business there are clearly areas of information which are highly technical. If these are not our own area of expertise, we become dependent on the judgements of others. Nevertheless, experts often disagree, so we may well have to acquire some detailed understanding in order to get a sense of who is likelier to be right!

The issue of Sunday trading is not a highly technical area, but it is a complicated one. The most cursory reading of the 1950 Shops Act is sufficient to demonstrate that. In order to be well-informed, one needs a good grasp of the current legislation, the standing of that legislation in the light of Britain's membership of the European

Community, and how it compares with laws in other
countries. One ought to be cognisant of the extent to
which shops currently open on Sundays, and how many
of those that do so succeed in staying within the law. One
needs to have access to the most reliable surveys which
have been done on the attitudes of both shopworkers and
customers towards Sunday trading. In order to see how
the facts can be differently interpreted, one should read
the literature both of the Keep Sunday Special Campaign
and the Shopping Hours Reform Council.

Stage two: consult the important sources of guidance

To have a mastery of available empirical information
is important, but that by itself does not settle ethical
problems. We need to know what value to give to certain
facts; we need to know how to assess and weigh them
aright. In short, we need guidance.

In many business situations, all the guidance which is
required may be available from entirely secular sources.
The ethical code to which either the company or the profession subscribes may accord a clear answer, or at least
a pointer in the direction of an answer. Alternatively,
guidance may be forthcoming on a personal level from
someone of self-evident integrity and reliable judgement
who has long-standing experience of the relevant issue.

But with many of the deeper, more intractable or more
wide-ranging dilemmas that are encountered, it is likely
that merely secular answers will not satisfy. We look
to specifically Christian sources of guidance. High upon
the list of these sources should be the Bible, though our
understanding of the Bible takes place within a wider
context of Christian thought. We are inheritors of 2000
years of church history which have built upon, developed
and sometimes deviated from ideas contained within the
Bible. This tradition is often enriching, though it can also
be restricting. Most Christians belong to a particular
tradition which influences, and to some extent filters,
the way in which we read the Bible.

In the course of this book I have repeatedly drawn on the rich vein of insight and inspiration which the biblical writers provide. I have highlighted central events or concepts like creation, fall and redemption which afford key interpretative tools for making sense of the world in which we we live. The theological motifs to which I have assigned different chapters provide a series of perspectives for looking at business scenarios. Which perspective is most relevant to which situation is something that will be discovered by a sensitive appropriation of these themes, nurtured by the lessons of experience; there is no easy rule-of-thumb that will decide it.

A mark of Christian integrity will be a concern to hold all these different perspectives together, and not to opt, in a one-sided way, for any one of them. During the course of the last few years I have met some businesspeople who have, frankly, been theologically imbalanced. There are those who are preoccupied by the doctrine of the fall, who gloomily acknowledge that business practice manifests the marks of a sinful world all too clearly but feel there is little that can be done about it. I have also met those who go to an opposite extreme. Taking their stand on a one-dimensional theology of creation, they end up with a bland affirmation of nearly everything business gets up to. I have rather had that feeling at some very prestigious meetings about business ethics which I have attended in London: the captains of industry reassuring each other that everything they do is thoroughly honourable. Where both these groups go astray is this: neither actually operates from a Christian (as distinct from an Old Testament) understanding. Whether one's theology is dominated by creation or fall and even if it contains elements of both, it also needs New Testament perspectives such as redemption, resurrection and future hope, if it is to display a truly Christian understanding.

But as well as the broad themes of Christian theology, it is also important to attend to particular texts. I have sought to do that in this book. I have examined passages from every part of the Bible, from Leviticus to Luke, Proverbs to Paul, Ruth to Revelation. The books of the law, the sections of historical narrative, wisdom literature, prophecy, gospels, epistles, apocalyptic . . . the Bible contains a great profusion of material on which to reflect and to aid one in charting a course of action.

The right use of Sunday is an issue on which there are relevant passages all through the Bible. They include, from the Old Testament:

Genesis 2:2–3   The statement that God rested from his work of creation on the seventh day, thereby blessing and hallowing it.

Exodus 20:8–11   The Fourth Commandment, forbidding the Israelites to work on the seventh day because God had rested then.

Exodus 31:12–18   Reiteration of the sabbath command, with emphasis on the fact that it is a sign of God's covenant with the people.

Numbers 15:32–36   The chilling story of how an Israelite was stoned to death for gathering sticks on the sabbath day.

Deuteronomy 5:12–15   A second version of the Fourth Commandment, in which a different reason for keeping it is given: remembering God's rescue of the people from being slaves in Egypt.

Nehemiah 13:15–22   Nehemiah's shutting of the gates of Jerusalem to prevent what had become the regular practice of trading on the Sabbath.

Isaiah 58:13–14   Isaiah's statement that if God's people honour the sabbath and make it a delight, they will experience joy, victory and prosperity.

Amos 8:4–8   The prophet's condemnation of those who cannot wait for the sabbath to be over, so that they can continue with their dishonest and exploitative practices.

The strict and solemn tenor of the Old Testament material on the sabbath is well captured by Jeremiah 17:21–22:

Thus says the Lord: Take heed for the sake of your lives, and do not bear a burden on the sabbath day or bring it in by the gates of Jerusalem. And do not carry a burden out of your houses on the sabbath or do any work, but keep the sabbath day holy, as I commanded your fathers.

The New Testament, however, poses a striking contrast. Material on the sabbath and Sunday falls neatly into three different kinds. First, there are several Gospel passages which describe the controversy caused by Jesus' activities on the sabbath, e.g.:

Matthew 12:1–8 (cf. Mark 2:23–28) The disciples plucking the ears of corn.

Mark 3:1–6 The healing of the man with the withered hand.

Luke 13:10–17   The healing of the woman with the bent back.

John 5:1–18   The healing of the paralysed man by the pool of Bethesda.

In all these incidents, Jesus displayed a liberalism of practice which devout Jews of his day found deeply shocking. He went out of his way to heal people on the sabbath, and encouraged his listeners to think of the day as a positive opportunity for helping others, not as a time when nothing could be done: 'Is it lawful on the sabbath to do good or to do harm, to save life or to kill?' (Mark 3:4). Although we do not have enough evidence to say Jesus regarded the sabbath as unimportant (he did, after all, attend the synagogue regularly on that day), it is interesting that the reports we have of his citing some of the Ten Commandments never include the sabbath one (see e.g. Mark 10:19).

Second, there are three references by St Paul to disputes within the early churches about whether special days should be observed:

Romans 14:5–8 Every one should be fully convinced in his own mind, but should respect the
views of others.

Galatians 4:9–11 Observation of special times represents a turning back to the slavery of legalism.

Colossians 2:16 Detailed questions like the sabbath
are not a matter for passing judgement on others.

The thrust of these passages appears to be that Paul
thought observation of the sabbath was no longer binding
on the Christian, although (at least in some pastoral
situations) he considered it a permissible option.

Third, there are two fleeting references to the early
Christians' habit of meeting together on the first day of
the week. They are:

Acts 20:7 Paul speaks to the Christians at Troas,
who have met to break bread.

1 Corinthians 16:1–2 Paul's instructions to the
Corinthians to save money for the Jerusalem
collection.

These references indicate that if any day was considered
special by the early Christian church, it was Sunday
rather than Saturday. This is because it was the day when
Jesus rose from the dead. But the transfer was far from
being total. In the world of the Roman Empire, Sunday
was a normal working day, and there is no evidence that
the early Christians refrained from working on that day,
nor that they sought to dissuade others from doing so.
Presumably the habit of meeting together was practised
early or late in the day, outside working hours.

There is one further New Testament passage which
concerns the sabbath, Hebrews 4:1–11. This is unique in
type. It does not pass any judgement on the continuing
validity of the institution, using instead the sabbath rest
as a metaphor for the experience of salvation.

Stage three: identify the vital principles

In virtually every business dilemma, there are important matters of *principle* at stake. Values such as honesty, safety, respect for human dignity and concern for the environment are under the ethical microscope. A principle expresses a moral quality which ought to be present, not just in one particular act, but across a whole range of acts. In analysing a moral issue it is important to identify what are the vital principles involved. These will emerge in the process of sifting the facts under the spotlight of the appropriate sources of guidance.

For the Christian, there are two primary principles which underlie all others. They were stated by Jesus when asked what was the most important commandment.

> Jesus answered, 'The first is, "Hear, O Israel: The Lord our God, the Lord is one; and you shall love the Lord your God with all your heart, and with all your soul, and with all your mind, and with all your strength." The second is this, "You shall love your neighbour as yourself." There is no other commandment greater than these.' (Mark 12:29–31)

Ideally, everything that we do should flow from love of God and love of neighbour. Yet it is not always obvious what that means in practice. The principle of love needs to be spelt out in terms of more detailed, second order principles if it is to be of practical assistance. These second order principles are the key considerations which best express the demands of love with regard to a particular issue.

In relation to many problematical issues, it is possible to identify not one, but several relevant principles. Assessing the Sunday trading issue in Britain in the 1990s, in the light of the biblical material, I suggest the following:

1. *Human beings function best if they have a regular rhythm of rest from work one day a week.*

This is not stated explicitly in the biblical material. Yet the link made in Exodus between the sabbath and God's rest after the work of creation suggests that it is part of the order he has instilled into creation – in particular, the biological rhythms of human beings. This is borne out by the lessons of history. When alternatives to the pattern of a day of rest after six days of work have been tried (as after the French and Russian Revolutions), they have not lasted long. Admittedly, there are exceptional individuals who boast of their ability to keep going seven days a week, fifty-two weeks a year, but they are a very rare breed, and 'workaholism' of this kind almost invariably takes its toll eventually – whether in work, health, or relationship terms. Love for our fellow human beings needs to take seriously the way in which we have been made.

That the sabbath was intended for human good is clearly implied in the famous saying of Jesus: 'The Sabbath was made for man, not man for the sabbath' (Mark 2:27). Its purpose is one of re-creation.

2. *Rest does not mean a cessation of all human activity*.
For most people, sitting around twiddling their thumbs and doing nothing is not particularly restful. Victorian Christians who forbade their children to play games or read books on Sunday were following the letter of the Pharisees, not the spirit of Jesus. Re-creation involves most of the activities we include under the word rec-reation: activities which provide refreshment, entertainment, even diversion. This will mean different things for different people: doing the gardening, playing golf or visiting a stately home are three common examples.

The weight which Jesus put on the urgency of meeting people at their point of need is also worth pondering. In citing the example of David eating the sacred loaves ('when he was in need and was hungry': Mark 2:25), he taught that ceremonial considerations should be subordinated to humanitarian ones. The Keep Sunday Special Campaign acknowledges that in 'Applying that principle today, concern to honour God by keeping Sunday special should not prevent shops selling prescriptions, petrol and basic food items which people are likely to need on an emergency basis' (Christopher Townsend and Michael Schluter, *Why Keep Sunday Special*, 1985, p. 24).

3. *The vulnerable should be protected from exploitation.*
Again, this is a concern which is tangential to the biblical material, but there as a factor nonetheless. In Deuteronomy 5 the Israelites are told to remember that they were slaves in Egypt. It is likely that during their time as slaves they had to work seven days a week. Any employee who is required to work every day of the week is being exploited through overwork, to an extent which bears some resemblance to slavery.

The prophet Amos criticised businessmen who did (technically) keep the sabbath, but whose minds were hellbent on making money at any human cost – trampling over the poor if necessary. Precisely the same motive in Western society can drive retailers into keeping their shops open all seven days a week. The 'poor' in this case will be low-paid shopworkers (and those working in ancillary services) who may have to work on Sundays whether they like it or not, because they cannot afford to lose their jobs. Justice demands that they be protected from exploitation, and love is always more, never less than a concern for justice.

4. *Which day is taken as the day of rest is relatively incidental.*
Sunday is a fitting day for Christians to set aside for rest and worship because it commemorates Jesus' resurrection, but observing it in this way is not obligatory, as was the Old Testament sabbath. If we take the implications of the second principle seriously – that allowance should be made for emergency provisions and recreational activities – it is clear that for people in some occupations, working on Sundays will be a regular requirement. If they work on Sunday but set apart some other day such as Wednesday as special, Christians who benefit from the services of a nurse, a service station attendant or an ice-cream vendor on Sunday have no justification in looking down on them.

However, the word 'relatively' in this principle should not be ignored. It is clear that there are advantages if the majority of workers do take the same day off. The more that a weekly day of rest is a *collective* affair, the greater the chance of it being a real source of refreshment. When shops are open, they attract traffic and generate noise. Sharing the same day of rest increases the opportunities for family and communal gatherings. If it is right to earmark any day of the week as special, then Sunday seems the obvious choice, because of its place in the customs and tradition of society.

Stage four: evaluate an order of priorities

Identifying principles is doubtless a splendid thing to do, but what is the next step after that? Different principles can point in different directions: it is clear that the first and third principles I have just enunciated point more in the direction of maintaining restrictions on Sunday trading, while the second and fourth point more in the direction of relaxing them. There is a danger that the highly-principled person may end up just as confused (perhaps more so!) than anyone else. But with a clearing of the mind and a holding of the nerve, this danger can be averted.

In many such cases, what is required is some subtly woven solution which incorporates all of the principles identified. Neither rigid Sabbatarianism nor total de-regulation are satisfactory approaches to the current situation. This is an issue where compromise is not something dishonourable; it is entirely appropriate. But it remains to be seen whether there is a compromise solution which is both acceptable and workable as far as the different parties involved in Sunday trading are concerned.

The Keep Sunday Special Campaign has made legis-lative proposals which are broadly consistent with the principles I have outlined. They describe their fourfold aims as protection of the special character of Sunday, prevention of hardship, the promotion of family life and

social contact, and consideration of the reasonable needs
of customers. They then suggest four categories on which
to base exemptions from the general law forbidding
trading on Sundays. These categories are Recreation (per-
mitting the sale e.g., of flowers, newspapers and sporting
equipment), Emergencies (medicines, prescribed drugs,
cycle accessories), Social Gatherings (drink, restaurant
meals, guide books) and Travelling Public (petrol, motor
supplies, books at stations). Together these categories
form the acronym REST – hence the REST proposals.
Keep Sunday Special argue that though the selection of
goods whose sale is permitted by the 1950 Shops Act looks
very arbitrary (so that it is legal to sell a pornographic
magazine but not a Bible), on closer examination it turns
out that most fit into these four categories. They seek
to bring this underlying logic to light and argue in
favour of a tidying up operation on the law (removing
its more glaring anomalies), rather than its wholesale
abandonment.

Rather than base the law solely on a list of exempt
goods, however, which is hard to enforce, they propose to
follow the example of some European countries and make
a list of exempt shops (e.g., chemists, petrol stations,
newsagents). The problem comes with those shops which
sell a mixture of goods which do and do not fall into
the exempt categories. Here the Keep Sunday Special
Campaign offer an 80/20 rule: a shop would be registered
by the local authority to open and sell its full product
range on Sunday if the authority is satisfied that the shop
sells 80 per cent or more exempt items as a proportion of
its aggregate sales throughout a twelve-month period.

It is easy to find fault with such a proposal: why 80
per cent, and would a local authority have either the
will or the capacity to assess the proportion of sales
accurately? Yet it is difficult to come up with a better
alternative. Clearly if a political pressure group is going
to be taken seriously, it has to descend into the fine detail
of legislative proposal and counter-proposal. To discuss
the ins and outs of exemption and registration thoroughly
falls outside the province of this book. I can only express

my hope that a compromise solution which gives concrete expression to worthy biblical principles can be discovered and made to work.

The fact remains that principles cannot always be held in a neatly synchronised balance. There is no way that one is going to be able to please everybody all of the time. Businesspeople have to make some hard decisions. Often the decision will involve putting different principles in an order of priority.

Is it possible to put moral duties in some sort of hierarchy of importance? I used to believe that it was, but I have made less progress with constructing such a table than I had hoped! The Bible does give a few helpful pointers in this area. For instance, although the Bible in general terms sets high store by the virtue of honesty, there are a number of biblical stories where individuals who make statements which were actually dishonest do so with divine approval. The Hebrew midwives perpetrated a fast one on Pharaoh (Exodus 1:19), Rahab lied about hiding the spies (Joshua 2:4–5), and Elisha misled the Syrian soldiers about his identity (2 Kings 6:19). The biblical writers see God as being on the side of the individuals concerned on each occasion. On closer examination, one notices a common thread which runs through all these stories. In each case life was imperilled if the truth was told. The message seems to be that in exceptional circumstances of extreme danger, the obligation to preserve life outweighs that to tell the truth.

This example illustrates the importance of paying attention to specific situations. The reason why it is difficult to draw up a plausible league table of moral obligations is that there are so many circumstantial variables. Take a chemicals company, forced to cut costs, which may have to choose between making staff redundant and reducing its pollution of rivers. It has to place two worthy objects, keeping people employed and contributing to a cleaner environment, in an order of priority. In a period of rocketing unemployment it might be more important to save the jobs; in an era of escalating pollution it would be better advised to clean the rivers. The context in which the decision is made rightly affects the evaluation of priorities.

The difficulty of reducing moral decisions to hard-and-fast rules is further illustrated if we translate the Sunday trading issue into the following practical dilemma. Roger and Barbara run a long-established DIY tool merchant store in a town shopping precinct. Some of the neighbouring shops open on Sunday. Roger and Barbara employ ten people, all long-serving employees, and pride themselves on offering a knowledgeable service to discerning buyers. A well-known retailer has recently opened a DIY superstore on the outskirts of town. It opens Thursdays to Saturdays for late night shopping, and this has already tempted away some of the couple's customers, with an inevitable effect on their profits. The superstore has now announced its intention to open on Sundays and customers are asking Roger and Barbara whether they will do likewise, making it clear that they would like the opportunity to shop on that day.

Roger and Barbara realise that their business is under serious threat. They put the problem to their staff, who indicate real disapproval at the prospect of Sunday opening, because they treasure their Sunday off and want to spend time with their families. The couple consider employing casual staff on Sundays, but they think it unlikely they would find the calibre required. Using 'spotty teenagers', as Roger calls them, could jeopardise their reputation for excellent service.

Suppose that Roger and Barbara agree with the principles on Sunday trading which I have outlined earlier. What should they do? Whether DIY products should fall within the goods considered exempt is in fact something Keep Sunday Special has had difficulty deciding. Whereas some people regard DIY as a tedious chore, others regard it as pleasantly recreational! There is certainly a case for including it in this category, along, possibly, with that of Emergencies. There may be times when a person doing a DIY job will run out of items like nails, screws, paint, or wallpaper, and it is vital that he

or she gets the job finished before returning to work on
Monday.

If Roger and Barbara can satisfy themselves on that
score, there remains the problem of the attitude of the
staff. Because the views of the staff are so definite and
so understandable, Roger and Barbara should surely
do their best to continue operating without resort to
Sunday opening. If they explain their concern for their
staff as their reason for not doing so, it is possible
that some of their customers will be sympathetic and
continue to buy from them. But if the result of their
principled stand is that the couple's store is threatened
with closure, what then? It will not be any help to their
long-serving staff if they go out of business. Roger and
Barbara might have to go back to their employees and
put the argument that, in order to remain competitive,
Sunday opening appears to be essential. If that happened
they would of course guarantee the staff an alternative
day off.

What has happened here is that the gravity of the
store's financial situation effects the order in which priorities are evaluated. It does *not* mean that principles are
simply sacrificed to pragmatism. The survival of stores
like those run by Roger and Barbara is an important
matter for concern.

Admittedly, there is a further complicating factor in
this particular example, which is the position of the
law. At present it appears that DIY stores (whether
large or small) which open in Britain do so illegally.
As law-respecting citizens, the response of Roger and
Barbara will rightly be to abide by that. They will also be
fully justified in urging their local authority to prosecute
the superstore which threatens their livelihood.

Stage five: take the decision prayerfully before God

Finally, the time comes when decisions have to be made.
Facts have been absorbed, guidance sought, principles
named, and priorities weighed. The issue is thought

through to a conclusion – albeit, in some cases, only a provisional conclusion.

The Christian businessperson is not alone in the making of difficult decisions. He or she does so in the context of a relationship with God. I venture to suggest four ways in which this can be tremendously sustaining:

1. Paul makes the mind-blowing statement that the person who is indwelt by the Holy Spirit has 'the mind of Christ' (1 Corinthians 2:16). Do we underrate the intellectual resources at our disposal? It may be that, in the process of prayer and looking to the Holy Spirit for guidance, a clear message which radically simplifies decision-making will come. There is no guarantee of this, and I do not believe that it is the normal way of the Spirit's working, but it would be unwise to shut ourselves off from the possibility.

2. Even when we do not seem to receive clear guidance, we need to remember that at the end of the day we are justified, not by works, but by grace. Our relationship with God and our standing before him do not depend on the rightness or wrongness of our moral decisions. God looks upon something more fundamental – that inner core of our being which the Bible calls the heart.

3. It may be that when confronted by a difficult moral dilemma, a Christian may sometimes feel that whatever decision he takes contains an element of sin. It is quite likely that in feeling this he is suffering from an oversensitive conscience, because he is actually trying to take the best course of action to extract himself or others from a messy situation which is not of his making. I have argued earlier that many of the compromises about which people are inclined to feel guilty can be excused as thoroughly honourable. Yet it remains true that if sin is felt, the wise thing to do is to confess it, and thereby be released from its sting. As Martin Luther once said (in a statement which it is crucial to understand in the

right way): 'Sin boldly, but believe even more boldly
and rejoice in Christ!' The key message is not to be
paralysed by guilt, but to have courage to go forward,
doing whatever one conscientiously believes is the least
evil (or most good) thing to do, confident in the promise
of God's forgiveness.

4. God gives us fellow-travellers on the way. Too often
when making difficult decisions we isolate ourselves from
the companionship, support and potentially good advice
of other people. I recall a business ethics seminar at
which I spoke in a flourishing church in the commuter
belt of the South of England. A very revealing aspect of
this experience was to discover how many individuals in
that church were in similar types of work (notably the
field of insurance) but how little they had hitherto talked
to each other about their work. They were grappling with
similar problems, but had failed to use their collective
resources in discussing those problems. Perhaps one of
the most important lessons the Japanese have to teach
stubborn, independent Westerners is the readiness to be
interdependent. Interdependence is surely as relevant to
wrestling with complex moral decisions as it is to other
areas of work. It is taking seriously the corporate dimension to our humanity implicit in the Pauline doctrine of
the church as the body of Christ.

CHAPTER 15

NOURISHING THE PEOPLE OF GOD

The Underdeveloped Role of the Church

Many Christians who work in business feel very lonely in their job as Christians. That is a clear trend which I could adduce much anecdotal evidence to support. This is despite the fact that the number of Christian organisations in the work-place seems, if anything, to be increasing. Many companies, especially the larger ones, have a Christian fellowship which runs lunch-time or evening meetings on a regular basis. In Britain, the ICF (Industry Churches Forum, formerly the Industrial Christian Fellowship) produces a stream of quarterly magazines and pamphlets; Christian Impact (in conjunction with the UCCF Business Studies Group) holds annual conferences for middle and senior managers; there are lunchtime services and talks at leading churches in the City; and 'prayer breakfasts' for businesspeople take place in many of the larger cities. Industrial chaplains continue to visit work-places up and down the country. These are only a sample of a wide range of Christian organisations which are active in the business world. However, such activity is patchy, and not always well publicised. Many Christian businesspeople do not work near these centres of fellowship, and have not necessarily heard of them if they do. The sense of feeling isolated and unsupported remains strong among large numbers of men and women.

It is also true that the fellowship to which the majority of Christians in business would probably look first and foremost for support is the local church which they attend Sunday by Sunday. But do they find support there? Here one has to acknowledge a highly paradoxical situation.

A paradox

I recently read *The Irrelevant Church*, by Robin Gamble.
He is the Anglican vicar of a working-class parish in
Bradford, and from a working-class background himself.
The question on the book's back cover sums up his
theme: 'How can the church discard its middle-class,
religious corsetry, and establish itself as a vital and
relevant force in working-class communities?' Gamble
passionately indites the church in England for conspiring
in the creation of 'two nations'. He writes thus:

> The one force or movement in society which is
> supposed to follow its Lord's commitment to the
> poor and needy, has in effect become a bourgeois
> institution. Jesus came and actually lived among
> the poor, but his twentieth-century followers prefer
> the semis of suburbia. Jesus was the God of the
> Incarnation, he actually became 'one of us', but
> today's Christians have opted for incarnation with
> a nicely trimmed lawn back and front. The kingdom
> was heralded by the Good News being preached to
> the poor, but in our churches it is preached to the
> middle class. (*The Irrelevant Church,* p. 117)

Although I would quibble with aspects of his thesis, there
is much painful truth in Gamble's analysis. His book is
full of fresh ideas for making the church less stuffy and
more dynamic. He is also correct in characterising it as
a predominantly middle-class institution.

People who work in management positions come, generally speaking, from the middle-classes. It might therefore
be expected that a middle-class church would suit them
down to the ground. Such a church would have their
concerns, needs and interests very much at heart. It
would pray for them regularly, provide preaching that
was highly relevant to their line of work, and celebrate
the task of wealth creation in which they are involved.
But businesspeople testify with an almost unanimous
voice that their weekly experience of church services

is nothing like that. The world of business, commerce and industry goes largely ignored. Here lies the paradox which I referred to earlier.

The truth of the matter seems to be that although most churches *are* middle-class, they have an uneasy conscience about the matter. They have tried to take to heart the message of people like Bishop David Sheppard, with his *Bias to the Poor*, or liberation theology, with its 'power for the powerless'. Although they still make relatively little impact in working-class areas, the prayers, actions and financial resources of the church are being focused increasingly on the more underprivileged sections of society. The Anglican Report *Faith in the City,* and the Church Urban Fund which it spawned, is a notable example of this.

Unfortunately, church leaders often operate according to some mistaken presuppositions in this area. They assume that concern for those who lack power and influence is compromised if one expresses sentiments which might be interpreted as support for those who wield power and influence. They imagine that managers and managed are likely to be at loggerheads, whereas the realities of a highly competitive world economy are that the two are often locked together in a struggle for survival. They look for wealth to be redistributed (rightly so), but do not pay sufficient attention to the fact that it has first to be created. Of course I am indulging in broad generalisations – to which there will be many exceptions – but it is attitudes like these which help to account for the fact that businesspeople's experience of their local church frequently leaves them feeling unsupported.

To support people, but at the same time to challenge them, is the dual task of the church in every generation, for every class of people. It is not uncritical support which businesspeople either need or, generally speaking, want. The attitude which hurts them most is when the church simply passes them by: when it makes no mention of or appears indifferent to their concerns. When preachers openly challenge specific trends in the business world there is at least a measure of engagement taking place.

Members of the congregation who work in business can either heed or respond to such challenges.

I shall suggest three particular areas of the local church's life, prayer, preaching and celebration, where more connections could be made with people's working experience.

Intercession for business

In exploring the link between work and public worship, we have used the following exercise during our seminar weeks at Ridley Hall. We have asked participants the simple question: How often do you recall people in the following occupations being remembered in prayer in church services? The answers given are remarkably consistent. They are, on average, as follows:

Quite often: Nurse, Teacher, Politician

Occasionally: Ambulanceman, Farmer, Policeman, Soldier, Union Leader

Never: Bank Manager, Broadcaster, Corporation Chairman, Design Engineer, Salesman, Solicitor

A clear message comes through. The people whom the church prays for most regularly in its public intercessions are those who work in the 'caring services' (e.g., doctors, nurses, social workers), in education, or in positions of political leadership. Every now and again it prays for those who are at the forefront of crisis situations (strikes, wars, droughts, etc.) or who have the task of maintaining law and order. It hardly prays at all for those involved in any type of commercial activity. Surprisingly enough, this remains true even when the country is caught in the throes of a severe recession, and when there are reports of companies having to close and more people being made redundant almost every day.

It would be unfair to say that the clergy alone are to blame for this. In many churches lay people are heavily involved in the leading of intercessions. As in many areas of life, a disturbing process of learned behaviour takes place, so that people unconsciously absorb messages from others about what is the acceptable way to pray. It is refreshing when someone defies the trend and breaks out of the conventional rut.

True, there may be a genuine uncertainty as to how we should pray when it comes to business. At one extreme, we are rightly wary about asking God to take sides in a takeover dispute or to give a boost to retailers' profits. At the other, 'God bless this' and 'God bless that' is open to the charge of being vague and bland. But this problem can soon be addressed with a little serious reflection. I hope that the contents of this book provide some fruitful material for thoughtful prayer. Examples might include:

* The vision of the market economy brought under the authority of Christ (see ch.2).

* The creation of companies which are genuine caring communities (see ch.3).

* A spirit of responsible stewardship in managing God's world, so that its resources are used fully without the causing of irreparable damage (see ch.5).

* God's sustaining love for those who take costly self-sacrificial decisions in the work-place (see ch.9).

Then there are blessings for which it is appropriate to thank God in a business context. In the West we often give thanks for the stability of our political system. Does it ever occur to us to express gratitude for the stability of our *banking* system? It should be possible to do this without provoking the assumption that this implies unquestioning support for everything the banks get up to.

Another curious anomaly is this. As already noted, the world's prime ministers and presidents do feature regularly on the church's intercessory agenda. Yet the chairman of many large multinational companies preside over larger annual budgets than the gross national

products of some small Third World countries. The men
who run Exxon, Glaxo, IBM, ICI and General Motors
have a formidable amount of power at their disposal.
Is it not important to pray for them, that they may
influence the many countries in which they work, for
good and not for evil? Another category of people who
wield formidable influence are the money market dealers
on the world's stock exchanges. On what became known
as Black Wednesday in October 1992, Britain's Conservative Government proved completely powerless to shore up
sterling in the face of the solid conviction held by the
foreign exchange dealers that the pound was overvalued.
The role which they play is a matter of public concern,
and therefore proper material for corporate prayer.

Helping people to pray

There is a personal side to prayer as well as a public one.
Businesspeople are not simply those who are prayed for
(or, more frequently, not). They are also people of prayer,
men and women who realise that setting aside time to be
with God is vital for their own personal wellbeing. But
here too there are problems which need to be addressed.

Barry, Fiona and Miles, the three businesspeople featured at the beginning of this book and in succeeding
chapters, are doing very different jobs, and are at very
different stages of their careers and Christian lives. Yet
the three of them share a common problem, one that
many other Christians admit to also: they find it difficult
to maintain a disciplined prayer life. The pressures of
their respective jobs, the length of hours which the job
consumes, the demands made by family, church and other
interests, all conspire to put the squeeze on a regular
time of personal devotion. One idea that clergy might
usefully pursue is a crash course on how to pray for
busy people, probably within the programme of regular
Sunday teaching. I am sure that there would be an
appreciative response from members of the congregation
in management positions.

The fact is that in the area of personal prayer, people

often have unhelpful burdens of guilt and unrealistic expectations. Because they feel that they ought to be spending half or three quarters of an hour every day alone with God, and they never manage to achieve this for all sorts of reasons, it is easy to feel a failure and give up altogether. For some it will be far better to set much more modest targets during the week (perhaps making use of slack moments during the day, such as time spent on travel), and to carve out a more extended period in prayer at the week-end. I have made a few practical suggestions in this area in my booklet *Living with Affluence*.

A wise pastor recognises that in prayer, as in other areas, different individuals operate according to different rhythms. The same pattern will not be appropriate for everyone. It is also crucial to help people to see prayer first and foremost in terms of *relationship:* cultivating a healthy relationship with God, keeping it fresh and vibrant. Prayer in its essence is not a task to be performed, but the condition of consciously being with God. Intercession, similarly, is being with God with people on your heart. If we care about the people whom we rub shoulders with day by day, it is only natural that we should want to bring colleagues, customers and even competitors before God in prayer. One of the skills a good prayer counsellor can teach is how to impose order and instil imagination in doing this while avoiding the condition in which intercession becomes a chore.

Preaching which bites

Wherever one goes in the church today, a common refrain is heard: that outstanding preachers are very thin on the ground. This seems to be the case even in the branch of the church with which I am most familiar, the evangelical wing, where the emphasis put on the preaching of the Word has always been strong. Why is it that people so often leave church feeling unnourished?

I suggest that sermons often disappoint on one of two grounds. In many churches the best attended time of

worship is a family service where the fare is deliberately
light and the message easily accessible to everyone. In
the hands of a gifted communicator who has a flair
for the unexpected and some good visual aids up their
sleeve, the result is sometimes memorable. Too often,
however, the talk says nothing which makes one think,
and fails to expand even the horizons of the children: it is
a pedestrian retracing of familiar ground. If this becomes
the congregation's regular diet, there is a danger that
its members will never 'leave the elementary doctrines of
Christ and go on to maturity' (Hebrews 6:1).

A second peril is the preacher who is the very opposite
of light. On the contrary, he speaks solidly for twenty-five
or thirty minutes and gives systematic, thorough expo-
sitions of the biblical text. He expounds the word very
conscientiously. The question here is whether he (less
likely she) engages effectively with the modern world.
Certainly, attempts at application may be made, but
these are usually in a highly generalised form. References to 'church', 'work' and 'home' never become more
specific. The consequence is that the sermon lacks bite.

I believe that it is possible to steer a middle ground
between these two approaches. It is possible, within a
time-limit of, say, twenty minutes, to say something
which engages honestly with the biblical text and makes
imaginative connections with life today. It is possible to
give a message which is succinct and memorable. It is
possible to *move* people: in particular to comfort the
disturbed and disturb the comfortable, as someone once
described the role of the preacher.

The use of illustrations which are specific but, at
the same time, representative, is a vital aspect of such
preaching. There is a telling example of this in one of
the pastoral epistles, where Paul is exhorting his young
colleague Timothy:

You then, my son, be strong in the grace that is in
Christ Jesus, and what you have heard from me
before many witnesses entrust to faithful men who
will be able to teach others also. Take your share of

suffering as a good soldier of Christ Jesus. No soldier
on service gets entangled in civilian pursuits, since
his aim is to satisfy the one who enlisted him. An
athlete is not crowned unless he competes according
to the rules. It is the hard-working farmer who ought
to have the first share of the crops. Think over what
I say, for the Lord will grant you understanding in
everything. (2 Timothy 2:1–7)

Here Paul draws lessons from three different spheres
of life, military, sporting and agricultural. Each makes
a slightly different point. The example of the soldier
teaches endurance and concentrated service, the athlete
teaches discipline, and the farmer teaches perseverance.
Taken together, they illustrate vividly what it means
for Timothy to be *strong* in the grace that is in Christ
Jesus (v.1).

Suppose that Timothy then made use of these illustrations in his preaching to the congregation over which he
had charge at Ephesus. After all, the apostle encourages
him to pass on what he, Paul, has taught him. The congregation would probably include a sprinkling of farmers,
soldiers and athletes. If not, they would be figures with
whom the church members were familiar and could easily
identify. The result: a general moral point which could go
down like a lead balloon is brought to life by the use of
specific illustrations.

More teaching of this type is needed in our church
today. Risky though it is, the preacher should venture to
suggest what a particular point of application might mean
in a variety of occupational situations. Men and women
who work in business should be able to recognise themselves in the people described, along with other church
members. One day, the preacher might make his or her
point with reference to the building society manager, the
housewife, and the probation officer; another day, it could
be the engineer, the check-out girl at the supermarket,
and the child in the school playground. It is all part of a
process of helping people see work as a place where faith
can be put into action.

Some parts of the Bible lend themselves to this process of horizon-bridging particularly well. Imagine a congregation which includes an unusually high number of individuals in senior business, political, and civil service positions. A sermon series on the Old Testament figures of Joseph, Daniel or Esther would present a fascinating challenge. They were all God-fearing people in high places, wrestling with questions of conscience in a distinctly pagan environment. To identify their crucial qualities of character, and to see (reading between as well as along the lines) what were the issues on which they were and were not prepared to compromise, could prove enormously enlightening for such a congregation.

For sermon read seminar?

The sermon in its traditional format still has great potential, but it also has its limitations. It is difficult for a preacher to engage in serious depth with complex social and ethical issues without leaving most of the congregation feeling rather frustrated. There will be points which need qualification, questions which are begged, bold moral judgements to which some will want to respond. Most sermons are a case of the preacher standing six foot above contradiction. Sure, individuals can take points up with him or her afterwards, but the wider body misses out on whatever constructive interchange may ensue.

Preaching which is a conscious grappling with substantive topical issues (as opposed to sermons where reference to those issues is more incidental) needs to incorporate elements of dialogue. Here one would like to see more churches being prepared to experiment; some are doing so. One possibility is for people to be invited to stay behind after a service to ask questions of the preacher and engage in discussion. Another is to try what has sometimes been called All-Age Learning or, in the United States, Adult Sunday School. Here the sermon is replaced by something more akin to a seminar or, very likely, a series of seminars. People choose one

from a number of different areas of interest to attend. A
seminar leader provides a certain amount of input which
serves to stimulate group discussion. The seminar might
take forty-five minutes (longer than the average sermon),
with the rest of the service probably being condensed to
allow room for it.

The church which I attend in Cambridge has run
programmes of this type for limited periods of time,
notably Advent and Lent. Seminars of particular interest
to businesspeople, such as 'Using the Bible in Ethics',
or 'Prayer and Work', have featured among the options
offered. The response has been very positive. A greater
sense of participation and depth of engagement are
achieved than is possible within the normal run of Sunday
services. A church can only sustain such a programme
all the year round, however, if it has a large group of
unusually talented and energetic seminar leaders at its
disposal. A continual diet of this sort would probably not
be desirable in any case. There is still a place for the
more proclamatory style of speaking associated with the
sermon.

A festival of work

A third area of church worship in which the theme of work
might be further developed is that of celebration. There is
already one well-established example of this, in the form
of Harvest Festivals. The origins of this go right back to
Deuteronomy:

> When you come into the land which the Lord your
> God gives you for an inheritance, and have taken
> possession of it, and live in it, you shall take some
> of the first of all the fruit of the ground, which you
> harvest from your land that the Lord your God gives
> you, and you shall put it in a basket, and you shall go
> to the place which the Lord your God will choose . . .
> (Deuteronomy 26:1–2)

Here there is an invigorating sense that work is God-
given, and the product of work part of God's blessing

upon his people. The church today still seems to find that easier to accept in relation to agriculture than to industry. There is an Industry Sunday celebrated in some churches, but it has never caught on widely in the way that fruit, vegetables and loaves continue to adorn church buildings every Harvest Sunday. But in societies where only a tiny fraction of the population is involved in agriculture, this state of affairs is becoming increasingly anachronistic.

I suggest there is scope in every church's life (urban and rural) for an occasional Festival of Work. This might well include both an all-together time of worship and a breaking up into smaller groups, along the lines of service experimentation suggested above. The aim would be one of celebrating and exploring the work – paid and unpaid – performed by the whole congregation. It could include such activities as:

* The bringing of an object associated with each person's work.

* Sharing a testimony about how the person sees it as God's work.

* Offering the object and ourselves to God in his service.

* Giving thanks to God for everyone's contribution.

* Sharing and praying about problem-areas at work.

* Collecting for a cause associated with a selected area of work.

* Praying more widely for the work situation in the country (to which one could add continent or world).

The focus in doing this would not be solely on business. But it is likely that an effect would be to highlight the positive contribution that commerce and industry make to the community.

Bread and wine, product of human hands

One act of celebration which already takes place on a regular basis is the service of Holy Communion. Here elements which human beings have played a part in creating (the bread has to be baked, and the wine fermented) are transformed into tokens of eternal significance. It will be appropriate on occasion to draw attention to this dimension of human labour, though the effect should not be to distract from the centrality of God's grace in the saving death of Christ. I once asked an ordinand to consider how the Communion might be handled in a service intended to highlight the theme of work. Using as her basis Rite A in the Anglican *Alternative Service Book*, and building upon published material from a variety of sources, the imaginative alternatives she came up with included the following:

Proper Preface:
    And now we give you thanks that through your Son we have an example to follow for the whole of our lives, at home and at work. In sharing our earthly life, he shared also our experiences of toil and labour, and entered fully into our human condition.

Breaking of Bread:
    Though our lives may be different, and our occupations varied, we are one in our Lord Jesus Christ. We come together, to share the one bread, product also of human hands, and so we share in the body of Christ.

Words of Invitation:
    Come, draw near with faith. Receive the body and blood of our Lord Jesus Christ, who shared our human life, its joys and its sorrows. Come, find rest for your souls, and refreshment for your lives in One who knew the toils and struggles of human life. Eat, drink, remember he died for you, and lives for you, and feed on him in your heart by faith with thanksgiving.

Thanksgiving:

Father of all, we thank you and praise you for
the gift of your Son to humanity: for his sharing
of our earthly life; for his work as a carpenter;
for his understanding of those whose jobs made
them outcasts, but also of those who held positions
of honour; for his own ministry, and that of his
disciples. And now, above all, we thank you for
feeding us with his body and blood. Send us back
into the world, refreshed by this heavenly food, to
work as he did, and, by the power of your Spirit,
to live our lives as witnesses to his life, death and
resurrection. Amen.

Blessing:

Christ whose family were carpenters, and whose
company was tax collectors, uphold you in your work,
give you a sense of value in what you do, and guide
you in your decision-making; and the blessing of
God . . .

There is some imbalance in the direction of a rather negative view of work in these selections (much about work as
toilsome, little about its creative aspects), and liturgists
could doubtless do some useful polishing up. But the
material has the virtues of relevance and freshness.
When Eucharistic liturgy comprises the same familiar
phrases week by week, it is all too easy for the congregation's concentration to wander. To emphasise a particular
dimension from time to time serves as a valuable stimulus
to thought about what it is that the gathered community
is celebrating.

Every member ministry

The plea of the chapter thus far is that people in the
local church in general, and businesspeople in particular,
be more satisfactorily nourished. This is not to belittle
much excellent work which goes on in lots of churches,
including the sterling efforts made by some clergy to keep
in touch with what the members of their congregations do

during the week. Overall, however, too many Christians are leaving Sunday and entering Monday feeling poorly fed. The body of Christ is supposed to be 'nourished and knit together through its joints and ligaments', growing 'with a growth that is from God' (Colossians 2:19).

Paul's teaching on the nature of the church, however, emphasises that relationships within it are mutual. Lay people should not be thinking just about what they can get from the church; they also have much to give. There are a wide variety of ministries in which they can play their part, and the development of this aspect of the church's life is a welcome feature of the last twenty-five years.

There are particular gifts which businesspeople may have to offer the church. They are accustomed to drawing up specific objectives, devising clear lines of account-ability, and analysing the effectiveness of new initia-tives. Churches are often surprisingly muddled in the way they go about their business; many lack even an adequate understanding of their own mission. While there are important differences between companies and churches as organisations (such as the fact that only a few individuals are employed by a church), many general management skills and techniques are relevant in both spheres of operation. Church leaders are wise to draw on the fund of experience in running complex corporate entities which is often available in their congregation.

There are also specific tasks in the church's life which may seem precisely matched to a particular business-person's skills or gifts. Perhaps the church membership includes an advertising executive who makes a superb editor of the church magazine, and an imaginative archi-tect who is marvellous at running the youth group. The message of the New Testament seems clear: 'As each has received a gift, employ it for one another, as good stewards of God's varied grace' (1 Peter 4:10). Nevertheless, two common dangers are to be avoided.

One is to assume that individuals who practise a par-ticular profession day by day necessarily want to perform its church equivalent outside their working hours. It may be important that an accountant does *not* look after the church's finances, and a hard-pressed teacher does *not* teach in the Sunday School, in order that they keep themselves fresh for their weekday ministry. It would actually be better if someone else has a go at being treasurer or teaching the children, and that the accountant and teacher use or develop another gift in the context of their involvement in the church.

The other danger is to ignore the considerable pressures experienced by most people in management positions in the present era. Often their work (travel time included) consumes twelve or more hours of the day; they come home with their heads buzzing and feeling thoroughly washed out. But work is only part of life, though for some it threatens to consume the whole. The home to which a businessman returns towards the close of a day may serve as a haven and a solace, or it could be a further source of pressure. The man's wife may resent the long hours worked by her husband. She herself may reach the evening hours exhausted by the demands of young children. She is keen to talk, having been deprived of intellectual stimulus for most of the day, and wants to know what has happened to her husband at work. The last thing that couple probably need is the demand of having to lead a house-group the moment he walks in. But it is all too easy for church activities to add to the stress felt by Christian people in demanding positions. Church leaders need to be sensitive to the existence of such pressures, and to know when – gifted as a particular individual or couple may be – asking them to perform a task might drain their energies or strain their relationship to near breaking point.

Called to account

A simple conviction on my part has motivated the writing of this book. Why is it so important to relate faith to work, to get one's theology sorted out so that it makes connections with the market-place? It is the belief and the hope that Christians have a crucial role to play in influencing companies, organisations and society for good.

The odds against their doing so are, in worldly terms, formidable. Christians often feel desperately outnumbered at their place of work. The distinctive contribution which they bring to bear on events may seem negligible. As they look back on their actions at the end of a day, or even the end of a career, they may well be inclined to ask themselves: 'Do not even pagans do that?' (Matthew 5:47, NIV).

The New Testament does not encourage a spirit of naive triumphalism. The forces of evil are powerful, and they are still alive and kicking. But the rise of the early Christian church, allied to the teaching of Jesus, gives grounds for hope that great things *can* develop from distinctly modest beginnings. Jesus talked about the kingdom of heaven as a mustard seed, the smallest of seeds which grows into the greatest of shrubs. He also uses the image of leaven:

> 'The kingdom of heaven is like leaven which a woman took and hid in three measures of meal, till it was all leavened.' (Matthew 13:33)

Christians who are truly worth their salt (which was after all another metaphor Jesus used about them) are infiltrators of the world in which they operate, permeating and purifying and penetrating for the forces of good and of God.

The nature of the world, however, is that Christians who betray their integrity, falling foul of the law or bringing disgrace on themselves, attract far more public attention than those who set a worthy example. They need to watch for signs of infiltration in a negative direction. Interestingly, Paul uses leaven as an image of how evil, not good, can be infectious:

> Do you not know that a little leaven leavens the whole lump? Cleanse out the old leaven that you may be a new lump, as you really are unleavened.

For Christ, our paschal lamb, has been sacrificed.
Let us, therefore, celebrate the festival, not with
the old leaven, the leaven of malice and evil, but
with the unleavened bread of sincerity and truth.
(1 Corinthians 5:6–8)

This book has said nothing directly about the task of
Christian witness, in the narrow sense of evangelism
designed to persuade one's colleagues to become Christians. I believe such a task is important, though obviously
it has to be undertaken carefully, sensitively, and with a
mind to what it is one is employed to do. No one has given
a better description of the way in which Christians should
witness to their faith than St Peter:

> Always be prepared to make a defence to anyone who
> calls you to account for the hope that is in you, yet
> do it with gentleness and reverence; and keep your
> conscience clear, so that, when you are abused, those
> who revile your good behaviour in Christ may be put
> to shame. (1 Peter 3:15–16)

The latter point underlines the importance of living a life
which matches one's Christian profession.

What this book has been concerned to explore is witness
in the wider sense: the way of thinking and type of life
which should undergird that readiness to talk of the
Christian hope. I believe that if Christians fail to clarify
their stance on crucial issues which lie at the very heart of
their involvement in business, they diminish the quality
of that witness. But if in contrast they can show how
their faith is relevant to tough decisions about values,
leadership, managing change, and coping with failure,
they will win greater respect for their convictions.

Christians are therefore *called to account*. They are
called to account by other people for what they believe
and how they behave. They should have no reason to
be defensive on such scores: it is possible to show that
Christianity makes sense, intellectually and as a way
of life. But the verdict of others upon them is not what

ultimately counts. Christians know that they are called to a different account, the account they will give of their life and work before God himself. It is his verdict which really matters, and him that they are principally concerned to serve.

> Whatever your task, work heartily, as serving the Lord and not men, knowing that from the Lord you will receive the inheritance as your reward; you are serving the Lord Christ. (Colossians 3:23–24)

The words were originally addressed to Colossian slaves in the first century, but they are just as relevant to individuals operating at many different levels of responsibility in the business world today.

BIBLIOGRAPHY

The following list consists of all the books referred to in the text, as well as some by other writers I have mentioned:

Adair, John, *Effective Leadership: A modern guide to developing leadership skills*, Pan Books, London, 1983

Archbishop of Canterbury's Commission on Urban Priority Areas, *Faith in the City: A Call for Action by Church and Nation*, Church House Publishing, London, 1985

ARCO Chemical Europe, *Because We Care*, Maidenhead, 1991

Bauckham, Richard, *The Bible in Politics: How to read the Bible politically*, SPCK, London, 1989

Benton, Peter, *Riding the Whirlwind: Benton on Managing Turbulence*, Basil Blackwell, Oxford, 1990

Brown, Mick, *Richard Branson: The Inside Story*, Michael Joseph, London, 1988

Bryant, Sir Arthur, *English Saga (1840–1940)*, Collins, London, 1940

Davis, John, *Greening Business: Managing for Sustainable Development*, Basil Blackwell, Oxford, 1991

Fowl, Stephen E. and L. Gregory Jones, *Reading in Communion: Scripture and Ethics in Christian Life*, SPCK, London, 1991

Gamble, Robin, *The Irrelevant Church*, Monarch, Eastbourne, 1991

Goyder, George, *The Just Enterprise*, André Deutsch, London, 1987

Handy, Charles, *The Age of Unreason*, Business Books, London, 1989

Harries, Richard, *Is There a Gospel for the Rich? The Christian in a capitalist world*, Mowbray, London, 1992

Harvey, A.E., *Strenuous Commands: The Ethic of Jesus*, SCM, London, 1990

Harvey-Jones, John, *Making It Happen: Reflections on Leadership*, Collins, London, 1988

Higginson, Richard, *Living with Affluence: Prayer, Prosperity and the Christian Business Person*, Grove Books, Nottingham, 1992

House of Bishops, a statement by, *Issues in Human Sexuality*, Church House Publishing London, 1991.

Jackall, Robert, *Moral Mazes: The World of Corporate Managers*, OUP, New York, 1988

Kanter, Rosabeth Moss, *The Change Masters: Corporate Entrepreneurs at Work*, Allen & Unwin, London, 1984

Lovatt, John, 'Jesus in the Workplace: Towards a Better Theology of Work', *MC*, Vol. XXXIV, No. 2, pp. 10–16

Macquarrie, John and Childress, James (eds.), *A New Dictionary of Christian Ethics*, SCM, London, 1986

Moltmann, Jurgen, *Theology of Hope*, SCM, London, 1967

O'Donovan, Oliver, *Resurrection and Moral Order: An Outline for Evangelical Ethics*, IVP, Leicester, 1986

Peters, Tom, *Thriving on Chaos: Handbook for a Management Revolution*, Macmillan, London, 1988

Polkinghorne, John, *Reason and Reality: The Relationship between Science and Theology*, SPCK, London, 1991

Preston, Ronald H., *Religion and the Ambiguities of Capitalism*, SCM, London, 1991

Roddick, Anita, *Body and Soul*, Ebury Press, London, 1991

Ryken, Leland, *Work and Leisure in Christian Perspective*, IVP, Leicester, 1987

Schluter, Michael, and Clements, Roy, *Reactivating the Extended Family: From Biblical Norms to Public Policy in Britain*, Jubilee Centre Publications, Cambridge, 1986

Schumacher, Christian, *To Live and Work: A Theological Interpretation*, MARC Europe, Bromley, 1987

Sculley, John, *Odyssey: Pepsi to Apple,* Collins, London, 1987

Sheppard, David, *Bias to the Poor*, Hodder & Stoughton, London, 1983

Smith, Adam, *The Wealth of Nations,* Penguin, London, 1986

Song, C.S., *Third Eye Theology,* Lutterworth, London, 1983

Thielicke, Helmut, *Theological Ethics Vol. I: Foundations*, Fortress, Philadelphia, 1966

Thomas, David, *Alan Sugar: The Amstrad Story,* Century, London, 1990

Thomas, Elwyn and Woods, Mike, *The Manager's Casebook*, Michael Joseph, London, 1992

Thompson, Peter, *Sharing the Success: The Story of NFC,* Collins, London, 1990

Townsend, Christopher and Schluter, Michael, *Why Keep Sunday Special,* Jubilee Centre Publications, Cambridge, 1985

Tucker, Graham, *The Faith-Work Connection*, Anglican Book Centre, Toronto, 1987

Volf, Miroslav, *Work in the Spirit: Toward a Theology of Work,* OUP, New York, 1991

Weber, Max, *The Protestant Ethic and the Spirit of Capitalism,* Allen & Unwin, London, 1930 (English translation)

Wright, Christopher J.H., *Living as the People of God: The relevance of Old Testament ethics*, IVP, Leicester, 1983

INDEX